To Be Hu
Is an Hon

C000294839

An energising glimpse of a young woman's life through a wide variety of experiences; starting in 1978, she sweeps you up and carries you with her. Sharing her emotions, her understanding of the world and her spirituality, she travels both physically and metaphorically around the globe. With her sympathetic approach to the people she meets, combined with humour, sadness, wisdom, love and occasionally bizarre happenings; you will become drawn into her world of trust and belief that everything happens for a reason, helping to create a beautiful pattern of life.

Written in 2015 this is Pam C.Golden's first book and her memoir. For fans of her *Tree Spirits in Time* series, it gives an insight into where some of her inspiration and ideas originated.

To Steve
with Best wishes

Pam C. Golden

Other titles by Pam C. Golden

For children

Tree Spirits in Time series

A Tree in Time (Book 1)

Mist in Time (Book 2)

Find out more about Pam and her books on her
website at
www.gentlepresspublishing.co.uk

Follow her on Instagram (goldenpamc)
Facebook (Pam C Golden author)

Pam C. Golden

To Be Human
Is an Honour

*Artwork for cover image
created by
Ben Davies*

Layout by Sara Simpson

Published by

GENTLE PRESS

GENTLE PRESS

Published by Gentle Press Publications

First published 2015
Second edition published 2021
Copyright Pam C. Golden 2015

ISBN 978-1-9163301-2-2

Dedication

To my wonderful parents and family

and everyone who gave me the best start

in life I could have asked for.

Contents

Preface

This is my recollection of events, which I have related to the best of my knowledge. To protect people's identity, some of the names have been changed or their identities have become combined with others. Thank you to all the real-life people portrayed in this book for being with me on my path through life and helping me grow.

PROLOGUE

Cheering and clapping erupted as the plane touched down on Israeli soil. Joy and excitement infused the air around me. A little bemused, on my first big trip alone, I gazed out of the window, wondering what lay ahead. Emerging into the palm-studded heat of the road leading from the airport, I felt a complete sense of being at home. Yet, with no Jewish connections and never having set foot on the soil before, there was no apparent reason for me to feel that way. I headed off towards the offices of the kibbutzim.

My childhood had been idyllic, in a comfortable home with loving parents and my older brother, Jeremy. Deeply loved, I was surrounded by a happy family, both nuclear and extended. Despite experiencing a tragedy, two years before my birth, I was unaware of their pain. Only in adulthood, have I truly appreciated what a wonderful basis they gave me for life.

Throughout my childhood, teenage and college years, I took every opportunity to participate in acting. It was like a drug to me. I loved it. As soon as one play was finished, I was looking for the next one. Quite a lot of people asked if I was considering it professionally. With the innocence of youth, I would reply, "If it falls in my lap, I will." Luckily, I allowed fate to decide. If accepted on the post-graduate Shakespeare tour of America, I would follow an acting career. If I did not, I would go to a kibbutz; hence, my arrival in Israel.

Little did I know, but this trip was the beginning of my spiritual path, which has taken me around the world, with an amazing variety of experiences. Many people's lives and stories have helped to shape the person I have become. As I tell my story, hopefully you can see a reflection of your own life in events or feelings. You can see the value in your story and how each of us is on a magical and amazing path through life. Sometimes it is easy, sometimes it is very hard and painful. Everyone we meet can be a gift, although occasionally it is a challenge to work out what that gift can possibly be!

CHAPTER 1

"Live life to the fullest... think of all the people on the Titanic who passed up chocolate dessert." Unknown

The dry, dusty office window looked out onto a street, blank with sunshine. "Could I go to a kibbutz in the desert?" I enquired. The man behind the desk looked at me and shook his head. The hard wall of bureaucracy resisted my request. "This organisation has no kibbutzim in the desert. You are assigned to another one, in the north." I was dismissed.

As my vision of staying in the desert receded, I felt a little lost. I stood, contemplating where I was going to end up. "Excuse me," said a voice behind me, "I overheard him saying that you are going to the same kibbutz as me. Do you know where we go?" A friendly looking young woman, about my age smiled at me. Her northern English accent made me feel at home. Suddenly it looked less bleak. I had someone to connect with.

As Judy and I travelled together to the kibbutz, which was in the fertile and lush growing areas south of Lake Tiberias, we exchanged our stories. By the time we had arrived at our destination, we had agreed to be roommates. My spirits lifted even more, as we passed leafy plantations of bananas, tall date palms and spiky grapefruit trees, before bumping down the dusty track into the kibbutz living quarters.

A few days later and we had settled into the routine of daily life, working, eating in the canteen and mixing with other volunteers from all over Europe. As the kibbutz was very large, the volunteers tended to socialise separately from the kibbutzniks. Looking back, I can hardly blame the more permanent residents, as a multitude of different young people would constantly be flowing in and out of their lives.

Everyday life was gentle and quiet, surrounded by nature, yet on the river edge, the towering, barbed wire fences told another story.

Judy and I both loved riding and soon she gleaned that a young man called Jacob was the kibbutznik in charge of the horses. Using her considerable charm, she engineered some rides for us. Unfortunately, one of the horses was only half broken in, as Jacob had had to go to do his National Service amid training him. Somehow, I ended up with that horse.

The ride followed the perimeter fence. Towering above us, rolls of evil looking barbed wire curled its way along the top. Beyond the fence was a minefield, full of untold horrors, then more cruel fences, before the River Jordan flowed, deep and swirling, forming the border. The irony was, we could see the Jordanian farmers, working the land on the opposite banks. As we rode our horses on the edge, they waved and smiled at us. That image has remained a strong motif in my life. Boundaries may be created by fear, but human love can go beyond that, melting the barbed separation, through the simple connection of a smile.

We started to canter. So far so good, we were going up a hill. My horse was slower and just about kept up with the others. Suddenly, the ground levelled off and he saw an opportunity. He took off. The ground whipped past me. Dust flew up. He would not respond to any of my efforts to slow him down. I tried not to panic as the distance lengthened between me and my companions. On unknown territory, I had never been this far from the settlement and was not sure where I was going. I had to stop the horse. The only thing I could think of was to shorten one of the reins and turn him back on himself, kicking up a cloud of dust.

It worked. Shaking a little, I waited for the others to catch up. No sooner had they arrived, then he took off again, but this time I had no control because he raced in amongst the grapefruit trees. There were irrigation pipes crossing the path and the plantation rows ran parallel to the main road. Being skewered by the nasty long spikes on the trees was not an appealing option, so I concentrated on staying on his back. After forever, he slowed to a stop. The horse's breath steamed over my shoulder as I slipped down from the saddle. With legs too shaky to remount, I walked back, leading the errant horse behind me.

In later years, I have reflected on the lessons that horse taught me. When someone loses their temper, I have discovered it is best not to

4

argue, let them rant on, until they run out of steam and eventually stop. If I react, it only feeds the flames till both of us end up out of control and saying things we may regret. (That's not to say that a good shout isn't very satisfying at times.)

As time went on, I began to rely more and more on Judy's good will for friendships, as I had been assigned work in the factory. There was only me with a kibbutznik, whilst everyone else worked in the banana plantations or the kitchens. Not only that, but all the other volunteers worked from six o'clock in the morning to twelve noon. I worked from twelve noon to six in the evening, so I was isolated, not meeting others easily. To make it worse, the work in the factory was anodising flights for missiles.

I started to think more and more of my earlier idea of living in a kibbutz in the desert. Having been in the system a while, I was beginning to work it out. Different groups of kibbutzim were managed by separate Movements. The Meuhad Movement was in the old communist style. That was the one I was signed up with. Most of its kibbutzim were in the north of the country. The desert was south. I realised I had to find a kibbutz in the desert, and then find out which Movement ran it.

In some of the long, lonely rest times I found myself reading a copy of the Jerusalem Post. In it was an article about Sde Boker, the kibbutz where Ben Gurion realised his dream of building settlements in the desert. The furthest kibbutz on the water pipeline, it was in the Negev desert. As soon as I read about it, I knew that this was where I wanted to be.

CHAPTER 2

"All religions, arts and sciences are branches of the same tree."

Albert Einstein

My departure from the first kibbutz was tinged with regret and a little apprehension, as I headed off to the city again. However, this time I knew what I was looking for and was aware of which office I needed to achieve my goal.

All alone again, I waited with other hopeful volunteers for my interview. Through conversing with them, I discovered I should have obtained a reference from the kibbutz I had left. It was too late to go back. I would have to bluff my way through. There were two options. One was a scary woman, who apparently gave everyone the third degree and the other seemed to be a gentle man, who was very pleasant. I hoped against hope I would get the man.

I got the woman.

My heart sank as I walked in and sat down. Her fearsome countenance glared down at me. "Why do you want to change kibbutz?"

I trembled inwardly. "Well, I really would like to visit the kibbutz that Ben Gurion had founded. It's amazing that it is at the end of such a long pipeline. I'm interested in seeing how it works and think it would be great to experience a kibbutz in the desert." I looked at her face. She gave nothing away. Had I said the right thing?

A pause hung in the air, then she barked out, "Where are your references?"

Using all my skills as an actress I looked shocked, "Oh no! Should I have got a reference? I didn't realise." I let the silence fall.

A gruff voice responded, "Well you should really have them but never mind, you can go to Sde Boker." A wave of relief flooded over me. I was on the way to the desert.

Sde Boker was much smaller than the first kibbutz, with a fraction of the volunteers. If the latter was like a town, the former was like a village. It was wealthier, with a more comfortable lifestyle for the inhabitants. Warm and sunny, there was the beautiful desert just beyond its edges. In my spare time I could wander there at will, luxuriating in the freedom and space, loving its colours, rock formations and silence. There were no factories making items of war, no barbed wire boundaries and my job was picking olives, milking the udder–like clusters, from the white-leaved dusty trees.

Here I learnt to love olives, avocadoes, and the desert landscape, but most important of all I met Marianne.

The two Swiss girls, who had been there several months, were learning Hebrew and had integrated themselves into the kibbutz life, befriending the kibbutzniks. They seemed separate from the newer volunteers. After a few days, one of these girls approached me. She smiled, then commented on my eyes. "They are very deep. Your eyes make you different from all the others. I think we can be friends." That was the beginning of our wonderful, spiritual friendship that has been extremely important in my life. We would chat a few times whilst I was there but lived out our own experiences separately. That pattern has continued. We do not need to see each other much, both secure in the knowledge that we have a deep connection, maybe even linking back through previous incarnations. Every time we *do* meet, marks a pivotal moment in our lives.

Quite soon after I'd arrived in the kibbutz, I opted to go for a hike in the desert with two of the kibbutzniks and a couple of volunteers, all males. Until that hike, I had never realised how precious and important water is. Growing up in Manchester, where the supply is frequently replenished from the skies, it was never that special. I took it for granted. All the guys were hardened desert hikers. "Water must be rationed on this walk. Only sip it when we tell you." I was determined to keep up their fast pace and not appear weak and feeble. Walking hard and admiring all the amazing rock formations in the dry and ever-increasing heat, I started to feel extremely thirsty. "Is it okay for a drink now?"

"No, you can't afford to drink anything till we are at least a third of the way on our route."

My throat stung, I tried to think of other things but all I could think of was how much I wanted that water. Finally, we stopped for a short break. I was all ready to guzzle down a large swig from my water bottle.

"Oh no, you don't," this Dutch guy said. "You must only sip it."

It was one of the hardest things I have ever done, having to sip the soothing, delicious liquid, that my desperate mouth craved. I savoured every drop, swilling it round on my tongue, making it last as long as I could.

A lot of self-control was learned on that walk, as well as the value of the amazing liquid that we use and abuse with no thought. In recent years I have read a lot more and subscribe to Viktor Shauberger's view of water. He argues it is a living being that holds memories, can transmit information, and needs to flow in its own path to be energised and alive. Think of a bright, bubbling, mountain stream chattering over rocks, as it follows a curving pathway. Now compare it with a stale limpid canal, forced into straight lines and held there by concrete blocks, and you can begin to see what he means.

A few times I have commented to people, "Look at water, it is amazing. You can feel rough, horrid, dirty and hot. Stand under water and what does it do? It transforms you. After a shower you feel refreshed, happy and altogether able to face the world again. How wonderful is that? A pair of hands that feel sticky can be placed in a bowl of silky liquid called water and come out feeling a million dollars. You can be feeling dry, thirsty and quite faint, one glass of this magical stuff and you are better again." Then I get a funny look as if to say, "It's only water." I suppose I must accept that they have never been without so cannot appreciate it in the same way. We have this wonderful gift in abundance, yet most people in the post-industrial world take it for granted.

In the desert we could never do that. We were at the end of the pipeline from the north and water was used carefully, being reused where possible.

I loved the apparent emptiness of the desert. Walking only a short distance from the kibbutz, I would look around and as far as I could see there was no other visible living being. I relished the space to be totally me, all alone in that vast landscape. What would you do in that situation? Imagine, pure freedom.

My favourite Shakespeare play is Macbeth. The rich language is pure power in its essence. Out there in the rocky landscape I would revel in repeating Lady Macbeth's speech, expressing her resolve and determination, performing purely for love of the words and my own satisfaction at expressing them. Returning to the kibbutz I would feel refreshed and empowered by the time spent alone.

Apart from experiencing the immediate environment around the kibbutz, we were taken further afield on minibus excursions, and we also travelled independently, hitching our way around the country. In that way I got to see quite a lot of Israel.

As a child I had been to Junior Church every Sunday morning and Sunday school in the afternoons. As I grew into my teenage years, this invasion of my free time became more and more galling. At the age of fifteen, it exploded into a blazing row with my mother outside church. I walked the two miles home and stomped into the house. I remember my lovely, quiet, calm Dad busy in his workroom. "Why are you home?" he queried.

"I don't believe in God. Church is a load of rubbish. I'm not going again."

"Church helps you to be a good person in your life," my father responded quietly.

"You never go!" I retorted, "And yet you're a good person. Anyway, I still don't believe in God!"

"It doesn't mean that I don't believe in God. It's very big headed to think there isn't a God out there." Those few quiet words, spoken by my loving, gentle dad, had more effect on me than any argument Mum could have presented. I never went back to church as a Christian. However, it has not stopped me appreciating people who do, or who follow the examples held in the pure essence and teachings of Christ. In fact, those values, learnt as a child, probably still underline everything I do in my own life. My long-suffering Mum finally accepted that her daughter was never going to come into the Church's embrace again. However, she loved me enough to listen to my beliefs and be happy for me. Eventually she ended up commenting

9

that I behaved in a more Christian way than many people she knew, who claimed to be Christians. I must have made it so hard for her. Brought up as a Methodist Minister's daughter, all her social life and friendships revolved around the Church.

In Israel, after years of rebelling against my Mum and resenting any part of me that resembled her, I began to change. It felt comforting to recognise her mannerisms or habits in my own actions. The miles of separation probably helped. I, also, allowed myself to feel a thrill to be in places I had heard about on Sunday mornings. It was a surprise to discover that Nazareth still existed, although we were not encouraged to go there, being a predominantly Arab town. I later discovered it was where some volunteers from the first kibbutz would go to buy strong, black hashish, brought over the border from Lebanon; not the idyllic town of bible lessons.

I preferred the Israeli name of Lake Tiberius, to the Sea of Galilee, and found it slightly incongruous to see coachloads of Christians coming to be baptised on the shores of the lake. They seemed disconnected, as if they came from another world. The scenery they were dropping into was host to the living Jewish culture which did not recognise Jesus as the Messiah; he was just another child of their race. In Jerusalem, I found the Stations of the Cross to be full of tacky stalls selling plastic artefacts and soulless churches full of idols and objects to buy. They left me cold. They were the symbols of what the edifice around the religion had become, not the true essence. Maybe Jesus would not have liked it either, thinking back to his attitude on money and idols in temples. I did like the garden of Gethsemane, which was beautiful, a peaceful oasis on a dusty hillside full of scrub bushes and goats.

I am ashamed to admit my ignorance, but I did not know, till I got to Jerusalem, that it was the centre of three religions.

For me, the strongest and most powerful place was the Wailing Wall. Here, generations of Jews have placed their prayers and dreams in the form of tiny pieces of paper tucked between the vast stones. It is believed that these stones form the original wall of the temple of Solomon. I stood by it and felt waves of love and feeling, as an almost tangible presence.

The other great religion in Jerusalem is Islam. The beauty of the mosque at the Dome of the Rock where Mohammed is believed to have ascended to Heaven is stunning. As in all mosques, there are no images of humans, prophets or otherwise. All the decoration is intricate patterns and designs, reflecting the divine patterns of life and nature. Again, it was a welcome relief from the tawdry statues of the Virgin and all the saints to be found in the Christian areas of the city.

Looking back, I can see that buildings hold the energy of the people who use them. My mum's church was very vibrant, loving and caring because the people that attended it were like that. My brother's church feels the same. In contrast, some churches I have visited feel cold and daunting. I suppose most churches in Jerusalem are not part of a living community, just part of a tourist route, hence the sensations I experienced.

In general, I loved Jerusalem, with the unique smell of orange and grapefruit juices pervading the ancient winding streets of the old quarter. In dark recessed stalls, sheltered from the relentless heat, street vendors plied their wares. Small cups of dark thick coffee were inevitably offered, alongside a wonder of items hanging from every corner to tempt the eye and imagination. My eyes feasted on the ancient stones surrounding the old town that had seen so much history. As I stood in the sunshine, I wondered at the Golden Gate; sealed for thousands of years, waiting for the day when the Jewish Messiah will enter Jerusalem.

As a young woman I was not particularly aware of politics or their consequences. Coming from England, it was odd to get on a bus and see soldiers sitting on some of the seats, with guns propped beside them, on their way home from National Service. Although for the Israelis, it was totally natural.

We were warned by the kibbutz to never accept a lift from blue number plates when we were hitching. This was because they were Arabs. The Israeli number plates were yellow. On the couple of occasions, we did accept a lift from the forbidden plates, we were pleasantly surprised to find the Arab drivers were courteous, friendly and very kind to us. The more I have gone through life, the more I have learnt that the individual is the person to respond to. It is no use judging anyone by their race, religion or looks. It is the person's behaviour that matters and the feeling you have towards them as a result. There are good and bad in every race, group or organisation. Everyone needs to be treated as an individual, not lumped together and judged.

One excursion that showed we needed to judge people by their actions, happened to me and another young woman volunteer. During my stay on the first kibbutz, some young Israeli soldiers visited and ended up chatting to us. A couple of them invited us to their homes in Tel Aviv for Shabbat. We innocently went along with it, thinking it would be great to experience a real Shabbat with an Israeli family.

Joining the good-looking men on the bus, we travelled back to the city. Eventually we ended up, not in a home with their parents, but in a flat in the middle of Tel Aviv. It was Shabbat eve, so everything was closed, there was no transport, and we suddenly became aware of the vulnerability of our situation. We did not really know these guys other than having chatted to them in the kibbutz. They could kidnap, rape, kill or do anything they liked to us and no-one would know. We had no clue where we were, we were surrounded by anonymous flats in an unknown city, we had no method of escaping and even if we did, we would not know where to start going. We could not speak Hebrew and might not be able to communicate with anyone. We huddled together in a quick conference in one of the rooms overlooking the other flats. I longed to be back in the safety and security of the kibbutz, where we knew the agenda and what was expected of us. I do not think I have ever felt so alone and vulnerable. Looking back, I cannot believe how naive I was, but that is how we learn. I see now that these thoughts were guided by fear.

We decided to overcome our fear and appeal to the better side of the young men. We did not know what their intentions were, and it was uncertain how they would respond to us, if they felt we were rejecting them or suspicious of them. We decided to talk to them, explain how we liked them as friends but did not want it to go any further than that. They responded surprisingly well. They respected our wishes and allowed us to sleep in a room of our own, where they said we would not be disturbed. All night I was restless and had never been so glad to see dawn. They saw us back to the bus the following evening and I was immensely relieved to return to the kibbutz and safety. We were very lucky, but it could have had a very different ending.

12

CHAPTER 3

"When I admire the wonders of a sunset or the beauty of the moon, my soul expands in the worship of the creator." Mahatma Ghandi

The beauty and variety of landscape in Israel is something I will never forget.

One place I really loved was Masada. The kibbutz took us there, but I also travelled there on my own. On the visit with the kibbutz, they insisted that we approached the fortress on foot. Walking up the four hundred and fifty metres from the Dead Sea in the blistering dry heat, we were encouraged to empathise with the inhabitants of two thousand years ago: the last Jewish defendants against the Roman Empire.

The Roman built fortress had large cisterns, underground stores and was very hard to attack. On one side was a four hundred and fifty metre drop to the Dead Sea, and on the other a very narrow approach, bridging a hundred metre drop. About a thousand people defended themselves there for a period of three years. Eventually they were facing starvation and defeat by the Roman army, so they came to a terrible decision. Rather than surrender to the cruelty of the Roman empire, they agreed that the head of each household would carry out a horrendous task. They chose to kill their own children, spouse, friends, then kill themselves. I cannot begin to imagine what they all went through.

The towering fortress resonates with the modern Israeli identity. It has become an important symbol of the determination of the Jewish people to be free in its own land. Maybe in the future they will realise that to be truly free they have to allow freedom to others as well. It is a difficult concept. They fought so hard to regain their homelands and suffered so much in the process, so it is very understandable that they feel as defensive of their territory, like the rebels of Masada. They are surrounded by peoples who are directly opposed to their beliefs and customs. However, we are now moving into an age where we need to choose love and respect, over fear and domination, as our guiding emotion. If everyone on the planet could choose that route, then I am sure things would work out better for everyone.

As my life has progressed, I have started more and more to choose the love rather than fear route, which has paid off in many ways.

After visiting Masada, we did the Dead Sea experience. It was wonderful at first to wade through the heavy water, then sit, feet up, in the sea. I floated around enjoying the sensation for a while, then decided it was time to return to the beach. I tried to put my feet down. They would not go. They just popped back up. I tried to swim, I could not. I began to get agitated, which was the worst thing I could have done. Splashing my eyes by accident, the salt-drenched water blinded me. Panicking, I managed to push through the water till, stumbling onto the beach, I staggered up to the freshwater showers. What a relief, when the health-giving salts were rinsed away and sight was restored to my stinging eyes!

* * *

Nowadays people often say they are going to Sharm El-Sheikh. At first, I could not believe how the place I knew could stand these large numbers of visitors. Then I looked on the web and saw what it is like now. What a difference!

I travelled there in the winter of 1978, with some friends from the kibbutz. At that time, it still belonged to Israel, shortly before Egypt regained the Sinai. Eilat was already a resort, so we decided not to stop. Staying on the bus, we journeyed down the long coastal road. The Red Sea glittered on our left, with the mountains of the Sinai rearing up on our right. Then it started to rain. One of the most magical experiences in the world is to see rain in the desert. The transformation was incredible. Like pebbles on a beach acquiring deeper beauty when the tide washes over them, the rocky peaks of the desert turned from a dusty cream into a multitude of colours: hues of red, brown, grey, yellow, cream, blue and green. I gazed from the bus window, transfixed by the scene before me. Israel was certainly giving me reasons to appreciate rain.

Further on, we saw groups of Bedouin tribesmen herding their animals, their black robes billowing in the wind. Along the route, we passed about three or four minor settlements which were no more than a handful of huts clustered round a beach. The odd back packer was in evidence at each of these, but we wanted to go all the way to the end.

Finally, the bus deposited us at the last of these settlements called Naama Bay, where maybe fifty or so tourists were camped out on the beach. A couple of huts were there to service them, shark nets were in evidence off the beach and that was it. As we were a mixed group of seven or eight young people, we decided it was safe to camp on our own, away from the main beach. Setting off from the bus stop, we walked around the headland till we were about three kilometres from the bay. No-one was in sight; we set up our tents and began to explore. The clear green-blue sea stretched in front of us and the bluest of blue skies formed a dome over our heads as we approached the sea edge. Everything above and below water was reef. There were a couple of shelves of dry reef, on which we were based and down which we had to step to reach the water. The third step down took us onto a shelf that was under water. When we reached the edge of that, the wonder of the coral emerged. I had never snorkelled in my life before and could hardly believe what I was seeing.

Pushing off the top shelf into the clear water, I watched as the cliff of coral dropped away, going down tens of feet below me. Hundreds of shoals of fish swam and darted around, swaying as one, in the movement of the sea. Brilliant colours assaulted my senses, some from the gorgeous fish, who almost nuzzled us as we swam, some from the myriad of colours and shapes which formed the living and swaying coral, and some from the brilliant snake like creatures that appeared to be nestled in the coral cliff. Beautiful but deadly, I learnt never to put my fingers or feet on the vibrant turquoises or blues; or the 'snake' would disappear, and I would be caught in the powerful grip of a clam.

Hours were spent floating and snorkelling in this enchanting world. The fish seemed to grade themselves according to size on different parts of the reef. Shoals of tiny brilliantly coloured fish darted close to the reef, slightly larger ones floated further away, and still larger fish swam and wove among the castle-like coral, towering up from the seabed many feet below.

As we were beyond the shark nets, we took turns to stay on watch duty for the tell-tale fin. One day, the look-out started yelling. We

15

hot-footed it on to the raised reef, fast. A fin was gliding past, about twenty to thirty metres out. At that distance, it wasn't clear whether it was a shark or a dolphin, but we weren't risking going back in. In my haste to get out, I inadvertently trod on some sharp coral which cut my foot. Six weeks later, it finally healed, after leaving Israel.

The day before, a young Arab fisherman had suddenly appeared over the crest of the dried-up reef. He surprised us. We had not seen a soul since our arrival and thought no-one knew we were there. After offering to sell us some fish, he wandered off.

The shark episode having put paid to further snorkelling, we decided to follow the direction we had seen him go. After walking across the barren surface for a good while, we reached the end of the peninsula. "That must be Sharm El –Sheikh." I commented to one of the others. It consisted of about eight or nine wooden huts. There did not appear to be a road. We did not want to venture into the settlement, as we were unsure of our welcome. A few men were wandering around in the distance, but there were no children playing or signs of any women. It seemed a very lonely and isolated place.

Looking at images of the resort nowadays, shocks me. I do not want to go there again, as the beautiful memory of that wild, desolate landscape with its vibrant coral reef would be destroyed. Sometimes it is best to hold memories in our heart and not revisit.

* * *

My saddest memory in Israel was of Christmas Eve. The kibbutz had been celebrating Hanukah. It is a festival commemorating the miracle of the oil. The festival reminds Jews of a time over 2500 years ago when Antiochus, a Syrian king, tried to make the Jewish people worship Greek gods. He had a statue of himself erected in the Jewish temple and the Jews were ordered to bow down before him. Their beliefs forbade the worship of idols, so they refused.

After three years of rebellion, they recaptured Jerusalem from the Syrians. The temple was virtually destroyed. Immediately, they set to work, cleaning and mending the temple so it could be rededicated to God. Lighting the Menorah lamp, which was a symbol of God's presence, was essential. Only one jar of oil was found, enough for one day. A runner was sent to collect more oil and it took him eight days to return. Yet, during all that time, the lamp stayed alight. This

16

miraculous event is celebrated annually by Jewish people all over the world.

On the kibbutz everything revolved around the celebration. For eight days, everything was cooked in oil. Delicious doughnuts were on the daily menu, the Hannukah song was sung before every meal. Every night the Menorah was brought into the dining hall with one more candle lit. Several communal events took place relating to the oil. Christmas Eve must have landed on the last day of Hanukah. Despite it being the culmination of their own festival, the kibbutz kindly arranged a trip to Bethlehem for the volunteers. I thought it would make my Mum's Christmas if I phoned her from Bethlehem on Christmas Eve, so I signed up to it.

As a grand finale to the Hanukah celebrations, the kibbutz organised a Family Relay Run of flaming torches. Unaware that we could go and watch, I stayed in my room getting ready for the trip to Bethlehem. On joining the minibus, I sensed a terrible feeling amongst some of the volunteers. At the back, some women were sobbing uncontrollably. It gradually emerged that an awful tragedy had happened.

One of the young boys had put his torch into the can of oil to replenish the oil and the torch had flared up, setting him on fire. The sobbing women had witnessed it. I felt a deep sense of worry and misery for the boy and his family, as we drove through the dark miles to Bethlehem. Understandably, I could not get them out of my mind. I felt utterly helpless.

On arrival we parked outside Manger Square and glimpsed the only view that meant anything to me that night. The hills beyond Bethlehem were lit by little clusters of light shining with some beauty and giving a little of the atmosphere I had imagined. The rest was a severe disappointment. To get into the square, we had to go through a barricade of armed soldiers, showing our passports to prove we were tourists.

The main service was going on in the Church of the Nativity, which was full of nuns who had signed up for years to get a place there. The service was broadcast onto the side of the police station wall. It was heaving with tourists and young Arab boys selling souvenirs and trying to get cheap thrill kisses because it was Christmas Eve. I struggled through the crowds and queued for a place to ring my Mum from the phone booth. Trying to put aside all the horrors of the night, I announced cheerfully that I was ringing her from Manger Square and wished her and Dad a Happy Christmas. I thought she would enjoy telling her friends at church that her daughter had rung her from Bethlehem on Christmas Eve. She then told me that Grandma, who lived in a flat at our house, was very ill. I cried all the way back against the dark windows of the minibus.

Grandma died a couple of weeks later, but I did not receive the news for many weeks. As it was pre-internet days, I had to rely on letters left at Post Restante addresses for communication from home. It was not until we were in Delhi that I finally heard.

CHAPTER 4

"When I do good, I feel good. When I do bad, I feel bad. That's my religion." Abraham Lincoln

Despite the sad times, I loved my stay in Israel and would have stayed longer than four months, but I had arranged to meet my boyfriend in Athens outside the main post office at twelve noon on the fifteenth January 1979. This is in the days before mobile phones and emails, so arrangements had to be made in advance and stuck to. He was travelling to Morocco first and then to Greece. I was a bit concerned about him managing it; as he had got lost going from Manchester to Cambridge, ending up in Wales. He had never been out of the country in his life before, so I knew I had to be there for him.

In the event, it was me who got it wrong. I waited outside what I thought was the main post office in Athens and was quite surprised to find no letters in Post Restante and no boyfriend.

Finding a cheap hotel for the night, I decided to try again the next day. After making enquiries, I discovered I had waited outside the wrong post office. On getting to the right place, I found a pile of letters for me, with a note from Aiden amongst them, telling me he was in a cheap hotel nearby. We met up. He was very relieved because he was nearly out of money. Again, it was in the days before cash points and credit cards, we could only get cash from traveller's cheques.

It was winter and colder than we had expected it to be in Greece. Ideas of camping on beaches fled before us, so we got a cheap flight to India instead. The Shah of Persia had been overthrown and the Iranian revolution was in full progress, so we decided to stay in India for a couple of months. The plan was to return overland when the Revolution was over. Looking back, I am embarrassed by my naivety.

Later, I learnt that I was not the only one to be oblivious to the implications. One of our fellow volunteers from the kibbutz, blithely went into Iran and travelled around during the Revolution, coming out totally unscathed or traumatised. She was a Norwegian girl, very blond, very beautiful and with a belief that nothing bad could ever happen to her. And it did not. We laughed about it afterwards. I think she may have had a male travelling companion who was, also, Swedish. Other travellers were having to sell overland vehicles, people were stranded in India, no-one dared go into Iran, yet they did and had a great time. In later years, I have learnt a lot of what we receive is from what we put out. Basically, we are still very animalistic. If we are fearful, we give out fear and attract negative situations. If we give out trust and love (in the widest sense), then we attract positive situations.

* * *

As we were leaving Athens, something happened.

Our money was in the form of cash and some traveller's cheques. I had given Aiden sixty pounds in cash to carry for me, which was a substantial amount in those days. He suddenly grabbed my arm, looking a bit green, "The money's gone."

"What?" I felt sick. We were on the verge of boarding the plane. It must have been a pick pocket who had melted into the crowd. There was nothing we could do. If we stopped and reported it, we would miss our flight and we could not re-book it. We had to go.

As the plane took off, we settled into the long journey to India, and I reflected on what had happened. To earn money for my trip I had spent the summer working in a garage. In those days, it was acceptable to display a different price on the board from the pump price. Effectively the petrol was advertised at fifty pence a gallon, but the pump charged sixty pence. We would give them ten pence back for every gallon. I had been brought up to be very honest and was diligently giving everyone their correct change. One day, a man raced in, put five pounds on the counter and raced out again. I tried to shout after him that he needed some change, but he had gone. I was quite upset and did not know what to do. Another cashier explained that when that happened you could pocket the difference. I was not earning a massive amount, so I decided that it was okay.

At first it felt bad, but after a while I began to look forward to the little bit extra. Then I am very ashamed to say I started to engineer

20

situations to create it. If the person did not look for change, I would not give it to them. If they did, I would. Sometimes I got it wrong. If challenged, I apologised and said, "Oh I was just getting it for you." My hand was always on the change, just in case. Once they were out of the door, it went in the 'pot.' Some was left in for the boss, so my takings were always up. The till never balanced. He must have known what was going on, but nothing was ever said. I started justifying it to myself. One man, a white South African, had just got off a plane and was obviously filling up his hire car. He had not a clue. He gave me the money and left. I thought to myself, well he lives in a country that oppresses other people and daily robs people of their birth right. Nelson Mandela was in prison at that time and violence against the black population was appalling. I felt his sin was greater than mine.

I now know that to abuse anyone, no matter what they have done, is wrong. It may be a petty crime, but it is still a crime to harm someone else and it brings harm back on oneself. The phrase 'easy come, easy go' echoed in my mind. I earned about sixty pounds extra over the summer and this was the sum that got stolen. I saw it as a lesson and learnt from it. I never did anything like that again and felt bad about it since. However, it gave me an understanding of how people can get drawn into crime and stopped me judging people too quickly. Given the circumstances, who knows what anyone will do.

CHAPTER 5

"Possessions are not really important to me. I love experiences that create unforgettable moments and memories." Unknown

India was unbelievable. It is hard to convey the multitude of experiences or impressions that assaulted our senses in that time.

Managing to get a train ticket each for two months, enabled us to travel anywhere in the continent for sixty pounds. We could sleep on the trains, which saved overnight accommodation. We calculated that we had fifty pence a day for us both. The average European was travelling on a pound a day each. It meant living a lot closer to the local people, which gave us a greater insight into their lives and how difficult it was. We had to bargain hard for our daily food and when we could afford to stay somewhere, sleep in basic accommodation. It was not a luxurious or particularly comfortable trip but that did not matter. We were young, could put up with lots of things and were having an adventure. It made me appreciate how affluent our lives are in this country. No matter how poor we think we are, we are in luxury compared with many others in the world.

We arrived in Bombay (modern Mumbai) and were instantly embroiled in the busy, vibrant life around us. People were everywhere. Life was lived on the street; you could get your hair cut, have your shoes polished, buy cooked food, have a shave or even a head massage. Standing on a street corner, I could have written a book, just by recording the events and activities around me. Nothing was wasted. People made toys from old roof tiles and paper bags from old magazines. There was always someone eking out a living, by reusing every item. I felt ashamed when I thought of the waste in our culture, which has grown and intensified even more since then.

The stations and trains in India were brilliant. In my dad's spare time he was a model engineer. He was always in his workroom building his latest model steam engine. I kept thinking how he would have been in heaven travelling on these beautiful beasts. The stations were faded grandeur from the past. Way above, the soaring architecture and inspiring lines were reminiscent of the grandest British railway stations, exalting the best of Victorian engineering. Lower down, the powerful steam trains caught the eye, clouding the air, chugging in to deposit their teeming passengers. On the human level was a world of activity. Porters were carrying huge trunks or parcels, often on their heads, their thin bodies belying the incredible weight they supported. Masseurs were massaging resting porter's (or anyone else's) heads. Multitudes of food and drink vendors were shouting their wares, their calls echoing through the crowded platforms. Many levels of Indian society bustled through, from the poor to the wealthy, marshalled and controlled by the inevitable station officials, intent on rule obeyance.

Our first destination was Goa. I suppose we were vaguely following the old hippie trails from the previous decade. Our accommodation was in a hut, next to the owner's home, which was, also, a wooden hut. The shower was in a round corrugated shed. We had to inform the owner when we wanted to use it. He would then stand on a block behind it and pour water into the shed for us to clean off. The toilet (an open-to-the-air-below-affair) was in a separate hut round the back. The next morning, perched to do my business, I heard a snuffling near my bottom. A bit shocked, I saw that the family pigs lunched off human excrement. No wonder so many Indians are vegetarian.

Looking back, it was a great system. Maybe we need to re-think our squeamishness to do with poo. It is a valuable resource and should be used productively, either to create compost or to feed other creatures, rather than polluting our valuable and beautiful water.

Goa was a very romantic place. Enclaves of hut-dwelling, leftover hippies, mixed with Indian tourists, who came for day trips in coaches to enjoy the beaches and bathe in the warm seas. I remember walking with Aiden, under the tall palm trees, on the beach, with ladies in beautifully coloured saris flitting about, looking like butterflies. At that time, the only buildings were a few homes, like our hosts, in the hinterland behind the beach. Now it is a totally different place. It has been 'developed' like Sharm El-Sheikh.

On route to our next destination, we met some fellow travellers. They got talking and offered Aiden a large piece of hashish that would have

23

cost a small fortune in England. They were desperate to get rid of it. The stuff was so cheap and readily available that they found it was too much; incapacitating them in their desire to travel. They were losing all will to do anything and decided that the best option was to give it away. I left the decision to him. I wanted none of it.

The great thing about travelling on the trains was the stops. At every station, as we pulled in, a cacophony of noise and smells hit the senses. Anyone and everyone were trying to sell fruit, cooked food and drinks. "Chai, Chai Chai Chai!" would echo across, as people leaned out of the windows or wandered onto the platform. At each station, the train would stop for a good ten or fifteen minutes, providing an opportunity to stretch one's legs. I loved it when the train started again. Unlike England where the doors shut and the train pulls rapidly out, the whistle would blow; the train would leisurely start and the passengers would equally leisurely swing onto the steps, walking alongside the moving carriages, then step on to the moving train.

We travelled to Bangalore and then down to the coast to Rameswaram where we would catch a ferry to Sri Lanka. We met many people on the trains and talked to them, learning much about their lives. One encounter that stuck in my mind was meeting a young girl who had just got married. She informed me she was twelve years old. I was astounded to hear girls were married so young. In turn, she was amazed that I was twenty-three and not yet married. She explained that she was living with her husband's parents. His mother was looking after her and teaching her the skills of looking after her home and husband. When she had a baby, her mother-in-law would teach her how to bring up the child. Despite being horrified at the young age of the girl, I could see the reasoning behind this way of living. If the family she was placed into were good, kind people, then the nurturing skills could be passed on effectively and there would be strong family links and bonds created. However, coming from our society and views, I found it extremely hard to accept her young age. She seemed quite happy with her situation, as if it were totally normal.

From twenty-first century 'western perspective' the whole idea is abhorrent, but looking at our society, do we do any better? It is now the exception, rather than the norm, for children to be brought up in households with their birth parents still together. I am not saying

24

whether that is good or bad, it is too complex and depends on the individuals, but does that give us the moral right to condemn other societies that are structured differently?

With the concept of arranged marriages, the girl's parents would have been involved in the marriage and one would hope they chose with care. I think the very young age is what feels so wrong. Her access to education is removed and she is vulnerable to abuse.

However, abuse can happen anywhere to anyone, no matter what the level or culture of the society. Our own society is rife with it. It is based on the mind-set of someone owning someone else or not seeing them as an equal.

I'm sure that forty years ago things were very different in India and things will have changed a lot since then. Often, we are very ready to judge other cultures and criticise. I think the only safe solution is if everyone makes choices in their lives based on love (in the broadest sense) and not fear or greed, then it should create a happier place for us all.

* * *

In Rameswaram, they were building a temple. It was astounding. I imagine it was like the way English cathedrals were built centuries ago. All the stone was being carved by hand. The scaffolding was formed from living trees that were supporting the structure. It had taken so long that the trees had had the time to grow. I think they said it would take another sixty years to complete. Monkeys chattered and leapt around the stonework, men toiled in the sun working with the calm dedication and ultimate patience that seemed so characteristic of the people of that continent. It was a very humbling sight.

The ferry over Palk Strait was very busy, with many people and lots of luggage. We stood on the deck, enjoying the cooling breeze, as the boat ploughed over the warm sea.

On arrival in Sri Lanka, we made our way to Anuradhapura. Magical and beautiful, a Buddhist moon festival was taking place. Candles lit the path on either side leading to the temple, while around us, nature's candles, in the form of fireflies, darted from side to side. Saffron robed worshippers glided gracefully by, with garlands of

25

flowers adorning the delicate statues of Buddha. Pervading everything was a sense of peace and well-being. I felt honoured to be there.

Every Singhalese whom we met, impressed me with their kindness and consideration. On our journey south, we chatted to people on the train. One man was particularly friendly. He told us he had been working up north and was on his way home. When we told him of our destination and asked if he could recommend anywhere to stay, he invited us to his house. I felt worried that we had imposed on him, but he insisted. Concerned as to how his wife would feel at having two complete strangers landing on her doorstep, I tried to remonstrate. "She will be happy to entertain you," was the reply.

Aiden and I were overwhelmed by the kindness shown by Jaya and his wife Ratna. She was a doctor, already trained in allopathic medicine and working at such, but she was, also, learning the traditional medicines, as she felt they were very important too.

They showed us the little scroll holder, hung around their necks. Inside was their horoscope, written at birth, showing their destiny. When anyone wanted to get married, their horoscopes had to be consulted and if they were incompatible, the marriage was not allowed. I think I understood from Jaya that he and Ratna were a love match rather than an arranged marriage. When they decided to get married their parents were not convinced, until the horoscopes were matched. Theirs were very compatible, which allowed the marriage to go ahead. They had three young sons who were delightful boys.

Jaya could not do enough for us. We did not understand what we had done to deserve such royal treatment. He took us on a tour of the local tea factory, where they gave us a packet of tea. I carried it with me for another five weeks before giving it to my mum. Even after being in a smelly backpack for that length of time, Mum said, "Well, I don't think I've ever tasted tea so delicious and fresh in all my life."

Next, he took us to the local brick making factory. I had never seen hand-made bricks before. The men collected the clay, filled a wooden frame with it, tipped out the block of clay then left it to dry in the sun. The sun was so intense that the clay baked into hard bricks in a very short time. The speed at which they made them was amazing.

Ratna was unbelievable. She would get up at five every morning. Then she would wash rice in coconut milk. You know the brown coconuts we get in this country? Well in the countries where they grow, no-one thinks they are fit to eat in that state. She would take the hard flesh from the brown shell, grind it by hand into flakes, then pour water over it, straining it through the coconut flesh. She did this about five times, pressing and squeezing the juice. Only on the fifth time did she keep the resultant milk. She then used this to cook the rice for our breakfast.

After that she would get the boys up and feed them. Following what amounted to a day's work in the home, she would go to work as a doctor, starting at about eight o'clock in the morning. She had no machines to do anything; everything was done by hand, washing, preparing food and cleaning. I told Jaya that I would like to help, but he was not having it. As Ratna could not speak English and Jaya was our host and translator, I felt I had to accept her kindness without argument, but I never forgot how much extra work we must have cost her.

One day as we were walking along the road, Jaya told us to watch out and stand back. He then indicated a young lad who was shimming up a tall coconut tree. My eyes widened in disbelief as I saw how high he was going, clinging on to the trunk with his legs and arms. No safety rope or harness was anywhere to be seen. Strapped onto his back was a sharp knife. As he reached the smooth green baubles hanging in clusters near the top, he paused, readjusted his position, retrieved the knife, and slashed them free. The green bombs rained down with tremendous force, thundering into the ground around the base of the tree. Jaya told us how dangerous a falling coconut could be. Apparently, a person had recently been killed by one. I could well imagine it.

Our time with Jaya and Ratna was ending, so with many grateful thanks, we took leave of our dear friends and set off on our travels again. On our return to England, we sent the family gifts to thank them for their kindness and have exchanged Christmas cards ever since.

On the ferry back to India, I noticed a large group of people who had been escorted on to the boat by the police. They looked very sad, huddled together. Other people on the ferry told us they were Tamils who were being expelled by the Singhalese. At the time I did not know much about the Tamils, only that they lived in the north and were regarded as being very different from the Singhalese.

After our stay in Sri Lanka, we headed up to Madras. There Aiden became very ill. He was sweating profusely and almost delirious. Very worried, I made enquiries and found a local doctor. With painstaking slowness, I managed to get him to walk along the road to the small, dark shack. He was diagnosed with paratyphoid and given a shot of medicine with the most enormous needle I had ever seen. The doctor told us to report back the following morning. By the next day, Aiden had recovered enough to be aware of the second jab. He nearly fainted when he saw the size of the needle. It did the trick though and after some days' rest, we set off again.

Our next stop was Calcutta (now called Kolkata), where my love of lassi was born. The milky drink was so refreshing, as were the slices of cucumber sprinkled with paprika. After Aiden's illness we felt he needed some treats. We eased up a little on our budget, deciding to sample some of the Indian sweets we had been ogling in shop windows. They were gorgeous.

Everywhere we went in India, there were beggars. Never have I seen illness and maimed limbs so openly thrust into my attention. I remember one man with no legs, scooting around on a slab of wood that had wheels attached. On a few occasions I noticed people begging who had elephantiasis, with large and deformed limbs. Another time a beggar came up to me pushing a badly damaged hand in front of my eyes, pleading for some money. At that time in Britain, disabilities were covered up, hidden away and 'protected' from the public gaze. Not so in India, everything was visible. In that sense, although I found it hard, I began to appreciate the openness and acceptance of people. Nowadays, there is a healthier acceptance of disability in our society. Thankfully we, also, have a system (although not perfect) that supports people to live, without having to exploit their disability to survive.

Leaving Calcutta on the train was an experience I will never forget. Looking round the platform, I could not believe that the numbers of waiting people would all fit in one train. It was so full. People were even sitting in luggage racks. In fact, we ended up doing so, as there was nowhere else to go. As the slow chugging started to pull us out of the station, Aiden pointed to the shadow of the train. It revealed that the roof was as full as inside. It was crammed. Health and Safety would have had a field day...but this was India, not Britain.

Gradually the train emptied as we travelled further and further from the city. Having seen it was possible, on subsequent journeys we often clambered up onto the roof. The main hazard was bridges. To avoid decapitation, it was essential to lie down, closing our eyes for protection from the smoke. It was infinitely preferable to being stuck inside.

* * *

As day grew on, the train emptied. One of the other passengers told us we were entering bandit country. A few stops later, he got out. Darkness fell and the lights in the carriage were not working. There were very few occupants now. We began to feel nervous when we pulled into stations. At the next stop, a man suddenly entered the carriage. Unusually tall and heftily built for an Indian man, he was wearing a large khaki overcoat. In his hand was a large stick. Two smaller men appeared to be his henchmen.

This was when it would have been useful to speak the local language. However, in India, a different language can be spoken even twenty miles apart, and in the seventies, although Hindi was the official language, the common language left over from colonial times was English. Normally we struggled by the best we could, using our own language supplemented with signs and smiles. However, this man was not the sort to respond to smiles. He towered over us. We looked back, unsure of what was happening. They spoke to us in Hindi, but we did not understand. The men gestured with urgency, telling us to get off the train. We did not know what to do. Were they the bandits? If we got off, would we ever get on again?

We decided to sit tight for a while. Then they tried to make us move with more gestures and pointing of the stick. I looked at Aiden, he looked back at me. One of the few remaining people in the carriage indicated we should go with them. It was a big moment of trust. We had to go with our feelings. Although they looked scary, they did not feel bad.

They looked at us, we looked back. Eventually we thought it would be safer getting out in a station, where we were, than maybe further on, at an unlit stop. We alighted and they escorted us further down the train.

Suddenly they opened the door of the first-class carriage and ushered us in. It was lit, bright and had other European travellers in there. We could not believe our luck. They must have been railway officials, concerned for our welfare in the bandit country. The gentleman with the large stick then stayed, guarding us all till we reached our journey's end. It was a lesson in trust.

CHAPTER 6

"Holi is the day to express love with colours." Unknown

Since being in India I have never complained about English toilets. I found the benchmark. Toilets do form a very important part of anyone's journey. Whether we like it or not, they are an inevitable experience and often affect one's judgement of a place.

When I was in sixth form, my option for P.E. was to choose yoga. Our tutor was always telling us how much better it is to go to the toilet in a crouched position. Apparently, our organs are then naturally in the right position to excrete easily. The root of a lot of bowel and digestive problems are because of the unnatural position we adopt by sitting on a toilet.

She entertained us with the tale of her new bathroom. Because a hole in the ground is not acceptable in our country, she was desperate to find a low toilet so she could be in the correct position. Hunting around, she eventually found a very low toilet. She was thrilled. She left the workmen installing the new bathroom and returned at the end of her day. "Eh missus, that toilet you found was right low," said the foreman. "We've done our best and worked hard all day to build it up on a platform, so you won't have to get down to it." I never did find out what she said to them.

Bearing that in mind, I often found the public toilets in India fell into two categories. There were normally two toilets with holes in the ground, then one toilet left over from the colonial past, which was a 'sitting' one for the British. As normal there were long queues (that never changes, whichever country you are in) for the hole in the ground. No-one was going in the 'British' one. The Indian ladies let me pass them, as I went for the sitting option. As I entered, two of the largest rats I have ever seen, ran up the pipe and along the cistern. I screamed and the other occupants ran to see what the matter was. "A rat!" I exclaimed.

"Is that all?" they responded, with a look of incredulous disgust that I could make a fuss over such a little thing. I felt like a pathetic little white girl who should really toughen up a bit.

One time I was in a crouching toilet and I remember being fascinated by a row of ants. As I watched, they started to carry a cockroach which was upside down and getting on for fifty times their size. The ants worked as an amazing team. They had bundled up its body and were passing it from one to the other along the line. The ones at the front were running forward scouting out the route, the ones at the rear were bringing up reinforcements and the ones in the middle were dealing with the body. The way they worked was incredible. It made me consider the insect world in a completely different light. We can learn so much from them.

The most disgusting toilet I ever experienced was on a railway station somewhere in the north of India. As I approached the block, I noticed there was an overflow. The whole toilet block was six inches deep in running sewage. In the heat, the rancid smell was intense with a cloud of flies hovering over the area. I was desperate to go but could not make myself paddle in it and further contribute to the stench. Hopefully, the public toilet system has improved massively since then.

* * *

One day when we were travelling on the trains, it was unusually empty. Normally every seat was taken, we had to book seats to ensure a place and at times even had to sit in a luggage rack. We travelled through a village and the train stopped for its usual ten or fifteen minutes. We got out and wandered round. Everyone looked as if they were dressed in their old clothes. "Look at that!" Aiden exclaimed. A bus was driving past with open windows (very few had glass in them, it was too foolish in that heat) and people at the side threw buckets of coloured dye all over the occupants! No-one seemed to mind, it was all in taken with laughter and good fun. We could not believe our eyes. Before we knew it, people in the village were throwing buckets of coloured dye all over each other. Soon the street was a blaze of oranges, yellows, blues, greens, reds and every colour you could imagine. We beat a bemused retreat to the train, as we had a limited supply of clothes and could not afford to get them ruined.

32

More was in store for us. I always liked to sit by an open window. It was so hot on the trains and the breeze helped to make the journey more comfortable. As there were so few people on the train, I had the luxury of a window all to myself. Imagine my annoyance, when a fellow traveller, who was a woman, sat opposite me and pulled the shutters down, tutting at me. We had no common language, so she could not explain. I was annoyed, so I pulled the shutters up again. She shook her head and pulled them down again. A pantomime ensued. She pulled them down, I pushed them up. Eventually, she gave in and sat by the window looking out. I followed her gaze.

Soon we saw a group of boys standing by the railway line. Instantly she rammed the shutters down. Seconds later, we were bombarded by the sound of rocks, stones and mud being pelted at the side of the train. If the shutters had been up, we could have been seriously hurt. As usual, the kindness of the Indian people towards us, despite our rudeness and suspicion, made me feel very embarrassed. All the time we were being watched over and looked after, even when we did not realise. They wanted us to be safe in their country, a country where they knew the customs and we did not. Often, they could not explain properly because of the language barrier but they would try through their actions to offer help.

Later we discovered it was the festival of Holi. It is an amazing day when all normal customs are ignored, and misrule takes over. The state of the trains as they all pulled into the central stations, had to be seen to be believed. They were covered in dents and mud. The festival marks the coming of spring. Very colourful, it is full of fun with lots of dancing and singing. On the first night, bonfires are lit and roasting grains, popcorn, coconut and chickpeas are thrown on. The next day, people of all ages go into the streets for fun and paint-throwing. Everyone gets involved with no distinctions between caste, class, age or gender. It is a free for all, with boys often getting up to every imaginable mischief. Some believe the origin of the festival lies with Krishna who was very mischievous as a young boy and threw coloured water over the gopis (milkmaids). This developed into the practical jokes and games played on Holi. The story of Prahlad tells of good overcoming evil and explains why the bonfires are lit.

Prahlad's father was an evil demon king who wanted everyone in his Kingdom to worship him. He had one son, a lad called Prahlad, who was a very good and pious child. His father was devastated when his

33

only son refused to bow down to him, preferring to worship Lord Vishnu. The evil father kept trying in many ways to kill his son, but each time Lord Vishnu would protect his faithful follower. Finally, the king asked his sister, Holika, to take the child with her into a bonfire to burn him to death. Now Holika had a boon that protected her when she entered fire, so the plan seemed to be fool proof. Unfortunately for Holika she did not realise that the boon only worked when she entered a fire alone. Tricking her nephew into sitting on her lap, Holika sealed her own fate. Prahlad, protected by Lord Vishnu, emerged from the fire unharmed, whilst Holika was devoured by the flames.

In some parts of India, images of Holika are burned on bonfires. The ashes from these fires are supposed to bring good luck. To me, it seemed to be a festival of cleansing the energies of winter ready to welcome in the spring renewal of life.

CHAPTER 7

"A day in a new place is like a month at home. Your senses absorb every tiny new impulse, hot-wiring your consciousness, making every second seem a lifetime." Author

We ventured north into Nepal where we encountered the first spring of 1979. That year we experienced three springs and no winter. Most people would say, "Oh how wonderful! You got to see three of the best season and none of the worst." Interestingly, the following autumn, I was very happy to feel the onset of winter. It felt such a long time since I had experienced it. Ever since, I have really enjoyed the changing seasons and understood how I need to go through winter to fully appreciate spring and summer.

Nepal felt very different from India. For one thing it was cooler, the people were more reserved, and the scenery was stunning. We only went as far as the foothills of the Himalayas, just beyond Kathmandu, but I had never seen terraced agriculture on such steep slopes and against all odds. The food that was being cultivated on the mountains was incredible, all by hand or with the help of a few animals. The mountains beyond were so tall that they disappeared in a haze of blue, with the white snow peaked tops reappearing above, as if floating above the haze.

My main recollection is of camping on a patch of grass near the roadside. About a hundred yards away was a small wooden building with a dark interior which housed a family. I remember rising early, as dawn approached. The sky was starting to lighten, and the cock was beginning its herald of dawn. At that time of day, a cold air hung around, shrouding the land below in a light mist. Breath showed in clouds, as a man swathed in blankets, quietly emerged from his home. Wood smoke from early cooking fires started to spiral around the valley, drifting into our nostrils, as we blinked into wakefulness. Later in the day I went to wash some clothes at the nearby stream. Watching the other women, I observed them beating the cloth on stones to scrub out the dirt. I tried to follow suit, managing relatively well, I thought, but from the looks on their faces, I was obviously a novice at this game.

Our money was beginning to dwindle, so we decided to return to India, visit Agra and then head home from Bombay.

In Agra we gazed on the tomb for Shah Jahan's wife, built with so much love and passion. Visiting somewhere that has been extensively photographed and written about, there is always the concern that it will be a disappointment. The Taj Mahal exceeded my expectations; elegant, beautiful, and full of the love that its creator had felt for Mumtaz Mahal.

An unexpected surprise was the acoustics. Under the intricately carved white marble dome, housing the tomb inlaid with precious jewels, only soft, gentle sounds resonate and echo. Any harsher sounds do not. I don't know how the building was created to achieve that effect, but it was a beautiful emphasis of the love that inspired it. Apparently, the Moghul Emperor was going to have a black marble replica on the other side of the river for himself, but this was never built. He was laid to rest beside her in a simple ceremony.

It truly is a Temple to Love, no wonder it attracts so many people to share its peace, harmony and tranquility.

* * *

Delhi is the city nearby. There, the letter telling me about Grandma, finally caught up with me. I remember collecting the post and sitting on a grassy area to read it. I burst into tears, which elicited the usual consternation from passing locals. Normally, when they found out the cause (which was usually exhaustion or frustration) they would dismiss me with a sense of exasperation. Elders are respected and revered in the Indian culture, so on this occasion, I was treated with a lot of respect and sympathy.

It was time to return. However, we had no money for the flight, having thought we could travel home cheaply overland when the Iranian revolution was over. Many others were stranded, like us. Land Rovers were being sold to get flight tickets, stories were rife of how people were trying to earn money to get a passage home and the hippie trail was finally broken. We listened to advice from other travellers. "Don't get money sent out through a bank. They hold on to your money for weeks saying it hasn't come."

"Get your money through Thomas Cook, at least they can be relied upon to get it through to you." We made a reverse charges phone call home and asked my ever-forbearing parents if they could send us a money order to cover a flight home. We caught up on our news, I told them I had only just found out about Grandma, and they said that she had left me some money in her Will that would just cover our flights.

A couple of days later we called into Thomas Cook's and collected our life-saving money. Then we decided to check out prices between Delhi and Bombay to get the cheapest deal. It did not cost us anything, as we could use our train pass and sleep on it, saving accommodation costs. Aiden decided to indulge in a head massage on one of the station platforms. He said it was like being in heaven. The masseur and inevitable group of bystanders told him he was a child of India. He liked that.

CHAPTER 8

"And in the end it's not the years in your life that counts. It's the life in your years." Abraham Lincoln.

The cheapest flight we could find took us to Athens. We luxuriated in seats that were cushioned and not wooden. Every piece of the airline food was consumed with alacrity. We were so hungry, it tasted delicious. Horrified, we noticed that some people were wasting theirs. Aiden even ate the marrow out of the bones. Having got used to living frugally, we were not taking any normal luxury for granted.

In Athens, we tried selling some of the beads we had bought in India to raise some funds. While standing on a street corner, with the beads strung over my arm, a woman approached me and asked me what we were doing. I explained. She asked me what I did in England. When she heard I was trained as a teacher she could not believe what I was doing. "You could earn a decent wage teaching English here!" she exclaimed.

It was not to be. We were both tired of travelling and ready to head home. After one last visit to the Parthenon, we decided to go to Delphi and then hitch home. In Greece, we experienced our second spring. Walking on a cliff by the coast, with fields of wildflowers nodding around us and the blue Aegean glistening below, it felt like heaven. The temperature was perfect, neither too hot nor too cold. Visiting the ancient sites, which I had studied during my education, gave me a strange feeling. It seemed as if I had stepped into a reality that did not really exist.

Our first lift took us over the border into Yugoslavia. Tito was in power and it was a communist state. I could not believe the difference between the Greeks and the Yugoslavs. The Greeks walked with a sense of pride, jaunty and confident. Some were rich; some were poor, but all seemed to have a belief in themselves. What I saw in contrast, on the road through Yugoslavia, were a people that were oppressed. They wore dull looking clothes and nearly all of them walked with their heads down. No-one looked lively or animated. We felt like we wanted to get through as quickly as we could.

It was about a thousand miles to Italy, and we had only picked up the lift later in the day. The lorry driver spoke some English and told us we could stay in the cab for the night at a lorry park. As there was a bed in the cab big enough for us both, we were very grateful. He disappeared off with a woman on his arm. We realised this was a regular stop for him, as they seemed quite familiar with each other. Drawing the curtains, we settled down.

In the middle of the night, we were woken by a loud banging on the windows of the cab. We froze, terrified we were inadvertently doing something illegal. Imagining the police were outside, we pretended the cab was empty, hardly daring to breathe. The banging came again. We stared at each other in fear. Then we heard the person climb down from the cab and walk away. Quickly, I peeked out of the curtains. It was a woman, another prostitute, who had been touting for business. The lorry park had numerous women who 'patrolled' it. With a sigh of relief, we dozed off again. In the morning, our lorry driver returned with his woman on his arm, they gave each other a farewell kiss and we were off.

He dropped us just over the border into Italy, where we picked up a ride with a Romany driver from the East End. He was hot tailing it home to see his wife for their anniversary the next day and wanted our company to keep him awake.

However, as we reached the outskirts of Milan, he seemed to want to be rid of us. We decided we had enough money saved from our daily budget to afford a small hotel for the night. Entering a plush, dark red velvet world, it felt very decadent after sleeping in cabs and camping by roadsides. As we finished registering our stay, a couple of men came to the desk. They were dark suited, severe-faced and cold. No words were spoken. The small, kindly looking patron passed them a bundle of notes and they left. We reckoned they were Mafia, collecting their protection money. I felt how awful it must be to live in a society where fear governed your lives, either from an oppressive regime or from Mafia style rackets. For the umpteenth time on my travels, I recognised the value of living in Britain. We complain over everything, but it has a lot of positives when compared with elsewhere.

A night in the hotel refreshed us like nothing else. With food in our bellies and a good sleep behind us, we were ready for the last leg home. We managed it in two lifts. The last lorry driver told me to lie on the bed in the back under a blanket, while Aiden sat next to him in the cab. He passed Aiden off as his driving mate and we got on the ferry for free.

After a mere three days we had made it from Greece to England. Arriving in London, we were almost unable to believe it. We were home. It felt amazing to be with friends who cared, who were thrilled to see us and who let us have a bath. It felt like the most luxurious bath I had ever taken. Christine made us feel so welcome. I almost cried with relief to be there. Refreshed from a fabulous night in clean sheets, we were ready for the last part of our trip home to Mum and Dad.

* * *

I opened the door. "Mum, Dad! We're back!" No answer. The house was empty. I pounded up the stairs to Grandma's flat. I called her name. Of course, she did not answer. Only at that point, did it really hit me that she had died. I broke down and wept my heart out. I loved my Grandma. She was a real character, insisting on wearing three sizes of heels every day, even into her nineties, so that it exercised her feet. She was full of tales of her interesting past. All sorts of treasures were secreted around the flat, salvaged from her cottage in the Somerset countryside. A forceful personality, she was a great role model to my teenage self, with an avid interest in everything and everyone around her. I think it is only in later life do we look back and realise how much the people around us help to mould our characters and views on life. Human beings are such a mixture of so many influences; no wonder we are such a complex and interesting race of beings on this planet.

Mum and Dad arrived home, devastated to find they had not been there to welcome us back. At the age of twenty-three, I had finally grown up and realised how much they meant to me. It was great to be in the security of my home again. I had experienced so much in those nine months, that I fully expected everything in my hometown to be totally different as well. I was quite disorientated to discover it had not changed at all.

CHAPTER 9

"You are not defined by your past you are prepared by your past."
Unknown

I still did not want to teach. Education for me had been one long treadmill. I was never happier than the day I finished full time education for good. We all drank rather a lot, took a punt out on the Cam with some friends from Trinity, fell in, got soaked and rode home on our bikes, in borrowed clothes. The sense of freedom was heady. I felt free to get on with my life at last.

Nearly a year later, I was job hunting for something different. In those days, the government decided that young people should have job creation schemes to get them into work. I looked through the list of things I enjoyed and ticked a variety of boxes. It perfectly matched the job of a Community Artist, specialising in Drama. I went for it and ended up working in Salford. Living with Aiden in his house in Chorlton, I cycled to work every day.

That house was something else. It amazes me what we put up with when we are younger, with no question. I started going out with Aiden in my teens. Mum and Dad, who could see further, made me promise I would never get married till I was at least twenty-five. They explained your ideas change so much from your teenage years to adulthood. They were so right. They never criticised, just guided. Looking back, I cannot ever be grateful enough for their wisdom, help and quiet support over the years.

Aiden was in work when I planned my trip abroad. He decided he wanted to join me on my travels and gave up his job. A year or so before that, he and another friend, Bob, who was unemployed, had decided to buy a house together. Aiden had the capability of getting a mortgage through his job, and Bob had his share of a house that had been sold when he split up with his partner. They bought a large three-storey Victorian house in Chorlton. Whilst we were travelling, Bob had run up an electricity bill of a thousand pounds, which was an astronomical amount in those days. The electricity had been cut off and there were summons to court awaiting Aiden's return. As everything was in Aiden's name, he had to 'carry the can,' go to court and agree to pay it off in instalments of five pounds a week.

This meant that we ended up living in a house with no hot water and no electricity. I suppose our experiences in India helped us. I was young, in love and willing to put up with a lot. It was called 'Paraffin land' by our community of friends. Aiden being the kind and gentle person he was, allowed anyone to come and live there, I cannot even recall if they paid any rent. Bob and his girlfriend lived on the top floor, whilst we had the two front rooms on the first floor. The back two rooms on our floor were occupied by a dodgy character, who seemed to have a lot of unsavoury visitors. Another friend inhabited the ground floor. I was the only one working and the only one who ever cleaned any of the communal areas. The bath was full of tea leaves deposited there by the back-room guy. Naturally, they had blocked the plughole and gradually began to smell more and more unpleasant. The friend downstairs had no concept of cleanliness. Rancid and half used milk bottles filled the kitchen, stinking the place out.

Occasionally I would go on the rampage, yelling and shouting at the men to clean up their act, boiling water on a camping stove and trying to wash everything. The lights were from paraffin lights that we suspended from the ceiling. No wonder I kept escaping to Mum and Dad's to do my washing and have a bath. They must have hated seeing me in such squalor, but they did not criticise, just supported me and were there for me.

Christmas really revealed the true characters in our circle of acquaintance. I tried to make it a festive and lovely occasion. Of course, I spent Christmas day itself with Mum and Dad. Aiden went to his parents. However, for New Year I bought in a lot of bottles of different booze. Word got out that we had alcohol. The hornets descended. Suddenly we were very popular and lots of 'friends' decided they would visit. As soon as the bottles were empty the 'friends' disappeared again. I learnt a lot about people in my time there.

Sometimes, we would go to clubs in Moss Side. One time Aiden and Bob told me that we were going to a shebeen. The Harp lager factory steamed jets of forced cloud into the air above us, looming large and threatening. Opposite, on the corner of the street, a block of derelict houses stood stark against the night sky. We pushed open the door, hardly supported on its frame, and mounted the stairs. Paint had forgotten how to peel from the walls, as our footsteps sounded loud on the bare floorboards. We passed a bare room, lit by a single dirty lamp bulb. Three men sat huddled round a game of cards, glaring at the intrusion on the stairs. We moved on to the top floor and pushed open a door. Clouds of sweet-smelling smoke wafted into our nostrils, reggae music reverberated round the walls and we found ourselves in a series of   rooms, which were long abandoned family bedrooms. An ancient yet lively old man danced up to us, shaking our hands and showing us where we could sit. We duly took our places and melted into the background.

Our friend, Bob, was familiar with everyone there. As the evening went on, he indicated the old man who had greeted us. Some young guys (from out of the area) were sitting in the next room, wanting to fit into the 'scene.' They were rather obviously trying to look the part but sticking out like sore thumbs. The 'wise one' as I started to refer to him in my head, danced over to them and held up bottles of beer, whilst the men drank from them. From the expressions on their faces, the young men obviously thought they were really 'in' with the old man. Bob turned to us. "See what the old guy is doing?" We nodded. "He's showing everyone else in here that these lads are babies, he's holding the beer bottles like he's feeding a baby." Soon after he pointed out another guy going over to them and patting them on the back, again they looked like they felt really accepted. "That guy is touching them to find out where their money is," our commentator explained. Sometime later, Bob reported that they had been relieved of their money and were so drunk, they had no idea.

I watched the whole process with the dispassionate curiosity of youth. I little cared for the victims, feeling it was their own fault for putting themselves in that situation. I was, also, conscious of being on a thin thread of hospitality, myself, based on our friendship with Bob. If things kicked off, the situation could become unpleasant.

Forty years on, I look back at my younger self and wonder if I would have been any different. I do not know. Lessons were learnt, thankfully from the safety of second-hand observation, which would serve me in future, giving me wariness. It, also, gave me an

43

understanding of how important it is to be known by someone, particularly when entering a community that has a history of bad treatment from others of my race. Hopefully, I have grown more compassionate since then. With luck, the lads did not lose too much or feel too stupid at being duped. Sadly, their underlying reason for being there was probably a basic human need to communicate and interact with others. Their only fault was not working out the unspoken rules for that situation. I believe that everything happens for a purpose. We are either enjoying life, appreciating the wonderful planet we live on, or learning a lesson to help us evolve.

* * *

During those eighteen months, I had quite a few contacts from my friends on the kibbutz. They came to visit me at Mum and Dad's which I still regarded as my proper home. A few Norwegian friends came, a Swedish friend visited and of course Marianne. She came to England and I went to visit her in Switzerland. Her home was in the Emmenthal valley, a beautiful place to stay. I was made to feel very welcome by her family. On that trip, I first came across how to eat muesli properly. We did not have it for breakfast; we had it for afternoon tea. The base was a very finely prepared oats and flakes mixture, soaked in milk, yoghurt and cream for half a day. Chopped up fresh fruit was added, just before it was served. We ate it with slices of bread and butter. It was delicious.

I had visited Switzerland once before on our family's first big trip abroad. My maternal grandparents had honeymooned in Lucerne around the turn of the nineteenth century and my Mum had always longed to do the same. However, when she and Dad got married it was at the end of the Second World War. In fact, their wedding had to be brought forward by three weeks because of D-Day. Over the years we often heard the tale of how Mum was not allowed to know the reason why; she lost two stone in weight racing round to change all the arrangements and her dress had to be remade. Their honeymoon was in the Lake District, Britain's nearest equivalent to Lake Lucerne.

When it came to their Silver Wedding, they decided they would finally get to Switzerland. It was our first holiday abroad. In the 1960s, travelling out of the country for a holiday was a relatively new concept for most people. A big adventure, it was planned for months in advance. Passports had to be obtained and all eventualities thought through. In preparation, we went round to my parents' friend's house for a slide show of what to expect.

On finally arriving there, it was very similar to the pictures we had seen. The massive snow-capped mountains were bigger than expected but the geranium-festooned chalets and the deep, blue lakes were mirrors of the slide show. The purity of the air and the tidiness of the whole country was almost unbelievable.

When visiting Marianne, I felt less of a tourist. I discovered the mountain pastures full of colourful wildflowers, the simple but beautiful pleasures of Swiss life and the kindness of my friend and her family.

Holidays like this, drives out into the Derbyshire countryside and frequent visits to Mum and Dad helped me to maintain a balance in those eighteen months in Chorlton.

At work, we initially trained with two permanent Community Artists, based in an area of Salford which was very close to the docks, whilst we worked from a community centre further up the main road. Driving there now, I cannot recognise any of the areas; it has changed vastly since those days.

Where we trained, was where the original Coronation Street was filmed before it was moved to a studio set. The local women used to tell me that they were quite disgusted by one of the leading male actors. They had all been standing watching the filming going on in their area and this man had yelled at them, "Haven't you women any housework to be doing, why don't you get back to it?" In reaction, the women did not mince their words.

Life was very hard for women in that area, at that time. They suffered a lot of violence and abuse from their menfolk. It was so bad that a lot of them had abandoned relationships with the opposite sex and turned to each other for comfort. The permanent community artists told me tales that opened my sheltered middle-class eyes. It gave me an understanding and feeling of compassion for people who had a very different deal in life than I had.

One child was regarded as an angel by his mother, but he was a complete devil away from her. Once she broke a woman's arm in a street brawl when this woman dared to complain about her precious Kev. The local priest spent a whole night reviewing his vows because if he had caught Kev, he would have killed him. The reason for the poor priest feeling this way was because the 'angelic' boy had been shooting at him and a group of others with an air rifle. Kev would go to town in an old pair of shoes, change his shoes in a shoe shop, come home in a new pair and his mother would never question what was going on. Kev was the terror of the area, everyone hated him, but no-one could do anything to change him because of his mother. Kev was twelve.

* * *

Where we were based, was a bit gentler. We worked with the children, making a film, creating activities in the holidays, painting 'murials,' reviving old street maypole traditions with broomsticks and ribbons, and generally having a great time. As the end of our year's contract was coming to an end, I thought I had better start applying for teaching posts to get my probationary year done. An interview for an Outward-Bound School in Aberdovey, gave Mum, Dad and I a lovely day out, but I didn't get the job. Half-heartedly, I applied for a few teaching appointments in England, but did not even get an interview. Then I started looking at jobs abroad. Seeing a job advertised in Switzerland, I applied for it, thinking that at least I knew Marianne there. I did not hear anything back.

Suddenly my employer contacted me to say that one of the permanent Community Artists was leaving and would I like her post? I was very flattered to be asked and accepted. He then said, "You won't give it up if you get a teaching post?"

"Of course, I won't," I replied. "I don't do things like that."

"I've known it happen before and it will happen again," he replied in a voice resigned to failure.

It came out of the blue, a month later. One of the schools I had applied to in Switzerland contacted me. They were holding interviews in Leeds and would I like to come? I decided to go along for the experience.

I got the primary teacher's job along with another girl, who got the P.E. job. I felt bad. I was in a real dilemma. Should I accept or not? I

46

felt I was letting everyone down, including all the community in Salford who had supported me to get the permanent job. I had a talk with lots of people including a lovely lady who was the local community matriarch. She kept a spotless house and mothered everyone. "You do it," said Ivy, "never give up a chance to better yourself." I have never forgotten her words or her kindness. I eventually decided to go. My employer sighed, but it did not surprise him, he was too used to people going back on their word. He almost expected it.

Aiden was upset but I said he could visit me there and that the two years would go quickly. Mum and Dad were thrilled. At last, I was going to use my teaching qualifications. It still would not count as my probationary year, but it was a start. A new life was waiting.

CHAPTER 10

"A little thought and a little kindness are often worth more than a great deal of money." John Ruskin

Only when I arrived at the school and settled into my room overlooking the lake and mountains, did I begin to see how different life could be. I was immensely glad to get away from that lifestyle in Chorlton but did not realise it, until then.

My arrival had been rather dramatic. In the dark, the school towered above me with its Gothic architecture. I waited, wondering if I had come to the right place. An older, very commanding lady with a white bun eventually answered the door, brusquely leading me through the endless corridors and up winding staircases till I reached my room. Secreted in the tower, it had a wonderful view over the lake. I was later to discover this powerful personality to be the Matron of the boarding house. First thing the following morning, I was escorted to another room where I recognised the Head of the English section who had interviewed me. He strongly resembled John Cleese. I half expected him to stand up and do a 'funny walk' around the room.

After I had got to know him better, I realised he was very aware of the similarity himself. He used to laugh about the time when he was interviewing a student for his misbehaviour. He made a move on his chair and then fell backwards, with his long legs and feet waving in mid-air!

"You are the only teacher in the primary section. I haven't a clue about primary education, so it's all up to you. There is a small library but don't get your hopes up. If you need any books, they will take six months to get here. Welcome to the school." With that I was dismissed. My first year in a classroom did not look very promising.

Over the summer I had done a three week intensive course over the summer in T.E.F.L.(teaching English as a foreign language) to prepare. I had an E.F.L. class and my primary class. On my first day, the primary class consisted of one pupil aged seventeen. The next day, another boy arrived from Venezuela, he was fourteen. That was it for the next few weeks, until two sisters aged twelve and nine arrived from Zambia. Finally, a few weeks later another boy arrived from America aged fifteen. My class of five was complete. I still do not know why they were a primary class. Maybe it was because they were of primary level in English? All I can say is that it was the hardest term of my teaching life.

I had never dealt with teenagers before and found the discipline difficult. With no guidance as to what I should be teaching, I taught three lessons for every lesson. The two girls did work based around their knowledge and interest while the three boys were taught whatever I could find in the sparse library that seemed relevant to their age group. My trusty First Aid in English supported teaching grammar and spelling rules. Haphazard or what! The second term things improved with their boundless energy being expended on the ski slopes three times a week. By the third term we had built a great relationship and were like a family, all looking out for each other. I have never forgotten my first class and often wonder where they are and what life has done for them.

Socially, I was having a great time. There were three new English teachers that year and three new Irish teachers. The Irish came over on one-year stagiaire permits, whilst the English had two-year contracts. Half of the total teaching staff were newbies. There was a high annual turnover of educators. I came to discover in my second year there, that a teacher of two years standing rose in status among the pupils, because of their sticking power. The teachers all got on well together. Most of us were in our twenties, in for experiences and up for adventures.

My mum said she had never seen me looking so healthy and well as when I lived there. The air was like nectar. After school we did loads of outdoor activities, such as water skiing on the lake and roller-skating along the promenade. In winter, we found a hidden lake in the mountain above us where we would ice skate, as well as skiing three times a week with the children. Living on school food was great for the figure, as it was not very palatable. Certain days were better than others. Boarding duties were on a rota, so on those days we had to work till 10 p.m. but otherwise we had no responsibilities, bills to pay or worries. Paid into our Swiss bank accounts, we used our monthly wages to make the most of our free time.

In my first term, I visited Marianne on quite a few weekends. Sitting with her friends, who followed a very different lifestyle in Berne, I would listen to the Swiss German, trying to develop an understanding of it. Marianne was always very good at translating or they sometimes conversed in French to include me. It was a lovely change from life in school, but gradually as I got more and more settled, I drifted away from Marianne. It was quite odd. In the two years I lived in her country; I was the furthest away from her spiritually.

There are a multitude of stories from my time in Switzerland; but many of them are not mine to tell. I did meet another extreme of life there. The children would come to school dressed in Dior. The teachers would all get our clothes from a warehouse clearance place down the road, where we rummaged in boxes to find bargains. It was fine; till one of the children commented that I was wearing the same outfit as another teacher.

One thing I noticed was that a lot of rich kids are often more emotionally deprived than poorer children. I remember on my first week, a gorgeous little girl arrived. I watched as the glamorous mother fussed over her young daughter and thought, "What a caring mother." As the year went on, that sweet little girl changed from being happy and confident, into a sad, uncared for child with nervous rashes developing on her skin. I did not know the details because she was not in our section of the school, but my instinct was that she felt abandoned. Her elegant mother hardly visited all year. She was seven. I have often wondered how she coped with her life later.

Some of the children were so vastly wealthy they had no concept of anything but money. I remember one of the German boys shared a room with two Turkish boys. The Turks had a hundred pounds a week pocket money. Nowadays it would equate to about five hundred pounds or more. Anyway, the German lad had spent months building a model, painstakingly saving all his pocket money (which was considerably less) and spending hours finding the exact match in paint to complete it. Barging in on their roller-skates, which they were not supposed to use indoors, his roommates collided into a table and sent his model flying. It broke. He was devastated. They immediately said, "Oh it's alright we'll buy you another one." They could not understand why he was still angry and upset. They had no concept that money could not ever replace the time and care he had put into the model.

I suppose being surrounded by all this wealth, made me see that having a lot of money does not make a good or wonderful human. In fact, it can often be an impediment. I realised it is not being wealthy that is important, but how one deals with others. If you are kind and fair with someone, no matter what your financial situation, then you can feel good about yourself. Often there is this glamour around wealth, as if money will solve all your problems. No. Often more money brings more problems. If I have enough to live on and not worry about paying bills, then I try to be satisfied. My brother is a very good role model for me in this. He is not wasteful with his money and as a result, he always has enough to do what he enjoys. He never hankers for more and appreciates being in a comfortable situation.

* * *

Another thing I learned was that the Swiss are very careful not to report bad news. Headlines always focussed on cycling in the summer and skiing in the winter. One of the boys in my class, told me about an incident the previous year. He and a friend had found a black bag on a mini golf course near the school. Being boys, they kicked it between them before deciding to open it. Inside was a severed head. Because the school was private, it was totally hushed up and not a thing was mentioned in the local papers. The decapitated body was found the following week in the lake. Several members of the public saw it, so it had to be mentioned, but it was hidden in a paragraph on the bottom of the middle pages.

Looking back on it, I should have talked to my pupil more about it, tried to counsel him and help him deal with it. It must have been very traumatic, but as he had mentioned it very casually, I did not think that it bothered him. I think with age and experience, I would have dealt with it differently.

A few months later, some friends told us that their house had been robbed. They were informed by the police that if they reported it to the papers they would be fined! Part of me applauds the Swiss for keeping their newspapers 'clean.' The more unpleasantness is dwelt upon, it does affect the nation's psyche. It makes people feel they live in a very negative place. However, I do feel that it is important for people to learn the truth about their world. (Not that all newspapers are renowned for doing that.)

Instinctively, I knew that if I stayed two years in Switzerland, then my relationship with Aiden would end. It did so, but we stayed friends for a few years after that.

My time in Switzerland was a lot of fun. I made some lifelong friends, learnt to ski and water ski in fabulous surroundings and loved the natural environment around me. However, as my contract was coming to its end, I had to decide if I wanted to stay or not. The school offered me a place if I wanted one, but I could not make up my mind. In the end, I wrote everything down in two columns, pros and cons. The pros ended up being linked to the environment and physical side of living. The cons were linked to my emotional and mental stimulation; the latter won.

I decided to try for jobs in London. After several failed applications, I was getting nowhere. By the time I had received the form, and then returned it, the application dates had gone. A couple of posts in different schools in the Borough of Ealing came up, one a week later than the other. The application forms were identical, so I inadvertently applied for the second job with the form for the first job. By a freak of fate, I had at last got the application in on time!

A few days later my parents rang me. They told me the Head of the school in London had been on the phone to them, chatting for ages about me. Then the following Sunday, I got another phone call from my Dad, "That woman's been on the phone again, she wants you to ring her." I rang her back, we had a chat, then she said she could not pay my expenses from Switzerland to come for the interview, but I could claim the train fare from Manchester. I said I was agreeable to that. "In that case could you be here for the interview tomorrow morning?" she replied. I felt it was my only chance to get a job, so said I would do it.

A few mad hours ensued. Attempting to buy a plane ticket, I somehow got through to the airport personnel's home number. I could hear her family in the background. Talking in French, she asked me if I was staff. Not thinking I replied "Yes," thinking of being teaching staff. I got a return ticket from Switzerland to Gatwick for less than the train fare from Manchester. Then I had to organise my teacher friends to cover me for two days of lessons, give them my plans and organise cover for my boarding duties. Next, I ran up the hill to the Head's chalet to let him know what I was doing and get permission to go, then see the Director of the school and tell him. After that I had to beg a lift to the airport (a good hour away) from one of the other teachers and pack.

From putting the phone down, to landing in Gatwick, was about four hours.

On arriving in London, I rang my dear friend, Christine to ask if I could stay the night. Hitching across the city, it took me several lifts, till I was finally dropped outside her door in a purring Jaguar. Christine said as soon as she heard the car and looked out, she knew it would be me. As usual, her warm welcome helped to calm my building nerves.

That night I phoned another college friend who was an expert in music teaching (it was a job in a middle school which required me to teach music). She suggested how to approach the interview and gave me ideas of what to say. I wrote it down and learnt it. The next day I had to negotiate my way across North London by tube. Arriving about ten minutes late for my walk round the school, I hoped it would be forgiven, considering what I had gone through to get there.

I got the job.

CHAPTER 11

"Be yourself; everyone else is taken." Oscar Wilde

Life in the big city raced in upon me and before I knew it, I was starting my new job and trying to find somewhere to live. A friend from home, Helen, offered to let me share with her, whilst I looked for my own flat. Despite all the changes, staying with Helen made me feel comforted and safe.

Money saved from my time in Switzerland, was soon deposited on a maisonette in Harrow and Wealdstone. The only way I could afford it, was to take in a lodger. He had the front room as a bed sit and I had the back room as a bed sit, with French windows leading onto the garden. There was a shared walk-through dining room to get to the kitchen and a bathroom beyond that. My entire wage was needed to pay the mortgage, so his rent paid for my food and bills. It was very tightly budgeted, but it worked.

I loved having my own garden to tend, awakening me to the necessity of needing a green environment. Very happy in my first proper years of teaching, I finally passed my probationary year. My colleagues were great and very supportive. I remember being touched by some of the comments the children made. One of the children was holding my hand as we skipped round the playground at playtime. "What do you want to be when you grow up Miss Colbran?" she asked. Then she looked at me quite shocked and said, "Oh you are already grown up!"

As I settled into my new life, I started to become more concerned about world events. My new colleagues opened my eyes to the issues of the day- discussions were lively and I was fascinated. My mind was alive again. I went on demonstrations. I joined busloads of women going out to Greenham Common. There, we linked hands in a massive fourteen-mile human chain round the American base. We were only there for the day, but I was in awe of the brave women who had given up everything to camp for months and sometimes years in the cold, damp conditions on the perimeter fence, to protest the nuclear missiles.

Things I'd never really thought about, suddenly became important.

I remember the day of Live Aid. Not having paid much attention to it beforehand, I was cooking a meal for some friends. Where I lived was only a few miles from Wembley Stadium and I decided to borrow my lodger's TV and watch it, as I cooked. I became engrossed. I ran outside to look up at the jet, as it flew overhead, taking Phil Collins from the concert in London to the other concert in the U.S. By the time my guests arrived, I felt unable to eat. All I wanted, was to be a part of this global event, coming together to help people, who through no fault of their own, were suffering. Little by little, I was starting to see how we are all one humanity together on this earth.

My social conscience was being drip fed these nuggets, while my social life was, also, widening my outlook. Interestingly, the church I had so railed against as a teenager, now provided me with some good companions. As well as Helen, I reconnected with my friend Lis, who was living in London. Friends from high school and college, introduced me to their friends and so the circle grew. Supplemented by visitors from my travels, I worked hard and played hard.

Having left Switzerland, I now missed skiing. At Easter and half term, I returned to the slopes and visited my friends over there. One time, after skiing with friends from my old school, I made my way over to see Marianne. At that time, she was working in a farm in the mountains. It felt like real Heidi country. Local children would ski past the house in the morning on their way to school. Going through a door from the kitchen, I was surprised to find myself in a warm barn smelling of sweet hay and cow dung. The deep snow outside meant the body heat of the cattle helped to keep the chalet warm, as well as giving them shelter during the winter. One of Marianne's jobs was to bottle feed the calves and she let me help her. I was surprised at the strength of those young mouths, as they tugged at the teats.

Although Marianne was a teacher, she would work for a few years, save all her money, then take a couple of years off to travel or live in different ways. Since my return to London, I had started to feel more in tune with Marianne again, and our friendship had revitalised.

As I was leaving, we were snuggled in warm clothes, on the back of the tractor, being driven down the snowy mountain slopes. Marianne asked me if I had ever read any books about Native Americans. She then recommended two books that I should try to get. One was about a man called Sun Bear and one about a man called Rolling Thunder. Those books were to have a massive influence on my life.

On my return to London, I ordered them from Waterstones. As they were coming from America, it would be some while. After a couple of months, I had heard nothing, so I went to the shop. The girl looked up the order. She went to the shelves. "I can't believe this," she said. "They arrived, but someone must have put them out instead of keeping them and they have gone."

I decided I must not have been meant to have them yet.

As time went on, I was feeling on a different wavelength from a lot of my friends and colleagues. No-one else seemed to get where I was coming from. I had just finished a relationship which had gone a bit sour. My friend's way to console me was to introduce me to her husband's friend, Matthew. I fell in love. Conversation was easy between us and everything was perfect. Understanding where I was coming from, he made me feel so comfortable. I thought I understood him too. He talked about having had a past life in Italy and because I so quickly felt in tune with him, I wondered whether we may have been together in that life; or at least had known one another in a previous life. The bond between us was very strong, or so I felt.

I was mad about Matthew; too mad.

A month or so later, a holiday to Florence had already been booked with several of my friends, so I went away. I could not stop thinking of him. I sent him an express letter, saying I was missing him. Big mistake!

The next six months were Hell. After having appeared too keen, I was advised by our mutual friend to back off, "Let him do all the chasing." We would meet up, have a wonderful time together, and then he would go quiet on me. Sitting by the phone, waiting for it to ring could be classed as one of the tortures of late twentieth century life. The first week would be agony. The second week it would be a bit better, the third week I would start to get back to normal, the fourth week I would be me and happy again. Then he would ring. We would go out, have a perfect time together and the whole cycle would start again. In the end I started calling him 'Once a month Matthew.'

Beginning to feel I was going crazy, I needed to stop it all. However, the result of doing so, seemed too great. I could not bear to lose touch with the only person I knew who shared my views on the world. On one of our monthly dates, Matthew lent me a book which linked in with our way of thinking. Deciding to find my own copy of this book, felt like the first step to regaining control of my life. At least then I would have a link with this world he had opened to me. After that, I could start to think about finishing the relationship.

I knew Waterstones would not stock this kind of book, so I went hunting in all the 'dodgy' bookshops in Soho. Opening the door, down a dark shadowy side street, I entered the fourth shop I had visited that day. Scanning the gloomy shelves, I tried to find the book I was looking for. As my eyes flitted across the spines, they suddenly registered a familiar title on the shelf. It was not the book I was seeking, but it *was* the book that I'd ordered from Waterstones and never received. Not only that, but *both* books I had ordered were there, sitting side by side on the shelf. It was finally my time to have them. To top it all, on the inside cover of the Sun Bear one was an invitation to a weekend workshop in London. I could not believe it.

Since then, I have learnt that when you are on your spiritual path, this is how things work, but at that point, I was new to it all.

To increase the synchronicity, Marianne then called out of the blue to ask if she could come and stay with me on her way up to Findhorn. It happened to be a couple of days before Sun Bear's weekend workshop. Immediately, I suggested she should come to the workshop with me. She declined, saying that was my path, not hers, but she would set me on my way. She did. On the morning she left, I had to go to school. On my return, I found the table laid, in the beautiful way that Marianne is so good at. Amongst the things she had left for me were candles to light my path, Swiss chocolates to sustain me, a quartz crystal to keep my way clear and a beautiful poem to inspire me.

The workshop was more than everything I had hoped for. After the first day, I was buzzing. It was so in line with everything I had been yearning to find out about for so long, but not been able to vocalise. In the evening, I went round to see my best friend, expecting her and her husband to share my excitement. I bubbled forth about what I had done and experienced. Their reaction was cold shock. I was upset they did not get it but tried not to let it bother me. I was way too high on my new-found life to let anything stop me now. Later, I discovered she thought I had been inculcated into some sort of strange sect, which explained her reaction.

The next day was even better. One of the activities was to visualise a beautiful rainbow in the centre of the circle. We had to place someone we wanted to heal from our lives into the rainbow. In went Matthew. It was so good to let him go from my mind. All the torture over the previous months evaporated. I felt my own power coming back. I was not the helpless little lovesick girl sitting by a phone anymore; I was a woman in charge of my life, choosing where I wanted to go.

At the end of the whole weekend Sun Bear passed around the pipe. We did not smoke it, but we had to think of a wish for ourselves and a wish for someone else, as we held it. (I have since learnt that what he did was not approved of by many First Nations people. I was in ignorance at the time, so I apologise for this.) I did not have to think what to wish for. All I wanted was to find out about my Spirit Guides. The pipe went round. We all thought our *silent* wishes. Sun Bear smoked it, explaining about the sacred aspects of the pipe, how the natural kingdoms are represented in it through the materials it is made from. Then he lit the pipe and told us that as the smoke went up, it carried our prayers to the Great Spirit.

That was the last session. As we were closing, a woman stood up and said, "If anyone wants to learn more about their Spirit Guides, I am running courses on it." I could not believe my ears. How instant was that! The woman was called Dr Helen Ford. Within minutes I had taken her details and arranged to go on her course. She lived in a place called Stourbridge.

Over the next few days, I felt my task was to finish the tortuous relationship with Matthew. I wrote him a letter explaining why, covered it in rainbow colours, collected up his book and drove to where he lived in London. That night I learnt a very valuable lesson. Asking my newly found guides to help me, I said, "If I am not meant to do this, make it difficult for me to find his flat." His flat was in a complicated series of one-way streets. Sometimes I negotiated them with ease. That night however, I got lost and kept getting lost. However, I was determined to complete my mission. Eventually, when I got there, I could see he was in, another rarity. His flat was on the third floor. Stubbornness pushed me on. I posted the book and letter through the door. I could not talk to him in case my resolve was weakened.

He did not get in touch, but a few weeks later, I heard through my friend that he had been furious. Apparently, her husband had never seen him so angry. Matthew could not understand why I had not talked to him, when he was in.

It was another year before I saw him again. We were both invited to our mutual friend's house for a party. Knowing I was going to see him, I prepared myself. Not wanting to show my intense nervousness, I decided to pre-programme myself. First, I meditated to achieve a calm frame of mind. Then I visualised the whole party, putting in the emotions I wanted to feel. I saw myself talking to him calmly and feeling calm inside. I felt reassured. The details were not important, as long as the feelings were there.

It worked. I highly recommend this technique for anyone going into a situation they are worried about. We spent the whole party chatting to each other, like we always used to. It felt so right and easy...until I left. Then all the emotions I had pre-programmed away, re-surfaced and I returned home to become a gibbering wreck.

We met once more, at another party a year later, by which time he had another girlfriend. Again, we seemed magnetised towards each other or maybe I monopolised him. I do not know and will never know. I have never seen him since, although I hear about his life from my friend.

The trouble is because I asked my guides for help, then ignored it; I ended up wondering for a long time afterwards, "What if I hadn't posted it through his door?" This led me to regret, which is not a healthy thing to do. I have followed a different route in life, and I am happy that is the right path. I do not know what would have transpired if I had listened to my guides that night, but if I had done it a different way, then I would not have had the doubt.

Since then, if I ask for help, I have learnt it is important to listen to their advice. They see the bigger picture and know what the consequences could be. It is not as if some thunderbolt will strike if I do not heed them, they are not like that. We have free will but with their help life flows more easily.

CHAPTER 12

"Just as a candle cannot burn without fire, men cannot live without a spiritual life." Buddha

Returning to the glorious beginning of my new spiritual path, I went to see Helen in Stourbridge. Helen was trained as a doctor and had worked in allopathic medicine but had decided to go 'alternative.' Alternative medicine felt very new back then. People had been practicing the different disciplines; homeopathy, acupuncture, herbal medicine and so on for hundreds of years. (My mum was brought up on homeopathy in the early twentieth century, as was the Queen.) However, many people did not seem to know about it, in the way they do now.

Helen had been on courses by a man called Francisco Coll to learn about and connect with her spirit guides. This formed the basis of the knowledge that she started to teach me. Initially she 'read' me. By clearing her head of her own thoughts, she tuned into her guides and listened. "You have thirteen guides who will work with you. If you work with people, you have more guides, because you need them. If you work with objects, for example like an artist who works with paint, you have fewer guides." I discovered that one of my guides was my maternal grandmother, one was my sister Jill, who had died when she was five, and one was a little boy who sat on my shoulder and got me into mischief. It felt very comforting to think that some of my guides were relatives. Jill's tragic death before I was born, always made me long for the sister I never knew.

Helen continued, "Our guides are always with us, but allow us free will, so won't help unless we ask them. Before starting this life, they make a contract with us. If we don't use them, they are unfulfilled as our guides." She taught me how to know when they are there. "You know the days when everything is going right for you and life just flows? You feel great and it all seems easy? That is when your guides are close to you. On the days when things are bad and everything is going wrong, that's when you are blocking your guides." She encouraged me to think of a happy time when I felt great. "That is the same feeling as when your guides are close. That's how to recognise it."

Since learning more about it, I like to explain it as follows. We all vibrate on a frequency, like radio waves. The guides vibrate on a higher frequency. When we are feeling happy, our vibrations tune up to their frequency, which is closer to the true energy that flows through everything and makes life work. When we are feeling like that, we are 'going with the flow.' However, when we feel depressed or low (there is a reason we use these terms), our vibrations are tuned out of their frequency. We do it ourselves, often triggered by events or feelings. Then our guides cannot vibrate on the same frequency. They are still there but we cannot feel them. Blockages appear and life seems much harder. The trick is becoming more aware of those times and learning how to lift ourselves out.

Helen went on to tell us that we all have four gifts. We are endowed with all of them, but in different orders. They are Intuitive, Feeling, Visionary and Prophetic. People who are 'Intuitive' as a first gift, work through sound. Music is often very important to them. Their psychic gift is clairaudience. They are very sensitive to atmosphere, and if they are unaware of it, will pick up any feelings in the room and think they are their own. For example, I might go in a room, feeling fine, and then if the atmosphere is bad, begin to think it is me feeling bad. As a result, Intuitive people need space to clear their energy and love being on their own, particularly when they are feeling rough. I am an Intuitive first, as was Helen. She confirmed this when she 'read' me. She told me the order I have the gifts and it made sense. The intuitive colour is red. An Intuitive is not bothered about the way things look; in fact, they tend not to be bothered about how they look to others.

My second gift is 'feeling' energy. 'Feelers' are very connected to the earth and animals. They love making things with their hands, particularly with clay. Their psychic gift is to heal, particularly through the medium of touch. They tend to be talented at massage and love the company of people. They are very strong inside and unlike the intuitive, if they feel rough, they need the company of people to feel good and boost their inner wobbliness. The feeling colour is blue.

My third gift is prophetic. 'Prophetics' have an inner knowing. A prophetic child is often misunderstood because they 'just know' things. An adult will ask them to explain *how* they know, but they cannot, which upsets them. They are often very dramatic and like to be the centre of the action. They love food and the pleasures of life. They have a strong sense of smell. Their psychic gift is prophecy. Upset Prophetics will comfort themselves by eating. I think the colour is orange.

My last gift is visionary. 'Visionaries' are very keen on the way things look. Their psychic gift is clairvoyance and they are often talented in art, relating well to visual representations. They can visualise how things should be and get very bothered when things do not look right. An upset visionary will go out and buy themselves new clothes to feel better. Their colour is yellow.

As Visionary is my last gift, I tend to be unaware of how things look. It does not really bother me. It drives my husband mad, who is a Visionary as a first gift.

To give a silly example to explain it all; an Intuitive will not bother if they have a rip in their clothes, the Prophetic will make it into a feature, a Feeler will just love the feel of the fabric and weave it around their hands and a Visionary cannot bear it and will buy a new piece of clothing.

Helen taught me how to 'summon' my guides. I had to pass my hands over my crown, then over my forehead. As I did so, I had to think of a phrase that felt comfortable about cleansing my soul and my body. I chose, 'May the Spirit of love cleanse my body, may the Spirit of love cleanse my soul.' She recommended that I did it repeatedly till I felt a tingly sensation. This was an indication that my guides were there. If you want to try it, just choose any phrase that feels comfortable and right for you.

She, also, taught me how to check if things are right. The hardest thing, when you are starting to communicate with your guides, is to distinguish between what are your own thoughts and what is from your guides (or anything else out there). The way to check out any thought or feeling is to make sure your head and heart agree. Your head is like the steering wheel and your heart is like the engine in the car. Your head will point you in a direction, but you need the energy of your heart behind it to make you get there. Sometimes an idea will come into my head, and I will think, "Does that feel right?" If it does, I will go ahead and follow it up. If it does not, I will not do it. Sometimes I have done it, even when it did not feel right and inevitably the decision ends up badly.

On one of the early weekend courses with Helen, we had to pair up and practice 'reading' each other. I was paired up with a chap, who was a little older than me. First, we had to speak about a problem we had. The other person was not allowed to speak, just listen. We each had two minutes to talk. Two minutes is a heck of a long time when you are speaking a monologue. It was very interesting. Outlining the problem did not take long. Then I started to go over it, thinking things through aloud and eventually before the time was up, I had solved the problem myself. The same thing happened when I was the listener. The man solved his own issue. Afterwards Helen pointed out that we all have the answers inside us. No-one else is as skilled as we are at knowing the solution to our own problems. All we need is the space to work it out. In normal conversation, the other person keeps adding their two penn'orth until the topic veers away and nothing is resolved. It was very freeing to know that when I wanted to help someone, the best way is to give them enough space and time to work it out for themselves. All I must do, is listen.

The next exercise was to close our eyes and see the other person, describing colours, landscape, anything we could see around them. What I saw for the other person was private and would not be right for me to share. However, I can share what he saw for me. Initially he described me as being a golden being, radiating light, with lots of children gathered around me. I could not take this, I was not some radiant being, I was just an ordinary person. Immediately I thought this, he said, "Oh it's all gone dark." I relaxed a little then and he said he could see me standing further away on a hill, still glowing, looking down at some children playing.

It was an important lesson in realising we only allow others to read us if we give our permission and that we can block anything we do not like.

Once I had been introduced to my guides, my first request was to see Grandma. I sat quietly meditating and in my mind's eye, found myself in a sort of no man's land. I got the feeling it was a halfway place where Grandma could come to meet me. Grandma stood quietly, tall and regal, whilst I danced round her telling her how much I loved her and missed her. Beyond Grandma, I made out a figure who was shadowy and more in the background. I realised that the figure was Grandpa, who had passed away when I was about ten.

As I registered who they all were, I suddenly felt an unexpected beam of warm, golden light pouring from the right-hand side. It was very powerful, very loving and determined not to be ignored. With a shock I remembered my other gran, my mum's mother. She had died when I was sixteen, after several years of dementia. I had forgotten about her true personality because the character that took over in dementia was unlike her own. My gran was amazing. She brought up a family of eight surviving children, (losing two more as babies) ran all the practical sides of a household and supported my grandpa in his role as a Methodist minister. He was very intellectual and other worldly, whilst she was totally down to earth and practical. As a girl at the end of the nineteenth century, she had gone to a Quaker School where she had learnt metal work and woodwork; unheard of for a woman in those days. She was the one that changed the light bulbs, wielded a screwdriver, and would get up at six every morning to bake bread. She had strong upper arm muscles from years of pounding washing in a dolly tub and kneading dough.

I was still a child when the dementia set in; from then on, I lost my name and was called 'the little girl' while her daughters were called by her sister's names. Her main carer was Auntie Phyllis, so the other sisters tried to support her as much as possible. Once or twice a week, Mum would take her and Gran up into the Derbyshire Dales to give them both a change of scenery.

One time, Mum and Phyllis had got out of the car to look at a Well Dressing. Suddenly Mum looked up to see the car sailing down the road with Gran sitting regally in the front seat. As Mum ran after the car, a coach appeared round the corner. Mum frantically waved at it to stop. The car crossed in front of the coach and bumped into a wall. Everyone in the coach glared at Mum, as if it was her fault. Gran had released the hand brake then sat back to enjoy the fun. Luckily, Gran was unhurt, and the car was not too badly harmed. After that Mum made sure Gran sat in the back. As her condition worsened, Mum and her other children, mainly the ones who lived locally, took it in turns to be with her and share the room with her at night. As Mum said, she had been such a wonderful mum to them all, it was the least they could do.

Following her death, Gran's house was put up for sale. The people who bought it told us that initially they did not like the house from the outside. However, when they walked in, they said they could feel the love and happiness that had been created by Gran and the family.

I reckoned that Gran had spent all her life giving and found it hard to receive. As a result, for her life to be in balance before she left it, she had dementia, to redress this in-balance. This meant she had to be looked after and receive from others. It is just my own theory, but it makes sense to me. Now she is in the spirit world, she is a wonderful loving force and looks after me and probably the rest of her grandchildren with the love and care she showed all her family in life.

When I told Mum of my experience in meditation, she said, "Oh yes, that's my mum alright. She'd be very upset that you had forgotten her."

* * *

I learnt a lot from Helen. It was a wonderful feeling to end the week at school and know I was heading north, sometimes to Stourbridge but even better, to North Wales. She had a beautiful cottage in the mountains that she had inherited. Working hard, she had managed to purchase land around it, so we felt an incredible sense of freedom on arrival there. We roamed around the hills, went skinny dipping in the pool under the waterfall, sunbathed in the summer by the stream, perched on the rocks dotted around the valley or just soaked up the wonderful views. From her cottage, the mountains rose to our right and behind us, whilst the stream fell away down a gentle valley, which then flowed into a bigger river. I remember days when I stood and gazed at the beauty, as the sun reflected on the shimmering river, glowing silver and gold, as it wound its way through wooded and green landscapes to the distant shining sea. It felt like looking at Hobbit land. If we walked behind the house, over the tufty moorland beside the tumbling, peaty stream, we would crest the hill and view the total opposite. Mordor greeted us, with black slate sheering every slope, loose and threatening to our every step. Even there though, nature was working hard to soften and change. Tiny pockets of green were clinging to life which would, in time, grow and transform this hellscape, into a garden of beauty.

Arriving exhausted after a long seven-hour drive, I would meet my fellow participants in the weekend workshop and inevitably be judgemental. Again, this was a big lesson for me. No matter what my first impressions were, by the end of the weekend I had changed them. If nothing else, I learnt we should never judge a book by its cover. Helen provided a space for us, normally in the cosy, sheepskin covered, stone floored room at the back. There we would explore our inner feelings, expose our souls and feel safe. Inevitably once you have been with people who have exposed their vulnerability, you cannot do anything but love them for it. I truly believe that everyone's soul is beautiful. The layers on top might be difficult to handle but the person underneath is pure and lovely. Everyone needs a chance to find that beauty in them and once unleashed it can do nothing but good.

During these sessions, everyone else seemed to have had a difficult relationship with their parents. My only problem was that I put mine on a bit of a pedestal. Other than that, I love them deeply, they were great parents, and I could not complain. I did try to find things, but I had done all my rebelling as a teenager. Adulthood showed me how lucky I had been. I was beginning to understand how important parenting is and how every little thing that is done to a child is embedded in their psyche, good and bad.

The longer I live, the more I appreciate that every child deserves the best love, care and attention if they are to flourish. Sadly, in our present world, this seems to have been replaced by the need to give materially rather than companionship and time. Children are ignored, as parents talk on their mobiles to important 'others.' Who could be more important than their own child? As teachers, we see the difference. Little ones who have been given all the loving attention they need from birth (and before) tend to be happy, confident and content. Frequently, attention seeking, insecure children have often been ignored or dumped on others, while parents are busy with their own lives. It is not rocket science, but I sometimes wonder why society does not value and encourage the early bonding, caring and loving relationship between parents and child more than it does. Preschool initiatives, to help struggling parents, get their funding cut. In contrast, nursery places are supported, encouraging parents to go to work and leave their child. The older I get, the keener I feel it. If we want to change and improve society it must start at home, with children being given attention, security and love. Simple, but then most solutions are. However, the benefits are long-term and generally politicians only want quick fixes.

* * *

As time went on, I met lots of interesting people up at Helen's. One man I remember was called Don, who was a dowser. He not only dowsed for water and metals in the earth, but he also dowsed for ley lines. Don explained, "If there is a bad ley (or energy) line in the earth then it can affect the people living above it, particularly if their house was built on one."

"I go to houses where people have asked for my help. A bad ley line can cause people to be unhappy or even ill. I dowse and realign it. Sometimes I do that by putting stakes in the ground at some distance from the property, where the ley line is. The line then changes direction and can be realigned so that it is safer. Instantly, people get better, start to get on and feel a lot happier in their home."

He told us that he belonged to the Fountain group in Brighton and described how it started. "From the mid-sixties to early seventies all the bikers and scooter riders would meet up every year in Brighton and have massive battles. There were horrific injuries and sometimes deaths. As residents of Brighton, we dreaded it. One year, we decided to do something. We'd noticed that the brawling was centred around the fountain in Brighton. Focussing on that, we dowsed the energy lines. You will never guess what we discovered."

"The lines reflected the same pattern that was under Nuremburg, at the time of the Hitler rallies. Working as a group, we realigned the ley lines. We thought they would spread out along the coast, but they went up the main road to London and stopped at a particular point."

"The following year, the bikers and scooters started the ride down to Brighton. However, the helmet law had been introduced that year and as no self- respecting biker would be seen dead in a helmet, few were wearing them. The police were out in force, which happened to be the same point where the realigned lines had stopped. They halted the riders, sent them home and the fights never happened again in Brighton."

In fact, Brighton has now become one of the focus towns of the New Age movement. I wonder how much of it is down to that original group of dowsers?

On my visits to Helen's, I began to build a friendship with a great person called Pat. She was lots of fun and had been with Helen from the early days of her ventures into alternative therapies. Kind and loving, her house became my base when I was in Stourbridge. Round the corner, was another lovely couple called John and Marilyn. John used to go to Helen's workshops and gradually over the years I grew to know and love them both.

John always says he initially remembers seeing me at Helen's first Healing conference. In those days (mid-eighties) Healing conferences were very new. Helen had a vision that she should do it and it turned into a magical, wonderful event. About seventy people attended talks, performances and workshops.

It was my introduction to Tim Wheater's playing; he gave a performance and transported us to beautiful places with the pure clear sound of his flute. Other speakers came on and talked of the power of crystals, aromatherapy, reflexology, and many other ideas, all very new to us at that time. Nowadays, it is hard to remember they were once regarded as whacky and weird. But they were. When I used to talk about these things, people would look at me as if I came from another planet.

I have accepted that I learn about things a bit ahead of the masses; not in the ground-breaking pioneer section, but in the bit that comes after that. I believe my role is to talk about things, not care what people think of me and get the new ideas out there till they become accepted. I am not alone in this role; there are hundreds, thousands, even millions doing the same. It is because we are all working separately in our own environments that we often feel alone. I have learnt to trust and know many others like me are all working towards a better way of being in the world.

The best speaker and one that has had the most lasting impression on me was a Buddhist monk. He stood at the front, a little round chap in saffron robes and said not a thing. He beamed at us all and then began to chuckle. His mirth was so infectious, that the whole hall was soon filled with laughter, but no-one knew why. He spoke very little, compared with the other presenters, but his main message was to find joy and laughter, which is very healing. I cannot remember if he got us to do this, or if we did it at a later conference, but everyone had to lie in a long line with their heads lying on the stomach of the person next to them. One person started giggling, and then it spread like wildfire, conveyed through our centres, wobbling with joy. We were exhausted afterwards but uplifted and refreshed.

After my weekends with Helen, I was so fired up and enthusiastic for my new life and beliefs, I could not keep them to myself. I am sure I bored everyone sick in the staffroom. There was no National Curriculum in those days, and we had the freedom to try out new ideas and ways of teaching.

I decided I would ask the children if they would like to have a go at seeing what pictures came into their heads when they were in a quiet space listening to music. They agreed to have a go. I told them to sit very still and find a quiet space inside themselves through breathing in and out gently. They closed their eyes, I put on some music, probably some Tim Wheater, and silently asked my guides to help them have a wonderful experience. For nine-year olds, they did very well, sitting in silence, listening to the music. When it was over, I asked for their reactions. The class exploded with hands, all eager to tell me of the amazing visions they had seen. Some had seen the ceiling open and angels come in, some had seen fabulous worlds, some had observed beautiful colours and one little chap put up his hand and said he had seen God and he had a blue nose! I asked them if they would like to have a go at painting what they saw. I have never seen a class so eager to get paint onto paper to express their visions. Fired up with their enthusiasm, it helped me to feel that what I was doing was okay, even if other teachers thought I was off the wall.

Over time, I learned to be careful about what I said about my new beliefs. Some people took exception to them, but mainly they were just sceptical and thought I was bonkers. Luckily, I did not care too much if people thought that of me. It was more important to express my truth. Not to do so would harm me, or at worst make me ill. The only thing that mattered was to be as kind, thoughtful and caring to others as possible. So long as people recognised that in me, I did not mind what else they thought.

CHAPTER 13

"This above all: to thine own self be true, and it must follow, as the night the day, thou canst not then be false to any man." William Shakespeare.

By now, I had been on my new 'spiritual path' for about a year and at the school for three years. It felt like time for a move, so I decided to look for a job in the East End. My tai chi class was over in Stratford and many of my college friends lived around the Stoke Newington area. I accepted a post in Bethnal Green, giving in my notice at Whit half term.

One of the teachers in my old school could not understand my ability to trust. It seemed to upset him that I had a house to sell and had not found a house to move to over the other side of London, with my new job starting in two months. The conversation in the staffroom often went like this:

"So, what happens if you don't sell your house in time?"

"I will."

"You may say you will, but there is no guarantee you will."

"I *know* I will sell my house and find a new one to buy before the end of the summer holidays."

"Yes, but what if you don't?"

"That doesn't come into the equation because I will."

"Don't you think you should have a back-up plan?"

"Why?"

"In case you have nowhere to live?"

"That won't be a problem because I will have a place," and so on. He could not understand how I knew it would all work out. My logic was thus: if I entertained the possibility of not finding anywhere to live, that would be creating a negative thought pattern and presenting it as an option to the Universe. That was to my detriment, why would I do that? I totally believed everything would work out perfectly and it did.

My new flat in Stamford Hill was a recently completed conversion of a large, terraced house into three apartments. I loved it. The use of space was imaginative and perfect for my needs. The gracious front room had windows to the floor, with a bathroom sandwiched between it and the bedroom. From the entrance space, some steps led down to the kitchen which opened into the garden. From the kitchen a separate flight of steps led up to my lodger's room which was directly above the kitchen. He was self-contained and so was I. As I came home, he would be setting off for his night shift at the BBC World Service. It suited us both perfectly.

By now the connection with my guides was growing stronger. Asking them for parking spaces was my way to practice. They are great at that, provided you give them enough time. If I ask as I am about to park, it is a bit unfair to expect them to create somewhere; but if I give them a decent amount of time, there will be several for me to choose from. It never ceases to amaze me. At one point I wondered if it were too mundane a thing to ask for. However, it was something simple and it could be easily verified. It helped to build up my trust and confidence in them, so it was fine.

One day I was changing the base plate on the distributor in my old blue Beetle. I had never done it before, so I got out the manual and started to take it to bits. All went well till I reached a point where I was really stuck. I did not know what to do. Dad was at home in Manchester. I could not ask him. No-one I knew in London could help, so I asked my guides to get me a spirit mechanic. Within seconds, I suddenly knew exactly what to do and completed the job successfully.

I loved that car. It was like a tank. I would use it to open the school gates, I would drive round London at high speed (because you had to, to keep up), cutting up taxi drivers, with my A-Z in one hand and my foot on the accelerator. I remember one of my friends from Switzerland, coming to visit me. He hid on the floor at the back, not wanting to see what I was doing. My driving has thankfully changed since then.

As my confidence grew, Helen encouraged me to start up my own groups, teaching about Spirit Guides. The sessions naturally engendered confidences, so it was hardly surprising that friendships grew. A young man, called Chris, answered one of my adverts, in turn introducing me to his friends and his cousin, Susie. It was not long before I was sharing the long journey up to Helen's with like-minded companions. One trip to Helen's was a particularly special one.

We decided to celebrate the Winter Solstice and Helen asked me to create the ceremony. I researched it. There was no internet in those days, so finding a few odd publications about tree-lore and old customs; I gleaned what I could from them. Combining that with intuition, a ceremony gradually came together in my head. The carol, 'The Holly and the Ivy' seemed to hold a potent message, particularly when I discovered that the Holly King takes over from the Oak King at mid-winter solstice.

I was driving up with one of Chris' friends in my Beetle. On entering Wales, it started to snow. The song 'Walking in the air' floated over the airwaves. Driving through gently falling snowflakes, which were starting to lighten the night-time landscape, I felt amazing, filled with pure happiness. Suddenly a deer ran across the road in the headlights and leapt off into the fields. It was as if the carol was coming to life. Immediately we noticed a copse of trees. Pulling over, we climbed out of the car and found what we had been looking out for, an oak log for the solstice fire. Arriving triumphantly at Helen's, we pulled up in front of the cottage. The stars blazed down on us through the frosty air, as we entered the warmth and companionship that had become so familiar.

The next day was the Winter Solstice. We drove down to a wooded part of the valley where Helen had arranged with the landowner to collect wood. There we found ivy, fuel for the fire and some holly. I told everyone to collect a leaf each.

Later, as dusk fell, we gathered round the fire we had built, outside the cottage. We placed a large circle of ivy around the edge of the fire. Flames flared up and we stood, absorbing the welcome warmth. Then I asked everyone to hold their leaves, "Speak into your leaf and tell it what you want to release from the old year." Quiet mutterings rippled round the circle as people thought of unpleasant things that they had dealt with and wanted to be free from in the coming year. Then we all threw the leaves on the fire, letting go of old habits, ways of being or emotions. The flames flickered as each leaf joined the inferno. Next, we turned outwards, our backs warmed by the heat, our faces looking out into the blackness of the night surrounding us. Facing the dark unknown, with the security of the light from the fire behind us, we welcomed in the New Year; asking for the qualities we wanted in our lives for the coming months. Turning back to face each other in the circle, we took hold of the ivy and carried it into the house together.

Once indoors, we placed it in front of a holly wreath we had made, which was lying by the hearth. One person carried a flaming stick from the outside fire which we used to light the yule log in the indoor fire. Then we sat down, ate, drank, and told stories. It was a great night. The next day, as we left, we all took a piece of the Yule log to carry with us into the next year. Many of us used it to light our Christmas fire the following year.

The familiar Christmas celebrations felt insipid and meaningless compared with the simple and lovely ceremony we had experienced in Wales. As the years have gone on, combining the Festival of Light to darken our shortest day, with the New Year to welcome back the longer days makes more sense. It feels that the simple Solstice ceremony would be so much better than the commercial hype that weighs down midwinter.

* * *

Through all the work I was doing and the self-knowledge I was developing, I realised that whatever you put out, you get back. One time I was driving very early to Brighton to a Healing Fair. I had a boot full of crystals. It was about five in the morning. Suddenly, blue lights appeared behind me. A police car pulled me over. In the past whenever I had even seen a police car behind me, I would panic and feel guilty, wondering what I had done wrong. This time I was not bothered. I got out and looked enquiringly at the police lady.

"Where are you going?" she queried.

"Brighton, to a Healing Fair." She did not know what that was, so I explained it to her. Then she asked what I had in my boot. "Crystals," I answered. In those days very few people knew about them, unlike today. She asked me why I had them, so I enthusiastically told her how they picked up negative energies and absorbed them, then how they had to be cleansed in running water, whilst visualising white light pouring through them. She looked a bit bemused as if she did not quite know how to respond. Then she smiled, commented they could do with some in the police station and sent me on my way. Even though she probably thought I was a bit strange, she responded well to me because I was true to myself, not hiding anything.

I truly believe that we are born to play a part in life's rich dance. If we were all to follow our dreams and do a job that we love to do, then society would work perfectly. Instead of rewarding jobs which have higher status in society, if we rewarded people for doing their job well, with love and enthusiasm, then we would all be a lot happier. Why should someone who enjoys cleaning, which is so vital to our society, have less value placed on their work, than someone who dislikes their highly paid job and is grumpy to everyone they deal with? Who is contributing more to society? If everyone were happier, the health care bill would reduce, social workers would be less stressed and over worked, teachers would have an easier job and so on.

Do you ever question if you are in the right job? If you do, give yourself an opportunity to sit quietly and focus on what you would love to do. Do not be limited by possibilities. Have fun drawing, sketching, or writing down your dream, then see how you feel as you write. If you feel fired up and excited, then it is for you. If you do not, then keep dreaming and drawing till something comes that you do feel good about.

If you feel you are in the right job but not totally happy with it, then have a go at the following exercise. Write down all the positives and all the negatives. Ask yourself, "Why do I feel those are negatives?" Can you turn them around to make them feel more positive? If not, what can you do about it? You have the power to create and change your life. No-one else does, you are the one in charge. Sometimes the decisions appear very risky, but if it feels right then it is the right thing to do. Later I will tell you of a technique I used to make one of the biggest decisions in my life, which felt very scary at the time.

One time when I was up at Helen's in Wales, I met a person called Jane. She asked me how I had come across Helen. I explained our connection at Sun Bear's workshop. She asked if I was interested in real First Nations Americans, to which I responded in the affirmative. We stayed in touch. She introduced me to a group of people who were part of an Indigenous American support network in Britain. I learnt that Sun Bear was not regarded very highly by this community. He, and others, were criticised for selling Native spirituality. I was made aware that everything else had been taken from them; their homes, their land, the animals they used for survival, their culture, their language and now this. Their sacred spirituality was being exploited for individual's profit. I began to understand how it must feel. Sun Bear was not as bad as some of them. His weekend workshop was twenty-five pounds. There was one guy, called Harley Swift Deer, who sold weekend workshops for hundreds of pounds (in the eighties) and was making a lot of money for himself and his devotees. I had an inner radar, guided by my pocket, which basically allowed me to steer clear of people like him. When I got to meet genuine supporters of Native Americans, not just 'wannabees,' I learnt that their nickname for Harley Swift Deer was Harley Fast Buck!

Through our common interest, Jane and I became friends. One day she informed me that a First Nations American Elder, called Janet McCloud, from the Tulalip tribe was coming to England. I offered my home for her, as I was aware that she would appreciate a warm, comfortable place to stay, and I felt honoured to be able to play host to her.

My usual approach to people did not seem to be quite so warmly accepted by Janet. Looking back on it now, I see she was very justified in her behaviour. I was probably putting her on a pedestal, as usual, and she was showing me not to do that to people. She complained about my pans which were aluminium and was disgusted to see tinned salmon in my cupboards. I learnt that she came from the Northwest coast where salmon fishing was the traditional food source for her people. In the Federal Treaty Rights, they had been given the right to fish, but Washington State kept saying it was illegal for First Nations people to do so. There had been arrests and her husband had been thrown in jail. To demonstrate her rights, she persisted in fishing and was, also, incarcerated. Meanwhile, the large canning factories and recreational fishing were decimating the salmon population, but the tribe, who fished sustainably, were being blamed for it.

75

By buying the tinned salmon I was contributing to this process, whilst claiming to support Indigenous Americans. I understood her anger. I began to start connecting my buying choices with the affect it has on the lives of others. In her short stay with me, Janet had a strong impact on my life. I had no idea who she was at the time. Later, I discovered what an amazing woman she was. She achieved a lot in her life to change the lives of First Nations people.

On her arrival, Janet had asked to see Stonehenge and Avebury. Jane and another friend Angie had arranged to take her in Angie's van. They asked if I would like to join them. Angie's son was to drive, so we were a party of five. I was thrown into a massive dilemma. They were going on a school day. I would have to bunk off work for a day, something I had never ever done before. I was brought up to be very conscientious and take my responsibilities seriously. It would feel terrible having to lie and say I was ill, but I was aware that this was a chance of a lifetime. How could I turn down the opportunity to visit ancient, sacred sites with someone who had more understanding of their significance and purpose, than probably anyone else I would meet in my life? I tossed and turned in bed, trying to make my decision. In the end, it was no contest. I would have to lie. I ended up feeling so bad, that I made myself poorly over it and was genuinely ill on the day after the trip. That aside, I have never regretted it. It gave me a unique understanding that I could never have achieved otherwise.

As we approached Stonehenge, Salisbury Plain glowered in a dull light. An army manoeuvre was taking place and two massive tanks were flying above us, supported between four helicopters. Everything seemed to reinforce the concept of Stonehenge being a masculine energy, protruding from the male dominated plain, connecting with the Sun. In many cultures around the world, the Sun is regarded as a representative of the male giver of life to the nurturing female Earth.

In those days, it was just after Stonehenge had been shut off from tourists wandering among the stones. As we were walking towards it, I remarked to Janet that it was sad that we were not allowed amongst the monumental stones anymore. "No, it is not," she retorted. "It is quite right. It is a very powerful place and if people who have no understanding or respect are allowed in it, then it can have serious consequences." As if to emphasis the point a young American woman screeched to her friend, "Photograph me, in this position, as if I'm the Heel Stone, with Stonehenge behind me." She threw herself into a posture and they all screeched and laughed raucously. Quite a few people were at the monument, but as we approached, they all seemed to melt away, including the American tour party. The half-light of the misty sun gave a calm, quiet feeling around us. Gradually all other sounds drifted off as we arrived near the perimeter fence.

Janet belonged to the Crow Clan. On the top of every stone, a large crow sat, observing us. As we came to a standstill near the stones, they all took off as one, flew in a circle around our heads and then flew away. "A welcoming party," she commented.

We walked in silence round the site and ended up at the Heel Stone. She then quietly proceeded to do an unobtrusive ceremony. I waited till she had finished, then asked her what she had felt. She told me that the stones were very powerful beings. She felt them lean over and sense her and who she was, before resuming their place.

After Stonehenge we moved on to Woodhenge, and then as the afternoon wore on, we neared Avebury. The village nestles amongst the stones, reinforcing the image of this circle being feminine, nurturing and protecting.

Wandering round the stone circle, Janet stopped and spent time with every stone. I wondered what she was doing but had learnt to wait and be patient. After she had finished, she explained that she was waking up the stones. At one point she found a stone that had been half buried. She told us it was anxious not to be overlooked and worried it would be forgotten because it was only partially visible. After a break for some tea in the van, night had fallen. It was full moon; the reason this particular day was chosen for the trip.

The stones glowed with a silvery light and I was eager to be out there amongst them again. Angie decided to stay with the van, so Jane, Janet and I walked to another part of the circle. It was a velvet night; we were by three stones that were separated from the others by a road and houses. They stood near us, seeming very tall and majestic, as we gathered ourselves in a group. Suddenly Janet said, "There are three women and three stones, we shall do a ceremony." A shiver of anticipation ran through me, as I felt honoured to be included. To this day, I cannot remember whether Janet sang in English or another language, but I remember the images conjured up in my mind as she sang. All the stones in the circle appeared to be glowing masses of white energy, pulsating with life; a much slower life than ours, but definitely alive. Emanating a pure sense of being, they enveloped us in their circle, including us as partners in their dance. I do not know how long we were there or how long it went on for, but it felt wonderful.

On the long journey home in the van, I closed my eyes, wanting to hold on to the vision and relive its beauty and feeling of oneness. As I drifted off, I felt myself back in the circle at Avebury. The stones were there, glowing white, pulsating with their living energy, the ditch around the circle was deep and I was on a horse riding round the circle, following the ditch. I wanted the horse and myself to be white, but the vision would not allow that. The horse and I were bright red. On my return, I discovered I had started my monthly period. I often used to dream of red at that time.

Sometime later, I saw Sun Bear again. I told him of my vision. He cited the large white horse carved out of the hillside in the chalky southern Downs and told me that the white horse is the Spirit of England. He interpreted my vision as the women (or the feminine energy) will be the ones to save Britain.

Seeing stones as living beings was a very new idea to me, but it made sense. Everything on this earth is living; it all vibrates at different frequencies, so why can't stones be the same, particularly stones that have been imbued with love and reverence over centuries. Why can't they be living, but on a slower speed than us? Many cultures believe the Earth is a living being, so should not the very stones that form her, be a form of life; albeit very different from ours? Some old legends of stone circles refer to them as having been people turned to stone. There is always an element of truth in old legends, pointing us to an understanding, long lost.

Several months later I was talking about my experiences to someone I had met. She related her vision, which gave a very plausible explanation as to why Avebury was formed.

She was told that the Earth wanted humans to recognise this area as special. A very valuable herb started to grow, that was only found there and nowhere else. It had amazing healing properties which caused people to travel from far and wide. Initially, the area was covered by the herb. Then it started to shrink. The people were worried, so they created a ditch around it to protect it. The herb shrank more, so a circle of stones was built around the plants. It shrank further, so an inner circle was created. Finally, it disappeared altogether. By then, Avebury had been established as sacred space for people to come to. I have not heard a more rational or better explanation. It feels true to me, so I have accepted this vision as my own understanding of how Avebury came into being. I leave it you to decide on your own views.

CHAPTER 14

"You are a powerful, unlimited eternal soul who is here to enjoy the experience of creativity and contribute to humanity's evolution."
Unknown

Every year Findhorn would hold a conference. Each year had a different focus. I noticed that afterwards, new ways of doing things would filter into the mainstream of society. For example, they held a conference on Management. In the successive years, business management courses were revolutionised. Managers started going on self-awareness and team building courses, unheard of in the early eighties.

The conference I attended was called a Healing Conference and it marked a personal shift on my path for me, away from my initial teachers, to one of my own creation. On a wider scale it marked a change in the attitude to medicines and healing. From then on it became gradually more acceptable for alternative remedies to be used alongside allopathic medicine, until now hypnotherapy, acupuncture and other traditions are accepted as complimentary ways of treatment alongside the mainstream.

Before attending any course or conference at Findhorn, they request that people take part in a Findhorn Experience week. This is for the participants to understand the context and meaning of where they are. I duly signed up for it.

It was a fascinating week, so great to be amongst others of my kind who believed in fairies, devas and the elementals of nature. We had to do something in every area of the community, working in the kitchens (we had to love the vegetables we were peeling), working in the gardens, (we had to love the compost and the earth) and cleaning (even the toilets had 'love me' labels on them).

We were also shown round the site, including the iconic Universal Hall. The tale of the building was related to us. "When the walls were halfway up, we ran out of money to pay the local builder. Members of the community had a meeting and agreed that they could do the job themselves. The task seemed long and laborious, when one of the members suggested *asking the stones* where they want to go." The result was amazing. From then on, instead of stones being cut and laid in rows, they were beautifully moulded and fitted into each other like a magnificent jigsaw puzzle. Not only that, but the task turned to one of joy and creativity, as they communicated with the stones, never quite knowing where the next one would go or how it would fit in.

We also experienced different workshops, one of which was a sweat lodge. Again, I have since learnt that it is not an activity to be undertaken lightly or for money. It is a very sacred ritual which forms part of the Plains tribe's culture. However, I did not know any better at the time and got a lot out of the experience. Sadly, not everyone does. I have heard of some cases of badly run sweats in Sedona, Arizona, which were led by white people posing as authorities on the subject, where people have died.

The one in Findhorn that I experienced was very beautiful. We walked a long way to the sparkling river and choose some stones. We were told that the stones would be sweating and giving of themselves for us, so we had to respect them and sweat to carry them back. We did. The sweat lodge was built with the fire in front. A fire keeper sat by the fire and his job was to tend to the fire and pass in the heated stones. The lodge represented the womb of Mother Earth.

We crawled through the entrance then sat in darkness around the pit of heat where the stones were placed. As we entered, we had to acknowledge we were doing this not just for ourselves but for all our friends and relations in both the human and wider animal families. I cannot remember all the details of the ceremony, but I do recall loving the heat, steam, darkness and sense of being a part of the earth. When it came to my turn to pray, I felt a deep sense of connection to the Mother Earth and took so long with my prayer that I had to be told to hurry up by the facilitator, because others were feeling the heat. Anyone could leave if the heat and steam from the water was too much for them. By this stage there were about two thirds of us left. Finally emerging at the end, we cleaned ourselves off in cold water. It felt amazing.

No other sweat lodge I have experienced matched that one. I now know it is wrong for me to run them, as I am not an Indigenous

American and it is not my culture. Several years later I learnt a very important lesson relating to sweats. A friend wanted me to run a sweat lodge. She told me to lead it. "You have been in sweat lodges you can do it."

"I'm not an expert. I've only experienced a couple. It would be disrespectful to Native Americans to assume I can run a ceremony from such scant knowledge and understanding."

"You can do anything, as long as you ask your guides."

I did not feel right doing it.

She continued, "Well I'm doing it anyway. You can lend your knowledge or not..."

I learnt a lot from what happened next. We went ahead with it, but in the lodge, there was a power struggle for control between us. The sweat lodge was cold. It was a valuable lesson for me in not going against my intuition. It also marked the beginning of the end of that friendship, which faded out after that.

As the Experience week ended, they asked me if I would facilitate a group in the following week's Conference. I felt very flattered to be singled out. I agreed.

The Conference itself was a real watershed for me. It marked the release of my early teachers and the moment where I 'came of age' in my spiritual development. Both Sun Bear and Helen spoke at the Conference, yet I did not choose either of their workshops. I was captivated by Caroline Myss and her remote healing. Amazed by her abilities to heal, I sat enthralled, listening to how she had cured even AIDs, which at the time was the new horror disease. Princess Diana was challenging people's attitude towards it and Caroline Myss was managing to heal people who had it. Her understanding of how people's mind sets could exacerbate or heal illness was fascinating. Even though I enjoyed her talk, I still did not feel the pull for her workshop.

At a break, I observed a woman singing a pure clear note of perfection into a crystal. The rock responded by glowing with greater clarity and purity. When she got up to speak, I knew she was the one I wanted to work with. Her name was Molly Scott.

Being an Intuitive, working with sound was perfect for me. I have never regretted it, using a lot of her ideas in school. We started by tuning our bodies up with sound. This entailed flopping over and starting with a low note, gradually singing our hands up our bodies till we were stretched up and at our highest notes. Next, we had to choose the name we wished to be called by for the workshop. Having chosen, we then went through different exercises to free up our voices and learn to let our voices sing with no inhibition. It was wonderful. Very rarely are we in situations where we can let our voices make whatever tune or melody we like. Once we had reached that freeing stage, we took it in turns to stand in the middle of the circle while everyone else sang our chosen names to us. It was good to sing, but equally lovely to receive. Molly stressed the importance of singing as a gift to that person, as one is very sensitive and vulnerable in the centre of the circle. Very few of us were singers in our daily lives. We improvised any note we wanted, yet we managed to create the most amazing and pleasing harmony. The bond we felt, having sung together, felt unique and special.

Each workshop had to report back to the conference about their experiences. Our group got together and decided we would not explain anything. Instead, we positioned ourselves around the Universal Hall. When it was our turn, we all stood up in unison and started to sing. This time we sang our free harmonies using Molly's name. She did not know we were going to do it and was very moved. We were greeted by a flood of appreciation. Lots of people told me afterwards that they wished they had chosen Molly.

Molly sang a beautiful song called 'We are all one Planet.' I loved the words and ended up teaching it to children in several different schools. It always got a very positive response. In the school in East London, there was a wide range of children whose families had originated from many different parts of the planet. Asking for volunteers from each language group, I got a little team together. We worked on translating each line of the song so that every line was in a different language. Finally, they helped me to teach the rest of the school their translations, so we could sing it in assembly. I hope it felt empowering to the children, with their own languages being acknowledged in that way. It sounded good when we all sang it, if a little disjointed!

On a personal level, I learnt how to sing the Earth, from Molly, which was to give me some very powerful experiences a few years later.

It was great to be in Findhorn with Helen and Pat, who were there in the second week for the conference. Pat's teenage daughter and one of Helen's teenage sons had come along for the experience. I loved their acerbic comments on the 'Love me' messages posted on the toilets.

One night Helen called us all together. "Guidance has told me to to do some rescue trance work. There are a lot of confused souls around Findhorn." We did a lot of rescue work in those days. Helen was very committed to helping lost souls who needed guiding home.

The souls were not the only ones to benefit. The members of the group taking part found it illuminating and helpful. We always fully protected ourselves before starting, ensuring that we were very firm with the spirits, explaining that we would only be available during the session and that we were to be kept clear at other times. Invoking our guides to surround us in light and protection at the beginning, we would ask for their help to assist the souls whom we were helping home. No-one ever left their body during this; we would just sit back and allow the soul to come in. At first the spirit would be given a chance to express itself, then the soul would be encouraged to look for the light and go with their angels to find peace.

Inevitably the 'lost' souls were caught up in thought forms that we had attracted because of our own 'hang ups.' Once they were in touch with their guides, the soul would then give us advice which was always very wise and helpful; to stop us falling into the same emotional traps in the future. It is a unique way to experience how someone else feels.

The way I understand it is that we are all energy. Energy never ceases to exist; it just changes its form. When we are born, our soul-energy attaches itself to our body. When we die, it leaves and returns to Source. All a soul ever wants to do is express itself, ideally in its clearest form, which is pure, universal love.

Energy vibrates at different frequencies. When we are feeling great, we are vibrating at a much higher frequency than when we are feeling rough. If a soul dies when it is not in balance, for whatever reason, then it can get caught in the thought patterns it had when it was alive. (This is why religions stress the importance of belief in life after death. If people have a strong belief that on their death they will go to heaven, that will over-ride any other thought pattern.) Its guides are always there, beside it, waiting. They are amazingly patient. The soul might have blocked out their guides through a negative thought pattern. Vibrating on the frequency of that thought, the soul is still on a plane of existence accessible to humans.

Along comes a human who is feeling rough and is on the same 'thought pattern' vibration. The confused soul thinks, "Oh I recognise this!" It slips in and uses that person to express the emotion it is caught up in. When it has expressed itself, it feels better and leaves. As the human expresses themselves they, also, feel better. They move out of the vibration of the soul and the soul loses the connection.

We have all experienced it. You feel niggled, then it builds, and you become irritated, then it builds, and you start to get cross. You express your anger; have a good shout or cry, then you feel a lot better. The way I understand it, the 'build up' is the souls we attract. When we express ourselves, they leave. However, it is not a long-term happy solution, as they are still not able to get home to the Source. They need to go there, where they can be nourished, replenished, and decide if they want another body or if they want to stay over there. The more we can work on clearing the confused souls, the lighter life will be for everyone. Then when people get upset, they do not have every other soul in the area latching on; they just have themselves to deal with.

The souls themselves just need a helping hand and the will to start looking, so that is what we provided. Sometimes the soul isn't aware they are dead. It comes as a bit of a shock when they receive the news. One time I entertained a soul who had been bent double in life and my body immediately bent in response. It made me understand what it feels like to be in a body in so much pain. When we put her in touch with her angels, the release and happiness I experienced through her was intensely beautiful.

Some people reading this will say, "Oh it's all in your mind, you just make it all up." I don't deny I used to question it for myself, thinking is it just our subconscious? However, one session really proved it to me that we do deal with real souls.

85

A friend called Lucy asked if she could sit in on a trance session. None of my other friends taking part in the trance knew of Lucy's circumstances. She had been close to a tragic incident in which a family had died. A couple of years after the event, Lucy showed interest in the spiritual work I was doing, especially the trance work. She said she was not confident enough to take part but wished to observe. The rest of us were experienced in doing it and happy to let her watch.

In trance three people work at once. One person, the sitter, releases the confused soul that has been attached to them. This is normally linked to an emotion that the person has been struggling with. One person goes into trance and takes the soul. They allow it to speak through them, experiencing similar emotions to the sitter, then help the soul to find its guides. Meanwhile the third person, the control, speaks to the soul and asks it questions, guiding it towards its angels and freedom. Then we would swop roles. It was a good way to build empathy. In this case, I released the soul, Susie went into trance and Chris was the control.

When the soul came through, he started getting very upset, talking about all the land being split up. He was in a terrible state. We finally calmed him down, managed to get him to see his guides and enabled him to go with them. As he was leaving, Susie saw him meeting his wife and the two children in a golden light. At the conclusion of the session, Susie turned and hugged me, "I didn't know you'd been feeling like that," she said. "It was terrible." I felt a bit of a fraud because I had not been feeling like that.

Lucy quietly took me to one side, "You do know who that was don't you?" she said. From what he had said, she recognised the soul. He was the father of the family she knew. Apparently, he had worked hard all his life and had gradually built up the land around his property. He was traumatised because he and his family had died in sudden and unexpected circumstances. He had not moved on, watching everything he had created during his life fall apart, with no power to do anything about it. Understandably, he had been caught in the emotion of chaotic panic, unable to see a way out. We were very pleased to know that the mother and children had already found peace and had come to help him go home.

Whenever we did this work, more souls would come and listen in. At the end of a session, we would give any souls who wanted to go, but who had not been given the chance to talk to us, the opportunity to leave. We would visualise a column of light and ask all the angels, or guides, to help them. It often felt like a hoover of souls! Finally, we would make it clear that if any souls had chosen not to go, they were not to attach themselves to the place where we were working, or the people who had given of their bodies for a time. We would then wrap angelic protection around all of us and clap to cut the energy.

I recently saw a television programme which is about haunted places. As I have refused to have a television for years, we only get to watch it on holidays or at friends, so I am not familiar with the programmes people talk about. Bearing in mind my work with trance, I was interested to see what would happen. The tale of a tragic story was told. As a result, the ghost of this young woman was reportedly haunting the pub. In the programme, psychics called on the woman or any other souls that were around, promising help if they appeared.

When they finally did make their presence felt; all the people ran off screaming. I was waiting to see the psychic talk to the poor distressed souls, expecting him to guide them to the light and rescue them. Not a bit of it. They had promised help, then run off.

I was appalled at how irresponsible they could be, especially to such a vulnerable and traumatised soul. It is like treating the souls as exhibits in a zoo. Imagine a small, terrified monkey, cowering in a cage. It tries to communicate with people now and again, to show it is there, throwing the odd nut out of the cage. All it wants is some love, affection and help to find itself a way home. Finally, someone with whom it can communicate stands by the cage. Calling out that he will help, he opens the door and entices the monkey to the bars to get out. The monkey gradually builds up confidence that this person can help. He tentatively approaches the door and throws a nut to show he is there, as the person asked him to. Imagine how he feels when the nut is thrown up in the air, people scream, the door is slammed shut and everyone runs away. The sense of betrayal must be so intense. Maybe in the future, when people have grown up a bit, then there will be agreements to protect the souls that inhabit the dimensions alongside ours and people will not be allowed to torment them in this way. I believe we are moving into a more enlightened age, so hopefully this will happen one day.

87

Back at Findhorn, Helen had asked if we could do some trance work. The community there were not happy, as people often get spooked by the idea, even though it does so much good. Helen's guides were insisting it needed doing, so eventually we found someone who was willing to let us work from her caravan. We did a session and discovered the place was heaving. One soul told us that they were packed like cotton wool into the Universal Hall. Souls tend to gather in clusters and the ones there were a lot of 'holier than thou' mind-sets. We did what we could that night. However, the souls we had cleared, explained that a lot more energy was needed to help the ones that were left. Helen decided on a plan of action. She would sit in the Universal Hall on the last day of the Conference and the rest of us would go out and find somewhere to send her the energy to clear the souls.

Pat mentioned she had found a stone circle up the road, so we headed there, with the two teenagers in tow. I had told them about my experience at Avebury. As soon as we arrived, Pat was off, checking out the energy of all the stones.

It was quite incredible. Each stone had its own feeling and personality; there was even a broken one that was virtually hidden by the grass, which was giving off a very sad energy because it had been ignored for many years. No-one else was around, so the teenagers got into the spirit of it. The vibrant green grass formed a cosy carpet under our feet, as we wandered round the stately stones with the warm sun on our backs. It was blissful being outside. Finally, we found a stone that resembled Helen's energy. It was the tallest of the stones, at the entrance to the circle, and it felt like a leader, strong and clear. We stood in a circle, holding hands around the stone. I cannot quite believe how we managed to convince two teenagers that it was a good idea, but I suppose they had both been brought up with parents who were of a similar mind-set. Whatever the case, they agreed to help and join in.

Pat then talked to the stone asking for its help and explaining the situation. I am not sure what we thought would happen, but we all visualised the same thing at once, which was not what we expected. A beam of light powered out of the top of the stone, flew over the countryside, and focussed in on Helen, who was channelling light up to the Souls in the Universal Hall. We stood there for a short while, then suddenly Pat's daughter hissed, "Some people are coming. Do we have to stand here holding hands? I'm not doing it anymore." Pat checked it out with the stone who replied we could leave, and the stone would continue to send the light. When the time was right, we needed to position ourselves in the same order and hold hands again, then visualise the light shutting down and returning to the stone. To the relief of the two youngsters, we were able to drop hands and walk casually away.

Normally I detest fast foods, but the younger pair were desperate for their 'fix'. After two weeks of intense living, with every meal prepared with 'full on love', the thought of food prepared with no care, no thought and definitely no love seemed quite appealing. I suppose it was a natural human reaction to any overdose. Anyway, the kids had been so good all afternoon, playing along with our antics, that the least we could do was take them somewhere they wanted to go.

The Conference finished at five o'clock, so we knew we had to shut the energy down then. On our arrival, we suddenly looked at the time and realised, a bit aghast that it was nearly five. "Oh no! We're going to have to shut it down here!" I remarked to Pat.

"We've got to do it," she replied, "we agreed it with the stone." We sat down, in the same positions we'd been in at the circle, and ordered the food. The waitress brought it over very quickly. In fact, it was on the dot of five. She arrived at the table and looked a little bemused to see us all holding hands under the table with our eyes closed. Luckily, she had no idea we were visualising the shut-down of energy from a stone circle up the road and thanking the stone. At best she probably thought we were praying for our food before we got it.

Pat and I encouraged the children to turn their mortification factor of five thousand percent into a thing to laugh about. They were miles from home, no-one knew them, they would never meet these people ever again, so what was the problem? It did not take long for them to get over it, particularly as the burgers had arrived.

When we do things like this it is very easy to think, "Oh, it's all in our imagination, nothing really happened, we're just good at visualising things." However, time and time again I get proof that it is not just our imagination, or if it is, others around me are imagining the same thing at the same time. On our return to Helen, she told us that she had been sitting at the back of the Universal Hall, quietly channelling light up to the Souls. She had been feeling she could not go on much longer when a sudden burst of energy had hit her. Totally rejuvenated, she was able to carry on till the end of the Conference. Comparing our experiences and the timing, we discovered that the moment she felt the energy was when we were at the stone. I am sure lots of people would try to explain it away with logic, but to me that is irrelevant. I know what I have experienced. It was very beautiful, great fun and extremely special in my life.

Good memories and experiences are probably some of the most precious things we can have. That is why childhood is so important. Our children need a wellspring of good feelings to support them in their adult life. Attitude and beliefs developed in childhood form the base stone for all our successive reactions to life. Love and nurturing are crucial for every future adult's happiness.

CHAPTER 15

"If you want to know what you did in your past life, observe your present condition; if you want to know what your future condition will be, observe your present actions." Buddha

The school where I was employed was a tall old Victorian building in the east End of London. I used to find a route to school that took me past every park I could find. The green spaces were like a breath of fresh air. One time I remember meeting a friend of a friend who was blind. He told me how he had been playing in a park as a child and had contracted an illness from dog poo that someone had not cleaned up. This caused his blindness. Every time I passed these parks, I would be reminded of him. I swore if I ever owned a dog, I would always clean up after it.

I always felt so sorry for the trees in London. I was grateful for their existence, but they looked tired and grey, a bit like the human inhabitants. It was always a relief to leave the buildings and drive up to Wales or out to the countryside. When I lived in Stamford Hill, it seemed to take so long to get there. The longer I lived in London, the clearer it became. I need to see green and nature around me. It is essential for my well-being.

When I first got to know about my spirit guides, my awareness of having had past lives grew. I was desperate to know more about it. Helen offered to ask her former husband, also a doctor, if he could help. He had done a lot of regression therapy. He agreed to try but explained he had never taken anyone to previous existences, only to earlier in this life. I was eager to give it a go. I was also aware of my strength of mind. At college, I went to see a hypnotist show. He told the audience to clasp our hands together, lift them over our heads and then try to pull them apart. Anyone who could not pull them apart, then went on stage. They were the susceptible ones. There was no way I was going to bend my will to his; I pulled them apart with ease.

I approached the whole exercise with Helen's husband with interest but awareness that I was in control. He asked me to visualise going down some steps. I had to count down and when I reached the bottom it was all dark. Then he asked me what I could see. At the time, it felt like I was making things up to keep him happy, but later when I looked back on it, I do not know where it all came from. I was a little girl in a front garden of a house. He asked me where I was and I said, "Estonia." He asked what my father did. I replied, "He's a merchant." I looked up at the house and saw a gable end, with a pointy roof. I got the impression we were in a town near the sea. My hair was a very yellow, blond colour.

When I came out of it, I did not know why I had come out with those things. I had no connection with Estonia and no clue where it was. I had to look it up on a map. In those days it was still behind the Iron Curtain, so information was sparse. I wanted to find out what the people looked like. Imagine my surprise when I eventually came across a National geographic magazine with an article on Estonia. There were photos of people with this same yellow-blond hair. I do not know to this day if it was a past life or not. I certainly would not have imagined myself there consciously. I had no knowledge of the place. Since then, I have had more of an interest in the country, although I still have no direct connection with it.

My urge to find out about past lives kept niggling, so back in London, I visited a clairvoyant. Chris said he fancied seeing one as well, so we went together. Chris himself was psychic, so I knew he would sniff out if she was genuine or not.

She talked about a young man 'who had come through' with long hair. Initially I could not think who it was. Then she mentioned he had been killed in bike accident. "Oh, it's Steve!" I exclaimed. Then I said, "No, no, that was his best friend. *He* was called Brian." It had been over ten years since Brian's death, and I had forgotten about it. I had lived in so many different places with such a variety of experiences that tragic though it had been, it was not foremost in my memory. "Oh, he has a lovely smile," the clairvoyant said. That was another thing I had forgotten. When she mentioned it, I remembered that Brian's smile could light up a room.

My teenage years in a local pub flooded my mind. Aidan would take me there to meet his friends, Brian, Steve, and several others. Always the wild daring one, Brian would do anything. He did not care. Aidan, who was very wise, used to say, "Brian's one of those who won't be long of this world." Sadly, he was proved right. A few years later, when I was away at college, Brian was riding his motorbike. For no apparent reason, he left the road and wrapped it round a lamppost and died. His mother was distraught. Aidan told me she had lost her mind with grief, wandering round the housing estate, looking in every garden for her son.

Here was I, years later, with very little contact with my old life, now being told that Brian had a message for me. Well, that was the last thing I expected. He wanted me to tell everyone he knew that he died at the right time. It was meant to be. When the accident happened, he had already left his body. The bike round the lamppost rationalised his death. Sadly, I did not know how to contact his mother, or even if she was alive herself. I told the few friends of his I still knew and hoped his message would eventually get through. However, I have been able to use Brian's story to comfort others at difficult times. He helped me to understand that there is always a reason, even if it is sometimes difficult to see. That convinced me. The clairvoyant was genuine. There is no way she would have known about Brian.

Often clairvoyants are portrayed as clever people readers and charlatans. I am sure there is an element of that. There are some who make vast profits, get side-tracked by their ego, and have an industry based around them. I would not trust them. However, there are good, genuine clairvoyants out there. In fact, I would argue that most people have a degree of clairvoyance, if they allow themselves to tap into it. The best ones have little or no ego about their work, insisting that they are a mere channel. The trouble is, our society is so controlled by the media, that unless someone on television states that clairvoyance is real, many people will dismiss it. It's often portrayed as a sensation for cheap thrills or mocked. This means that some very gifted people end up ignoring their own talents.

Returning to my clairvoyant in London, I asked her about my past lives. The answer was immediate and quite sharp. "Your guides do not want you to know about your past lives. You have had many, in many parts of the world and they have often been traumatic. You do not need to know about them in this life." That shut me up. Suddenly all my hankering to know about them left me and I had peace.

On different occasions since then, I have had odd glimpses of one or two lives. In a workshop session at Helen's, it once came out that I had been a fisherman. I had caused someone's death by my carelessness. That is why in this life, I have become over thoughtful of others, trying to compensate. That made sense.

Since being in a weekly meditation group, more snippets have come out. In one, I was in a vast church and singing. I loved to sing, but then war came to the region. I got the sense it was in the Middle Ages. We all ended up starving to death. Maybe that is why I appreciate my food in this life.

Who knows what has happened to our souls over the ages? We cannot truly know till we leave this body, but I have arrived at an understanding of life and death that is comfortable. It helps me when someone I love passes on and, I hope, helps me to comfort others. I do not have a fear of death and in fact when it comes, I am sure I will welcome it. However, I have come to recognise that incarnating is such a big thing that it is not to be given up on lightly.

First there is the difficult job of choosing the right parents and circumstances to help us with what our souls need to experience. Then there is getting born (and in the process forgetting the reason why we have come here). After that there is growing up, with all the teenage angst. Next, we have to discover in our conscious minds why we are here. Finally, we must find our path in life and try to stay on it with many distractions. I do not want to do it all over again till I have completed what I am here to do this time. It is far too much effort! I will know when the time comes, and go happily, but I think I have a bit more to do yet.

My mum always taught me to think of others and put myself in their place, so I could understand them. She used to explain that helping others was the best thing anyone could do. You can never feel sad for yourself when you are focussing on someone else. Over the years I have had to learn to get a balance in this view, as sometimes you need to look after yourself as well. It served my mum well though. She lived happily into her nineties, surrounded by loving friends and family, and is very fondly remembered by many people. It is rare for a ninety-three-year-old to fill a large church for her funeral, as she did. I still miss her a lot, but I know she is with me when I think of her.

CHAPTER 16

Fear less, hope more; Eat less, chew more; Whine less, breathe more;
talk less, say more; Love more and all good things will be yours."
Swedish proverb

Parallel to all the work I was doing with Helen, I was also, learning
tai chi. Weekly sessions in Stratford taught me the short form, then
after a year, I began to learn the long form. I loved tai chi. Stresses
from a day teaching would melt away, leaving me calm and relaxed.
Our teacher, also, organised occasional weekend courses or outings.
One of these was in a large country house. We would rise early, do tai
chi on the lawn, do some sitting, then some more exercises focussing
on different elements. In Chinese beliefs, there are five of these, Fire,
Water, Earth, Metal and Wood. When we focussed on fire, we did fast,
hot breath movements that burned up the energy inside. Water
movements were flowing and smooth. Earth movements were
grounded and firmly connected to the Earth. Metal helped us to move
with consciousness and Wood meant precision. The idea was to get all
five elements in balance in our form.

The most important thing was to practice daily. I took this to heart
and have practiced the form every day since, apart from a year or so,
when my son was a baby. I do it outside, whatever the weather,
resulting in some funny looks now and again. I have never forgotten
visiting my sister-in-law's family in a tiny hamlet in Northern
Ireland. I went outside in the morning to do my tai chi. A car
appeared and drove past. A short while later it returned with more
people in it. Soon it came back again with the occupants gazing out,
trying to look as if they weren't staring at me. Apparently, I caused
quite a stir, as they had never seen anyone do tai chi before.

On these courses I learnt how to do basic massage, focussing in on the
chi I was using and channelling it to heal people. We did exchange
massages for each other. I was paired up with a lovely Chinese lady.
We had to do a face and head massage, gently moving our fingers
over the delicate muscles and bones in the face, then channelling chi
through our fingers to the skull. She turned to me afterwards and

said she had felt she was in heaven. Her words made *me* feel amazing!

Sometimes our teacher would take us out to Epping Forest to do tai chi, then one day he got us to complete his dream, which was to do tai chi in the City. We grouped together in a big white stone-slabbed square, surrounded by towering concrete and shiny glass to perform the silent, flowing synchronised movements, while suited bankers raced past with their briefcases. It did make a few of them slow down and look at us. Who knows what we did? It felt good, doing the calm, gentle movements in the middle of such a busy, frenetic world.

Our teacher had been taught by a man from Thailand, called Chu. He was amazing. He had moved to Greece where he decided to hold a week-long workshop to include the Harmonic Convergence. This was an event that happened on the 16th and 17th August in 1987. It tied in with an alignment of the planets. Thousands of people around the world meditated in the world's first globally synchronised event. It was believed that this would move us on from millennia of war to a time of peace. Interestingly, a lot of major world events leading towards peace happened in the few years after that. In 1989 the Berlin Wall came down, 1990 Nelson Mandela was released and between 1987 and 1991 the Singing revolution happened in Estonia, Latvia and Lithuania that led to the restoration of their independence. These are some of the major ones, but I know lots of different organisations have set up since then, all promoting peace and better ways of being. There has been a marked change towards the way we treat children in schools, since then. They are afforded more respect. Although the cane had been phased out in primary schools before I started teaching, it wasn't made illegal in State secondary schools till 1987. (Private schools did not ban it till 1999). It is frowned upon to shout at children and an agenda that addresses their emotional needs is more prevalent. I am not saying that people did not do all these things before 1987, but it was not commonplace.

When I heard about Chu's workshop I was determined to be there. No-one from my tai chi class was going, so I travelled on my own and had fun at the airport trying to assess my fellow travellers, working out who was a likely candidate for the workshop.

Our first few days in Greece were intense fire exercises, to cleanse us. We moved with force and speed, punching the air with our arms and breath combined. Every impurity in our muscle tissue felt as if it was burning away. Chu said very few words to us; mainly demonstrating what to do. After a day or so, he commented to us about our movements. He told me I had a lot of Earth and Water in my form. How he could read that was a mystery to me.

On the day of the Convergence, he led us down to the sea before sunrise. I will never forget that morning. A mist shrouded the beach, with the chill of pre-dawn. We stood in our lines, spaced apart, expectant. Slowly and gracefully, we started the form, moving in harmony, our friends nearby appearing as stronger outlines, while the ones further down the line faded into indistinct shapes, but still moving together. A few early morning walkers were startled, as they stumbled into our space of mist and saw the silent figures.

There is something very special about moving in total silence and harmony. As we completed the form, the sun started to rise over the sea, breaking the threads of moisture and clearing the air. We concluded the form and stood silently, relishing the moment. Suddenly Chu plunged forward and waded into the sea. Those who felt like it followed. I was one. The water was alive with gold, the brilliance of the sun reflecting around us. We splashed and rolled, relishing the silky joy of water on our skins. Finally, the sun rose completely. We returned with amazing memories and a feeling of having been part of something momentous.

The previous summer I had experienced meditation in a Thai monastery and practicing tai chi in Taiwan. My brother, Jeremy had gone out to work in Taiwan for a year, so his family were there with him. I jumped at the opportunity to travel again, spending four weeks in Thailand with two friends, Lu and Mel. Then Lu had to return home, while Mel continued with me to visit my family.

I loved Thailand. The people we met were so gentle and kind. I was impressed by the fact that the young men do not do national service, instead they must be monks for a year and pray for their country. How brilliant is that? Every morning we would see them in saffron robes walking round with their bowls. People would fill them with food, knowing that the men were doing spiritual work for the good of everyone. The Buddhist temples were beautiful. It was explained to us that we must never sit with the soles of our feet pointing towards the Buddha, as this is regarded as extremely disrespectful.

We did all the tourist stuff, went down to Koh Samui for a few days, swam and sunbathed on the idyllic beaches, sleeping in wooden huts sheltered by the towering palms, and waking to the turquoise sea lapping on the shore. In those days there were no air-conditioned hotels, only the basics. A variety of larger huts were the beach restaurants. We tried each one out, eating whatever style it presented.

On the way down to Koh Samui I had come across a Buddhist monastery that was open to tourists, allowing them to come and take part in meditation and monastery life. I really fancied going. Mel wanted to come with me, but Lu had met someone. She decided that romance on a beach outweighed meditating in a monastery. I am sure most people would agree with her. We split up for a few days, arranging to meet up soon.

The lush green vegetation surrounded the walls of the compound, as we arrived at the beginning of a ten-day silent retreat. The monks were very accommodating. I explained we could only stay for a few days and that was fine. All we had to do, was respect the silence. We were shown our accommodation, in dormitory style rooms for the women, the men were obviously in separate areas. In the centre of our courtyard was the well. We were instructed how to use it. It was imperative that the water and the bucket were not polluted. We had to draw water, and then tip it onto our flannels or into smaller bowls from which we could wash. We were warned never to put them into the bucket, as this would contaminate it and the well for everyone else. Having never had to live with water from a well, I had not realised the importance of this.

Again, I was reminded to appreciate the value of water and its wonder. It is such an amazing substance. No other liquid on this planet revives and enlivens like water, yet we do not appreciate it, polluting it with our faeces, thinking we can waste it because it is 'only water.' Live without it for a few days and see what it means. It is a magical substance, which I am grateful to have in abundance.

The routine was very simple. We woke before dawn, and then walked through the dusky bamboo to the meditation hall where we would sit for an hour. Being in a sacred Buddhist space we were not allowed to kill mosquitoes. A gauze-like cloth was essential to cover my head and arms, to prevent painful distractions from my breathing. Having learned to follow my breath through tai chi, the peace of the monastery created a wonderful space to go deep within myself.

Initially, my head was full of all the petty things one normally says. Having to be silent, puts into sharp relief the facile nature of much conversation. I loved letting go of all that. The chatty voice inside my head could be still for a while. My friend found it hard. She kept trying to whisper to me, as we went about our daily chores after breakfast. I had to deal with my annoyance because I was enjoying the silence. The rest of the morning was an hour's sitting, an hour's walking and then another hour's sitting meditation. Then we had lunch. In the afternoon there was another hour sitting, and then walking meditations followed by a talk in the hall, then supper and bed.

To someone who has not experienced it, it sounds quite boring. It is not. Giving oneself the time and space to sit or focus on walking, watching each step, releases much that we push aside with busy lives, trying to suppress and ignore. Normally everything sits in our body, collecting in our muscles, giving us aches and pains or even making us ill. It is not always comfortable looking at our inner selves, but it is very healing. The lovely thing is, we can do it for ourselves. No-one is telling us how to think or what thoughts should be there. We look at the thoughts that are ours, love them (no matter how horrid) and let them go.

We were only in the monastery for four days, but it is a stronger memory than any other because I lived in the 'now' for much of that time. I found a deep sense of peace and learnt the value of a simple existence. Sadly, I have not managed to live so simply in my own society, but I know I can do it and enjoy it if I need to. The monastery opens its doors to show tourists another side of Thailand, to show that it is not all sun, sea, and sex. I was grateful to them for giving me the chance to share a little of the spiritual life of that beautiful country.

Re-joining Lu, we travelled north, visiting Chang Mai, where we trekked on elephants into the Golden Triangle amongst the hill tribes. It was but a brief tourist-geared view of the people's lives, but it gave me another glimpse of how different peoples on our Earth live. Like the monks, they live with such a minimal footprint on their environment compared with ours.

Further north, by the border, we met up with a little boy who was being sponsored by my mum's Sunday school class. We were taken round the school, treated very well, and taken out for lunch by the Mekong River. I felt terrible because the head teacher and all the children were so beautifully dressed, having made a lot of effort for us; whilst we were in our back packing clothes, which had all seen better days. At least I was able to make the connection, take some photos of him and his school mates (pre-internet days) and try to be not too much of a disappointment for him.

Soon it was time to leave a country I had taken very much to my heart, say goodbye to Lu (who had to return to work) and head off to Taipei to see my brother and his family. They lived in a flat in the city. I soon discovered that many of the Taiwanese would go to the central park every morning to do their exercises.

On my second day there, I got a bus downtown, emerged in the park and was entranced to see the activity there at six o'clock in the morning. There were some groups dancing, other groups doing every possible form of martial art, people walking, jogging, in fact people were taking part in so many different activities I lost count. I wandered round and tried to find a space to do my tai chi. I managed to find somewhere not too obtrusive and went through the form. Afterwards I decided to walk around. A group of students were having a tai chi class and they encouraged me to join them. They were so lovely and warm, welcoming me, although we had limited shared language. Their English was more extensive than my feeble Mandarin of two words, 'thank you' and 'hello' but it was still difficult to communicate about when they would be there again and if I could join them.

Each day I would go to the park, hoping to see them. They watched my form and commented that it was more like a dance. Their form was closer to the body with less stretching. I learnt a little from them, but mostly enjoyed their bubbly companionship. As my time there was ending, I told them my next day was to be the last.

The following morning, I got on the bus as usual, and then I noticed an older man behind me. He started up a conversation and discovered where I was going. He told me he knew a special teacher who could help me with my tai chi and asked if I would like to meet him. At first, I was interested, as I was keen to improve my form, but as the morning went on, I began to feel uncomfortable. I did not know how to leave him without appearing rude. He watched me do my form, and then started to guide me to the edge of the park where there were some shops. I realised he was trying to get me into a building away from the openness of the park. Every antenna in my body started screaming at me to escape. As we neared the entrance of the shop, I hurriedly made some excuse and darted away. By then a lot of the morning activity was disappearing from the park.

I raced around looking for my student friends. Finally, I found the remnants of the group. They had already finished, and some had gone. I felt gutted that I had lost my last session with the kind, young people. I tried to explain what had happened and they looked very worried that I had been waylaid by this man. They warned me against people like him and I felt very relieved to have escaped his clutches. He may have been totally innocent, but it did not feel like that, and by now I had learnt to trust my feelings.

It was wonderful staying with my brother and his family. They took us to the National Palace Museum in Taipei. Here, on display, were all the treasures that the Emperors of China had collected over thousands of years. It was an incredible sight. The intricacy and craftsmanship, with amazing attention to the finest detail, was something I had never seen before. There was much to absorb, but one object has always remained with me. It was a carving, out of a walnut shell, of a whole scene. People, structures, and patterns were carved into it in miniscule detail. It was so tiny, that the museum had placed a large magnifying glass in front, so that people could see it. The Chinese ability to create beauty through carving and sculpture was amazing. Heather, my sister-in-law, told me that they had been to a dinner party where carrots had been carved into flowers, whilst other vegetables and fruit had been transformed into peacocks, fish and all manner of fantastic beings.

Most of the Taiwanese people that we met were kind, eager to communicate and very friendly. There was one incident though, where I felt dreadful. Jeremy had taken us to the Taroko Gorge. It was a spectacular sight. The river has carved through layers of rock, much of which is marble, to form an awe-inspiring gorge. At the entrance was a deep azure pool, created as the river emerges from between the towering white, grey cliffs. Lots of Taiwanese families were bathing there and we decided to join them. I was swimming in the deeper part. A little child, who was with her parents, looked at me. I naturally smiled back at her and she started to move towards me. As she came, she was moving out of her depth and then she started to struggle in the water. With a sense of horror, I grasped that she could not swim. I could not get to her fast enough and she started to go under. It all seemed to take ages, but I think it was probably only a few seconds. Suddenly her father noticed and managed to grab her, pulling her to safety. I felt awful, as if I had enticed her into danger. At that time, not many Europeans visited Taiwan, so we were a novelty. The child was maybe intrigued by my skin and hair colour. Perhaps she was coming for a closer look. I do not know, but her father gave me a bit of a glare. I can't say I blamed him.

* * *

Every time they went to the beach, my nephew was mobbed. He was a baby with blond hair. Heather was quite alarmed at first, particularly when lots of women would congregate around them, then put their arms out, take him, cuddle him, then wander off with him to show their friends! Eventually, they became used to the attention and I am sure it contributed to making him the very sociable and amenable young man he is now. My six-year-old niece was equally as charming to everyone, enchanting people with her use of Mandarin.

Something we noticed was the treatment of the children. They were very loved and cared for. We never saw any parent shout at or ignore their child. However, if a child fell over, the parents never made a fuss. They virtually ignored the accident, obviously cleaning the child up if there was blood, but not cuddling or fussing over them, as we do. Consequently, the children never made a big deal of falling over. They would pick themselves up, dust themselves off and carry on playing. I thought about how children behave here. I have watched children in this country fall over in the street, get up, and then start to walk home. Initially, they are fine, but as they near their home, the tears start to build, the sobs are caught between breaths, then the tears start to flow, till finally the child enters their home and the full storm erupts! How much kinder it is to our children not to give the negative stuff attention, but just the positive. However, I know it is not easy to put into practice.

My brother recommended visiting some of the islands off the coast of Taiwan, so we'd booked flights prior to leaving England. On arrival in Taiwan, we heard that a typhoon had recently devastated the islands. After some deliberation, we decided we not to cancel. We would assess the situation and if our presence caused any problems, we would leave immediately.

On the small plane, we were the only foreigners. They made a special announcement in English purely for us. Other nations are so kind to us, whereas, as a nation, we treat visitors to our country so badly by comparison. As we left the plane, two businessmen made our acquaintance, offering to show us round the island and take us out for a meal. They had gone to the island to buy lobsters, for which it was famous. They were very kind, plying us with a surfeit of lobsters and rich sauces.

The next day we were dreading bumping into them again, as the thought of lobster was making us nauseous, but luckily, we found ourselves chatting to a group of soldiers. The island was inundated with troops, helping in the aftermath of the typhoon. They were great fun. It felt as if we were escaping the clutches of the men and lobsters, to enjoy the youthful exuberance of the army lads. Their energy was very light and respectful. There was no sense that they wanted anything more from us, than the pleasure of our company and to learn a little English.

They, also, invited us for a meal. We explained we were not very keen on lobsters, so they said they would take us for a traditional Chinese meal. They ordered the dishes. Pointing to the relevant culinary words in a Mandarin/English dictionary, they thoughtfully ensured that we knew what we were eating. In the traditional style, we were presented with dish after dish. Each one was delicious. Luckily, we had eaten very well and were not so hungry, when a rather strong-smelling dish arrived. It had rubbery looking circles in it and was a greyish colour. One of our new friends mimed a pig, so we realised from which animal it came. Then his friend pointed to the translation... bowels. At that point I rapidly discovered that I had eaten so much that I could not possibly eat another mouthful. My friend very bravely tried some, but she told me afterwards it tasted as bad as it smelt.

We are so spoilt in our culture, limiting our diets to only very few parts of the animal and only a few creatures. Our ancestors ate a lot wider range of meats and vegetables than we do, as many other humans around the world still do today. I know the Chinese diet is a lot healthier, and most of it is extremely tasty and beautifully presented. However, I really could not make myself ingest certain foods, for which I am not very proud of myself.

Finally, my six-week summer of travelling was nearing its close. I hugged my family and set off home. The long flight took its toll. My lovely mum and dad were waiting at the airport and drove me home. They had come down, stayed in my flat, got it ready for me, brought my car back (that they had been looking after for me) and met me from the plane. For the hundredth time I felt so lucky to have had such kind, thoughtful people as my parents. The next morning, I dragged myself out of bed, crying with exhaustion, having to go into school to start a new term. I never did that again. Leaving it so late, it wrong-footed me at the beginning of the year and I never caught up. If you are a teacher, you will know what I mean.

CHAPTER 17

"With each new friendship, we build more firmly the foundation on which the peace of the world rests." Mahatma Ghandi

This school year was to trigger another new direction in my life. In the previous term, the old head teacher who had employed me, retired and a new head started at Whit. She was a fabulous woman who cared deeply about the children, was an excellent teacher and had lots of innovative ideas. I.L.E.A. (Inner London Educational Authority) was our local authority. In those days, money was no barrier. Inspirational courses were in abundance and we had fantastic resources at our fingertips. As soon as she started, Penny gave an assembly about how she wanted to be called by her first name. We younger teachers embraced the idea and happily changed to our first names. Some of the older ones were appalled and by the end of the summer term, six of the 'old-school' teachers had left. One just packed her bags and walked out without even resigning.

New teachers arrived and fresh energy swept through the building. It was a great time to be teaching. One of Penny's friends was a very entertaining children's poet and he used to come and take a few assemblies for us, which were brilliant. Penny encouraged me to work with the music adviser who was, also, very inspirational. From her, I learnt some excellent techniques and have repeatedly used her ideas.

The Authority appreciated that to be effective teachers we needed to develop as people, as well as increasing our skills. One anti-racist course that I attended, sticks out in my memory. As part of the course, we were presented with a picture that had been covered over. The image was exposed in stages. Before each section was shown, we were asked to guess what it was. This revealed a lot about our assumptions and personal views on the world.

Initially all we could see was the sky, which was black and the land which was red. Most people commented it was the desert at night. Then an astronaut was revealed. Immediately it was assumed we were now on another planet, maybe Mars. Then another cover was moved down a little, revealing the top of a thin white stick. As a result, people commented that it was probably the aerial of a space dog or a marker to place a flag. The facilitator then revealed the final section of the picture.

It was a slim African man, sitting cross-legged, wearing nothing but a white loin cloth and holding a stick. I immediately put up my hand. "That guy has astral-projected himself onto the planet. He is looking at the astronaut, and saying, it's taken you a long time to get here and why do you need all that stuff on?" Everyone else laughed indulgently at me. Then they went on to expound their own theories; the main one being that it showed the difference between the rich and the poor countries, with the African being the poorer.

The facilitator then turned back to me, "You were the closest," he remarked. He then went on to explain that the poster was a representation of the Dogon tribe in Mali. He told us that the tribe plants their crops and have their ceremonies following the cycles of a distant star, Sirius B, that cannot be seen with the naked eye. The star was only discovered by modern telescopes in the mid-twentieth century. He explained to the others that their assumptions were in fact quite racist. They assumed that because the man was not wearing an expensive space suit, the culture that he came from was to be pitied.

When writing this, thirty years later, I thought I would use the internet to research this tribe. A computer programmer called Laird Scranton, who has developed tools to dissect and analyse languages of computers, has used the same tools to examine the Dogon language and cultural beliefs, which are closely aligned with that of the Ancient Egyptians. He has written a book called 'Hidden meanings' in which he explains what he has learnt. On his You-tube video he states that the symbols and drawings in the mythology of both the Dogon and the Egyptians, include evidence that they have a clear understanding of quantum physics and string theory. In fact, the Dogon drawing that matches present-day knowledge of string theory is more sophisticated. It shows knowledge than does not yet exist in science today. These symbols and drawings date back thousands of years.

He suggests that these symbols were encoded in the tribe's myths and kept as sacred truths for millennia, until the rest of the world were ready to regain long-lost knowledge. The same symbols are repeated through many ancient cultures and beliefs of native peoples around the world. He indicated that if there are any quantum scientists out there trying to puzzle out the conclusions to string theory, then they might find some clues in the Dogon drawings. It was interesting to find out more about the culture I had been introduced to so long ago and how it continues to fascinate and inspire people.

* * *

For the summer term at school, I was planning a topic about 'Moving on.' I was working with an educational support worker, who had organised a Romany gipsy and a Palestinian refugee to come and talk to the children. Then I heard from Angie and Jane that a man from the Hopi Nation, called Tom was coming over. I asked them if I could book him to speak to my class.

I learnt a lot from the visitors. The Romany was a lovely young woman who showed photos of her caravan, stressing how important cleanliness is to her people. She was trying to break down the prejudices people have. I always remember the slides showing pristine glass ornaments of shining crystal. Sadly, because the police kept moving them on, the Romany community had to settle for any scrap of land that they could be given. Our visitor showed us the terrible site they were living on. It was a slab of concrete between three massive flyovers. She told us how one day, she had just left the toilet block when a lorry fell off the road above, directly onto the toilets. A few minutes earlier and she would have been killed. They all went to help the driver, who I think survived, but I went home that night and tried to imagine the fear of living with that threat, noise and pollution encircling my home. It gave me a completely new feeling of empathy and understanding towards Romany people. I hope it did the same for the children in my class.

Equally, it was fascinating to hear the story of the Palestinian woman. Again, she transformed my mind-set, particularly as I had been in Israel and seen it from the 'other side.' I found it hard to understand how the people who caused such terrible suffering to her and her family were the same race of people who had undergone so much suffering in the past. A long time ago someone told me that all the fighting in Gaza is over the large underground reserves of water. The land above the ground is very poor, that is why the Palestinians were originally allocated it. However, what is underneath the earth, has become of paramount importance. As always, wars are often fought over what is under the surface.

I understood from Angie, that the Hopi, also, have been made to suffer for what is under their ground. The Hopi have lived in their stone villages in the desert, farming successfully there for over a thousand years. They are surrounded by the Dine (Navajo) tribe, who were settled there, in poor desert land, by the federal government. No·one was interested in any of this land. Then, in the last century, coal and uranium were discovered in the earth below. The Hanson Trust was involved in exploiting the coal, washing it down a pipeline hundreds of miles to the west, where it was used to fire coal power stations to feed the electricity hungry homes and industry of California. Not only was this process damaging and polluting the atmosphere, but it was also using up the precious water table in the desert, which the Hopi had nurtured for a millennium to grow their life·giving crops. To add further insult to injury the old natural enmity between the two tribes was being manipulated to enable forced movement off the land, so the Hanson Trust could get their coal smeared hands on it.

Having learnt all this, I felt it would be very appropriate to ask Tom to come and talk to my class. When he arrived, he came with two more people. Husband and wife, Hassan and Jacqui, they were his hosts and chauffeuring him around. Jacqui was half Indigenous Canadian but had been mainly brought up in London. I asked Tom to talk about the enforced movement for the tribes, but he showed the children pictures of many different tribes, with their variety of different clothing and homes. He wanted to break down the traditional concept of Native Americans being a homogeneous group, stressing the differences and variety between the numerous tribes of North America. Looking back, he was probably right; children could understand that more easily than the difficult concepts of land ownership and conflict.

Over lunch, Tom told me that the Hopi were thinking of having teachers to come and visit, to learn about the Hopi way of life. I was hooked. In an instant, my next goal in life was fixed.

I knew I had to keep the link with Tom and that Jacqui would be my point of contact. Jacqui and I got on well together, so we exchanged phone numbers and addresses. Before they left, she told me about an all-night vigil that was to take place outside the American embassy in a few days. "Will you be going? It's against the land partitioning of the Hopi/Navajo lands. Tom's going to be speaking." Eager for further contact with my new friends combined with my desire to support the issue, decided me. As it was a school day, I could attend in the evening but not stay overnight.

Contacting Jane, I discovered that she was going to the vigil, so we went together. About twenty or thirty people turned up. We stood outside the embassy on the pavement, milling around. I talked to Jane and Jacqui, then Angie who was there. Several other people whom I did not know chatted to each other and moved around to keep warm as the evening drew on. Tom gave a speech. Suddenly, I glanced round and noticed a tall, attractive Native American man. He was walking around the edge of the group, but I did not dare speak to him. He looked far too distant and remote.

Little did I know then, but this man was destined to be my soulmate and future husband.

After Tom's visit, my friendship with Jacqui and Hassan grew. She introduced me to new ideas and perspective on Indigenous people. Looking at the real issues began to give me some concept of life for First Nations people. On reflection, I can see it was important preparation. If I had floated over to the reservation with all my innocent but wannabee attitudes, I would not have been received well. Over the next year, I wrote a few times to Tom and his partner Patti over in Arizona, but I had not heard a thing back. I kept on asking Jacqui if he really meant it, "Am I fooling myself? Am I dreaming about something that will never happen?"

She reassured me. "Often Native people won't reply to letters, but it doesn't mean they aren't thinking of you." Jacqui and I bonded, not only from our love of Native culture and people, but also because of her links to the 'other side.' She had committed herself to her guide at a young age and was a very powerful psychic. I loved to hear of experiences and messages she would get.

During the summer, my friend Marianne turned up in England. I was really looking forward to seeing her again. We had not seen each other since her long stay in Findhorn, where she had had many enlightening experiences and met a husband. She was now in the early stages of pregnancy and going to visit friends in Glastonbury. We met up at my brother's house in Bristol, as by this time, he and the family had returned from Taiwan.

Mum and Dad were also there, so it was decided we would all go to Glastonbury to drop Marianne and me off. She was planning a long visit, as her friends wanted her to look after their premises whilst they were away, whereas I was merely there overnight.

There was only space in the car for one child as Heather did not want to come. We decided that Carrie, the older one should come with us and Thomas, the toddler should stay. As we were about to leave, both children started crying. Carrie, because she wanted to stay and Tom, because he wanted to go with us. Thomas snuggled in next to us for the journey down.

On arrival, we went to the Chalice Well gardens. For Marianne and I, the gardens were sacred, beautiful keepers of the red, healing water. The red water in the well is high in iron content, giving rise to its colour. To the rest of the family, it was an interesting and peaceful place to visit and spend the morning. I was fascinated by Thomas' reaction. The little toddler raced in circles around the garden with a look of pure joy on his face. I instantly knew that from his reaction to that special place, not only was he physically related, but he was also, related on a soul level. Marianne and I collected some water from the well.

After the others had left, she and I visited the white water well on the other side of the road. There we collected some more water. After that, we walked to the flat over her friend's shop, which was called 'Starchild.' Even in the eighties, Glastonbury was an established venue for the New Age movement.

Marianne wanted me to make her a flower remedy from the Glastonbury Thorn, to help with her pregnancy and birth. A few years ago, I had learnt from Helen how to make a mother tincture. To make up a remedy, I would use a few drops from that, diluted with spring water and brandy. To create the mother tincture, we decided to combine the red and white waters and sit them in the Glastonbury Thorn for a few hours. In those days very few people went up there, so I was not too worried about leaving the jar of water in its branches.

110

Whilst placed in the Glastonbury Thorn, the waters would absorb the energy from the tree. The next thing to decide was the timing. Guidance told me to place it there at ten past ten at night and collect it at five to five in the morning. Luckily, it was summer, so it was not too dark, either to place or retrieve it. Marianne and I went together, then returned to snatch some sleep. I drifted off. Just before four o'clock in the morning, I woke with a clear voice in my head, "One day you will carry a Starchild." I thought I heard it because of where I was staying, the fact that Marianne was pregnant and because I was making the remedy.

I stole out in the misty pale morning light. No-one was around, as I made my way up to the small hill where the thorn stood, tiny in a strongly windswept landscape. I collected the water, carrying it against me and returned to Marianne. Deciding to call the remedy 'Starchild,' I made up the remedy for her, then took the mother tincture back home with me. She later told me it had been very helpful and wanted another one for her therapist. I was very surprised and pleased to hear that it had worked so well.

Whilst we were together, Marianne told me of a dream she had. I've often retold it to help people understand that we don't need to be slaves to work in this world.

In the dream she was watching a man on a stage in a theatre digging. All around him were lots of others who were digging. They all were working hard, fearful of their 'Master' whom they believed would strike them down if they did not keep at the hard toil. Suddenly, the first man threw down his spade. "I've had enough!" he shouted. "I don't want to do this anymore." The others looked round in fear. Surely God would strike him down with a thunderbolt for being so disobedient and not toiling so hard. Nothing happened. Slowly and hesitantly, one by one the others joined him. Soon all the people on the stage had thrown down their spades and were beginning to look less oppressed and happier. A sound came from the darkened auditorium. It was the sound of a giggle. Gradually, the sound increased and increased until the space was filled with happy laughter. Suddenly the lights came on and there was God with all the angels. They were clapping and cheering, "They've got it at last!"

Around this time, I read a book which finally put the Christian religion into perspective for me. One of the reasons I had rejected it

111

as a religion, was because it never seemed to make sense logically. There were too many contradictions with too many bits that seemed to be missed out. I objected to the fact that the care and nurture of the Earth as our mother was never mentioned. Animals and the earth were referred to as objects for us to have dominion over, with humans being looked upon as superior beings. This attitude has contributed to the mess we are in today. It has given moral permission to abuse creatures in the name of science, farm them in factory conditions, fish wastefully, bringing stocks to near depletion and treat our brother and sister animals with a total lack of respect. No one can deny that our behaviour as a species has reduced many others to near or actual extinction.

Interestingly, earth care finally seemed to come onto the Christian agenda towards the end of the twentieth century. Now I am very happy to see that many Christian movements, in addition to their historic support for people's rights, are positively campaigning for environmental issues and animal rights around the world. Looking at the religion now, it seems to me that its values and approaches to the world have improved from when I was younger.

Sadly, it has a long history to shake off. 'The Holy Blood and Holy Grail' by M. Baigent, R. Leigh and H. Lincoln helped me to get an understanding of how the power of the Roman Empire worked. It took the burgeoning religion and used it to its own ends. Turning genuinely good concepts promoting equality, love and understanding between people into a tool of manipulation and control, it enabled the power of Rome to endure for two thousand years after the fall of the Roman Empire itself. Much was hidden, suppressed and twisted which was why I, as a child, felt that the Bible didn't make sense.

Later in my life, I met someone whose friend was working on the translation of the Dead Sea Scrolls during the nineties. Apparently, the Catholic Church still has a person who fulfils the role of the Chief Inquisitor, although his title has changed. No-one working on the translations could see more than a small section of the Scrolls. They were not allowed to confer or find out what anyone else had translated. The only person to have sight of the whole document was the 'Chief Inquisitor.' There was and possibly still is, a lot that needed to be concealed and suppressed.

My other difficulty with Christianity was the way that some Christians were always trying to convert me to their way of thinking. I appreciate there are good beliefs in the religion, but there is in any religion. I liked the Sikh religion when I visited a Gurdwara with the children from school. The beliefs were rational, kind and caring towards others. It was originally formed to try and bridge a link between Hinduism and Islam. When I asked if anyone converts to Sikhism, our guide replied, "If you like the Sikh religion, we don't encourage people to convert but to look for the same values and understanding in your own belief systems. Every religion has good in it."

Having said all these things about Christianity, my own extended family, whom I love very deeply are all Christian, as are many people whom I like and admire. They live their lives as truly as they can, following the idea of love and care for others in everything they do. When people live their life in this way, I have nothing but respect. Most of my favourite head teachers have been committed Christians. They live the good values promoted by the religion but do not push it down anyone's throat. Penny was one of those.

The next year at school was amazing. Penny asked me if I would like to float round the school, teaching music to every class, with the teacher present, so I could cascade my skills to them. The school was able to afford two floating teachers. The previous year, another colleague had been freed up to counsel and support children. Her work was excellent. A child in my class had experienced the death of two people very close to him, within a year. Naturally, he had a lot of anger which he found hard to control. The counselling teacher had experienced a close bereavement, so she could identify with his feelings. It was exactly what he needed. He found a way to express his grief and deal with it, which helped him to settle down and start learning again. I wish schools nowadays could all afford to have such a service for children. It is incredibly valuable.

That year we had two artists in residence and Penny asked me to work with them. One woman did an amazing Creation project with the children, while another did a beautiful glass mural with them, to go on the drab brick wall on the street outside. It is still there. Then Penny called me in to say the National Theatre had asked if the school would provide children for the rats and children in a production of the Pied Piper. That was right up my street. The current Doctor Who, Sylvester McCoy, was to play the Piper. I had a great time. I initially prepared the children then watched in awe as the professional choreographers transformed and improved their performances beyond belief.

Finally, our school's turn to perform came nearer. We had to go across the city by Tube for rehearsals. The children were so sweet and innocent about it. They had no idea how important the National was in the world of theatre. They were very excited when they saw their play's name in lights above the river. "Oh, look that's our play!" they exclaimed. Another child had come rushing into school one day to tell us he had seen the play on Ceefax, hardly believing that anything they could be involved in would be mentioned on telly. Even the secretaries commented with surprise, "It was as good as a West End production!"

The backstage crew loved our children because they were so unassuming. Apparently, children from schools in the West End were very different, with their mothers all in the wings, trying to push their children on to be closer to Dr Who. Our children just had fun and enjoyed every moment for what it was. Their performances were amazing. Penny came to watch it and wept with emotion; she was so proud of them.

When I was backstage, I received a bonus. Walking past the dressing rooms, one of the doors opened and a friend from college walked out. I could not believe it. She told me she was in a play there and asked if we could meet for a coffee to catch up. We did so.

It was very healing for me. For years, I watched people I had acted with in Cambridge, starting off in small positions, then gradually becoming more and more well known in the world of theatre, film and television. I kept thinking I had made the wrong decision and should have tried acting, as I might have been able to make a career of it like they had. I did notice however, that it was mainly the men, not the women, who seemed to rise with apparent ease.

It was great to see Brenda again, as I always felt we were of a similar talent, and I knew that if I had followed an acting career it would probably have been similar to hers. She told me how she had worked in the theatre since leaving college. Although she had not been out of work that much, she explained that acting was not an easy option. I could see, with the benefit of her wisdom, how my life could have been if I had gone that route. The trouble with an acting career is that you can work very hard and be great at your job, but unless your face fits the part (or you have some influential relations) you do not easily make it. It does not take much to feel insecure. You need to have a very strong sense of your own identity and know that even if you keep being rejected, it is not you, the person, that is being overlooked or ignored. Before I went on my spiritual path, I was not sure enough of myself. Facing a lot of rejection, I know I would have gone under.

There are some who make it big and for them, life looks great, but there are thousands whom we do not see, who struggle along barely making ends meet from one job to the next. At college, I had a friend who was a couple of years younger than me. She is an incredibly talented, funny and brilliant actor. She has been successful but has not achieved the same heights of fame as one of her contemporaries; unsurprisingly, the latter's father was a TV producer.

After meeting with Brenda, I went home and looked at what I had achieved in my life. I had a lovely flat, I had led a fun life, full of interesting experiences, had met lots of great people and was learning to know myself and be content with who I was. The final niggling doubt about wishing I had been an actress had been laid to rest. I cannot thank Brenda enough for giving me that peace of mind. I was ready for my next big adventure.

CHAPTER 18

"Doing what's right isn't hard, knowing what's right is." Lyndon Johnson

I decided to go to America, visit Tom and learn about the Hopi, as he had suggested. He still had not replied, but Jacqui told me to go and see what happened. My next big decision was whether to sell my flat or rent it out. Helpful advice echoed around me. "Don't sell, prices in London will never go down." "That flat will be a winner, keep it on." The future was an open book. I had no idea what I would find in America, or even if I might end up living over there. I had outlived London and wanted adventure. I could end up anywhere.

In my Easter holidays, I was going skiing in Switzerland with friends from my old school, then on to see Marianne. Her baby had been born and I was looking forward to meeting him and seeing her again. I decided that Marianne would be able to help me make my decision.

Her new baby was beautiful. When I first caught sight of him, he lay sleeping in his cot. As I stood by the side, he suddenly woke up and looked at me. This has never happened before or since, but the minute our eyes met there was recognition between us. Marianne noticed it as well and was thrilled to see our connection. Although Marianne has been over here, I have never met him again. If I ever do, it will be interesting to see if we still know each other. He is now a young man in his twenties. I am sure he will not recall that look. Nevertheless, it was a very special moment.

Marianne was very busy with her son and although we had some great catching up chats, I did not feel it was right to burden her with my problem. I decided to go off for the day, follow my spirit guides and see what would happen. Hopping on the first train that felt right, I headed up into the hills.

Dismounting at a station, I took a breath of the beautiful air and looked up at the the woods covering the hillside. A pathway beckoned me. Not a soul was around, as I wandered off. The trees towered over me, and the sky was a dull grey. Very few sounds penetrated between the stately pines, as my steps padded along the soft, needle strewn floor. I was unsure where I was going or what I would find. Finally, I stopped. No-one was in ear shot and it suddenly popped into my head to try singing, as Molly Scott had taught us. My voice sounded strange at first, but gradually I felt more confident. Soon, I began to lose my inhibitions and started to sing to the sky, letting the earth choose the notes. An amazing feeling of freedom filled my senses. As I sang and looked above me, a tiny crack appeared in the clouds, exactly where I was focussing my attention. I could not believe it. I sang some more, the crack turned into a hole. I continued letting the earth sound herself through me. Soon the hole had turned into a large blue patch, directly overhead. I stared at the sky, gradually clearing and felt a complete sense of peace and amazement. I had not solved my problem, but I had had a beautiful day. I had achieved what I came out to do. I'd allowed my spirit guides to lead. Leaving my mind open, they had given me this. Many people would say it was purely a coincidence. They are probably right. It did not feel like that though. All I can say is try it yourself and see how it feels.

Only once, have I tried it again. We went to Conway for my birthday a few years ago. My son and husband wanted to go round the castle. Happy to let them explore the building on their own, I took the dog for a walk. The day was dull as I wandered up the hill, moving through some mixed woodland. No-one was around and I felt like the world was mine for the day. Emerging from the woods, I was on a grassy knoll with fabulous views of the estuary and the hills beyond. Noticing that I was totally alone apart from the dog, I decided to have a go at sounding the earth again, like I had all those years ago. It was brilliant. As I sang, the sun came out from behind the clouds and started to light up everything on the hill. It was a magical moment. Again, it is most likely a coincidence, but at the time it felt like I was connected to everything around me, and it felt good. The best birthday gift ever.

Returning to Switzerland in 1988; I took my leave of Marianne, still with no decision made. It was the end of the Easter holidays, my notice was handed in, I was going leaving to go travelling in July and still I had not decided whether to sell or rent. A decision had to be made. All my financial wealth was in my flat. If I got it wrong, I stood to lose a lot of money. It was not a little thing I was risking. It was my home. I knew if I could interpret the message correctly from my guides, they would put me on the right track, it was just how to do it.

A technique that someone told me about, came to mind; drawing pictures to access your Higher Self. The way I understand it is like this. The all-understanding universal Love (my way of referring to God) is like a massive force of love and golden light. This light extends out in branches. At the end of each branch is a living creature, humans included. Humans can choose to open the connection or ignore it. They can open it wide or just a little chink.

When connected to this fabulous energy, it is like being linked to everything. The guides and angels are also part of these branches, but closer to the Source than incarnated beings. On opening my connection, I can access knowledge and understanding held in that beautiful Source of all life. To have a fully open connection, I think I would have to train for years as a Buddhist monk or something similar. I am not sure. I think you would have to be very clear and pure to access that level of Love.

My problem now was how to access that connection so that I knew it was the right message and not my imagination or something else.

Time was pressurising me into action. I sat on the plane home and took out a piece of paper. Focussing my mind completely on selling, I let my hand draw. First mountains appeared, then a chalet by a lake. It felt beautiful and wild. Next my hand drew an avalanche falling down the mountain. Above in the sky, I drew an eagle. I interpreted it as being risky because there was an avalanche, but it missed the house. I decided selling would be okay. The eagle represented freedom. The whole picture felt right and good.

Then I took another piece of paper. This time I focussed on renting. It felt the safe, cosy option, so I drew a bunny. Then I drew the rabbit hole behind it. Next a tree appeared, and then I found my hand drawing a man placing a ferret into a hole under the tree. I saw that if I was doing it purely for reasons of security, there was no guarantee it would be secure. I recognised the decision had to be made from what felt right, not what felt safe; the choice guided by love, not fear.

Returning home, I put my flat on the market. It sold easily at the top price as people were scrambling to get properties before a new law came in, restricting friends from sharing a mortgage. I paid off my mortgage, invested my money (interest rates were at thirteen percent that year) and set off on my big adventure into the unknown. Two months later, the economy crashed. Properties in London did the previously unthinkable and plummeted in value. Many house owners found themselves in negative equity, unable to sell without making a terrible loss. Surprisingly, all the people who had previously mocked me were suddenly interested in my guides and intuition, now that they had proved to offer good financial rewards. I felt this was rather a sad comment on our society. Before anyone will recognise an idea as being of any value; it must prove itself monetarily.

I felt sad to be leaving the children at school and all my friends there. The children wrote some very deep thoughts for me. One girl had once commented out of the blue, "Pam, why are you so good?" I was shocked. I never thought of myself as being good, so I was really surprised by her comment. She gave me a fabulous letter about growing on and away from each other but that I would always be there in her heart. Equally, she has always remained in my heart. Then one of the boys came in and said he had had a dream about me, "Oh Pam," he said. "It was awful. I saw you in the dream standing by a horse with spots on. You looked so happy, and I knew you were never coming back and I was so upset!" I was incredibly moved by these and many more comments from the children. I have never forgotten them all and often wonder what has become of them in their adult lives.

CHAPTER 19

"Life is not meant to be easy, my child; but take courage-it can be delightful." *Bernard Shaw*

I sold everything I had apart from a small transit van of furniture that I left at Mum and Dad's. Letting go of my possessions felt very freeing. Mum and Dad were so brave. They were really going to worry about and miss me, but they did not let me know that. They wished me well, reminded me to keep writing, gave me a massive hug and sent me off smiling. I had no clue what my future held. It was totally exciting, like I was on a mystery trip with my guides as the bus driver. By then I was much better at listening to them and working out how to stay on my path. Even so, I decided to let myself into it gently. I was starting my trip by staying with two separate friends, before leaping into the unknown, on the reservation.

My first stop was with my old school friend in Georgia. It was wonderful to see Kitty again and meet her family and friends. Situated in some beautiful woods, her home was in the hills north of Atlanta. Nestling under the tall trees, with strong-scented pine needles carpeting the ground and spiky branches rustling against the sky, her house was constructed of wood. Wrapped in a wide veranda, we could connect to the outdoors in comfort.

Her nearest neighbour in the woods had built a Dome house. I was fascinated by their home as I had never seen one before. Kitty took me round to meet them. Inside the dome they had set up a sound chamber for healing. They asked if I would like to experience it.

I lay on a bed that was suspended from the ceiling, to allow as little interference from anything, other than the sound waves. In the bed were specific crystals. Each one was related to a different chakra and positioned so they would align with them. As the music played, the sound was transmitted around me and through the crystals into my body. It was an amazing experience. I felt wonderfully relaxed and totally at peace. Although they ran it as a business, they did not want any payment. They gave me this special gift to mark the beginning of my magical journey. I have never forgotten their kindness.

Kitty was brilliant, sharing all her special places in the area with me. I felt very nurtured on the first step of my path. We went to a beautiful waterfall that tumbled over a steep cliff and experienced gold panning in a local disused mine, interspersed with visits to her friends. When Kitty had been in England on a previous visit, she commented on how slim everyone was, despite stuffing their faces with high fat fish and chips. In America they had low fat everything, watched their diets and still piled on the weight. She concluded it was all down to walking. In America, there are fewer opportunities to walk. You need a car to get anywhere. The only time people walk is when they go to a specially designated area in nature. This is limited to a set path, guided on a carefully laid out route. The opposite extreme is a massive wilderness trek, alone in the vast landscape with extreme survival skills a necessity. Later in my trip, I would get to meet people who did this. Mountain men they were called. There did not seem to be anything much in between. It felt so different from home where I could walk anywhere, with footpaths crisscrossing the whole of our landscape. Another part of the weight problem might be the growth hormones fed to cattle which inevitably finds its way into the food chain.

Over the years since then, more British people have grown larger. Probably it is due to our country adopting more and more of the American lifestyle, more out of town shopping areas, more fast food outlets and less walking.

Interesting and enjoyable as my time with Kitty was, I felt it was time to move on to my last safe haven before embarking on my unknown adventures.

As a child, I had always looked forward to the Christmas parcel that came from another world. The gifts in it were exotic to a child in fifties and sixties Britain. That was enhanced by the wait, as it was always late because it came all the way from America, the distant place of Disney. The names on the parcel were just as exciting. They came from the mysterious lady called Priscilla and her family. She had been my Mum's penfriend through the Camp Fire girls, a movement that always held much more interest for me than the Girl Guides. I was gutted that there were no opportunities to belong to

Camp Fire girls over here. My mum had been one in her teens in the 1920s and involved as a leader into her young adulthood. It was loosely based on Native American lore, although I get the impression from what Mum said, it was a romanticised view. Priscilla had been Mum's friend for decades, but they had never met. I was now travelling to Albuquerque to meet the giver of magical gifts from my childhood.

Finally meeting Priscilla and her family felt like a dream coming into reality. She was so kind. I got the impression that she had been saving up for a while for my visit. She took me to Native American museums and art galleries and looked after me very well. A few days after my arrival, my friend Jacqui rang.

Before I left England, Jacqui had told me she was travelling to America for a holiday with her twelve-year-old daughter and some friends. I was astounded when she said she was flying into Albuquerque. Before leaving England, we arranged to meet up so I could travel with her. I was aware that I had a much better chance of being accepted on the reservation if I arrived with Jacqui. She had done a lot more support work than I had. Tom had stayed with her, so she knew him better than I did. On top of that, I knew we'd have fun travelling together.

Searching in the local phone directory, I found a very reasonable motel for them to stay in, booked it and arranged to meet up with them the next day. Priscilla seemed a bit upset that I was leaving so soon. I felt awful about it, but I knew I had to go then, or an important chance would be lost.

Imagine my horror when we met up the next day and I discovered I had booked them into a brothel! Jacqui still laughs about it today, although she was not laughing at the time. All night there was constant traffic outside their room. People kept banging on their door, there was a lot of noise and drunken men on the corridors. None of them slept and they were desperate to leave at first light.

I took my leave of Priscilla and William, feeling guilty I had not been able to stay longer. I promised to keep in touch and did call back in to see them whenever I went to Albuquerque. I think she felt responsible for me, which was very sweet of her, but I was on my big adventure and wanting to be free.

CHAPTER 20

"When the missionaries came to Africa they had the bible and we had the land. They said "Let us pray." We closed our eyes. When we opened them we had the bible and they had the land." Desmond Tutu.

Jacqui, her daughter Nazima, a young friend called Steve and another woman who had decided to join them, had hired a car and we set off into the desert landscape. The reason we left so quickly was that we wanted to catch the Intertribal Ceremonial in Gallup, New Mexico. It was my first introduction to the drum, singing and dancing. I loved it. Many different tribes from all over North America were represented, dancing and singing in their traditional outfits. I found it interesting to note that when the American National Anthem was played, several Elders were remaining sitting, as we did. I did not realise at that point what a powerful statement that is in America. Over here people have a very different response to things like the flag and the anthem. We did not stand because we were not American and did not see the point of it. I suppose the Elders felt the same way.

Whilst at the Intertribal, we met a Dine man called Ron. After the ceremonial, he took us out on the res to visit his family and walk on the red, rocky landscape that I would soon grow to love. He taught us how to drink from rainwater pools on the tops of rocky outcrops, how to understand the stories the land holds and to appreciate and respect the beautiful earth we live on. His family lived in a trailer home, as many indigenous people do. It was surrounded by rabbit brush, tumbleweed rolled across the expansive plain and the red rocks formed the horizon. His kids were glued to the television, like many children around the world, whilst we could not get enough of this new environment and ways of being.

After leaving Ron, we decided to visit Sky City or Acoma. Turning off the main highway, the road climbs a steep hill, and then at the crest, a spectacular vista opens. The hill slopes down to a plain that stretches away to a distant mesa, rising from the dusty desert bowl. The mesa holds the village of Acoma. Like the Hopi, Acoma is part of the group of pueblo people. Pueblo means village in Spanish.

Traditionally their homes were built from stone, on top of the tabletop red rock mesas rising from the desert floor. The villages have been there for hundreds of years, in some cases millennia, and hold a sense of timelessness.

As part of the tour of Acoma, it was explained how the church was built. It shocked me to the core. On their arrival, the Spanish priests tried unsuccessfully to convert the villagers. Seeing that they were getting nowhere and being aware that to control a people, you must control their minds through belief, they resorted to a terrible thing. They ordered some of the men to be killed at gunpoint, then used their blood to make the first bricks. Under threat of death, they forced the rest of the village to build the church. That church felt terrible. It was soulless and barren of any spirituality. To me it was an awful example of how buildings hold the energies put into them.

Although I knew horrendous things had been done in the name of Christianity (particularly in the Spanish Inquisition), I had not realised what had been done in America. As with other big world religions, many things which are offensive to the true believers have been done in the name of the religion. This was another nail in the coffin of a 'man manipulated' belief system. No further confirmation was required to follow my own spiritual path.

Now I am secure in my own beliefs, I can appreciate the good things that are being taught through the world religions. I accept other people find what they are seeking through them and I would never put anyone else down for what they truly believe. There are some amazing teachings in the big world religions. However, I now have the confidence to pick out the good bits and reject the rest.

I find it hard when the religion expects their followers to be told how to believe, from an authority figure, like a priest in the church. I know these people can be very good and act as spiritual guides to others; but I also know that some individuals can abuse that power, manipulating and controlling others. For many years, the established church was used as such, particularly when people could not read and had to rely on the priests to tell them how to interpret 'God's words.'

I truly believe we have our own connection to the living energy that is in everything (God, or whatever name people want to call it). The name I am most comfortable with is the one that the First people of

America use, which is the Great Spirit. It denotes no gender and is referred to as the 'Great Mystery.' No-one needs to tell us how to talk to this Special Being. Going inwards we can find that beauty within ourselves, which is the point where we are connected to this fabulous, pure energy of love. The Dine have a saying which resonates with me, 'Always Walk in Beauty.' It is so simple but can be understood on so many levels. My interpretation is that 'Beauty' is connecting to the pure, universal love. When in that space, it is impossible not to behave with care, thought and love for our beautiful Mother Earth and everything that is a part of her. It is an aspiration, something to keep aiming for. I would be the first to admit it is hard to be like that all the time in daily life.

* * *

After visiting Acoma, the white hire car had to be returned to Albuquerque, so we set off into the dry desert landscape. It was getting late, so we decided to camp on a picnic site in a pull off area.

Jacqui could not get over my sleeping bag. It was a white sheet made into a bag, the weather being far too hot for anything warmer. "You don't half give me the creeps with that thing," she kept saying, "it's like a shroud." Amused by her comments, I lay on the earth and was more than happy to look up at the stars and drift off. Little chipmunks ran around and over me, as I gazed up at the multitude of brilliance above. The other woman lay on a picnic table whilst Steve camped on a bench. Jacqui and her daughter Naz were having none of it. "We're in the car, we can't sleep out here!" they exclaimed.

I was just dozing off when the car door suddenly flew open and Jacqui leapt out. "The bloody car!" she yelled, "Look at it!" She got out her camera and took a photo. "I was just falling asleep when a horrid feeling came over me. It was like something wasn't right. I tried to ignore it thinking it was my imagination. Then the car started rocking. I grabbed my keys and camera and got out! You're not getting me going back in that thing to sleep." By this time Naz was awake so we got her out of the car.

"We need to move away from here," said Jacqui.

All thoroughly awake and feeling slightly apprehensive, we drove off to find a motel.

125

In those days we had to wait for photos to be developed. On returning to England, Jacqui examined it. There was the white car, there was little Naz's face looking out of the back window and above the car is a massive white figure, arms outstretched, leaning over the car.

She still has the photo and none of it has faded with time.

Travelling with Jacqui was never dull. There were more strange things to come…

CHAPTER 21

"This is my simple religion. There is no need for temples; no need for complicated philosophy. Our own brain, our own heart is our temple; the philosophy is kindness." His Holiness the Dalai Lama

Thankful to be rid of the hire car, we took the train to Flagstaff, which seemed to take forever. On the journey, an Apache Elder ended up sitting down next to Jacqui. Over the many hours of travelling, he eventually engaged in conversation with her and invited us to visit the White Mountain Res in a week or so, where there was going to be a pow-wow. Feeling honoured to be asked, Jacqui nodded our appreciation.

Just then, the slow train finally arrived at our destination with a loud clunking of carriages. I could never quite believe the length of the trains as they progressed with stately dignity through the level crossing in the centre of Flagstaff. We took our leave from our new friend and set foot on the platform.

Looking around Jacqui said she would find us a motel, while we waited with the luggage. After my efforts in Albuquerque, they were not going to trust me again. A short while later she returned, "They say they're full," she said. "I think I look too Indian. You go Pam and book us in." I did so and was successful. I was so angry. This was the second case of blatant racism. Earlier in our stay we had been in a restaurant with Ron just off the res. The waitress had come and taken all our orders, apart from Jacqui and Ron's. In her best English accent Jacqui had said, "Excuse me, but you've not got our orders." Ron had blushed and told her not to make a fuss; he was obviously used to it. "No, you haven't," I repeated loudly, "there are two people you have left out." Their order was taken but with bad grace. I was all for getting up and leaving but we did not want to embarrass Ron any further. The same story would probably have been repeated elsewhere.

We hired another car and found our way to Tom and Patti's house. On arrival, I was astounded that Patti had been expecting me. "Told you so," was the look Jacqui flashed at my surprised face.

In my life there have been a few occasions when I have met someone for the first time and instantly known that they would turn out to be important to me. This was one of those times. I looked at Patti and knew we were going to be good friends.

The hire car was soon to be handed back, so I said I wanted to buy a van to live and travel in for the duration of my stay. We went to a large car dealer in Flagstaff. There, a keen young salesman showed us a green van. It had beds in the back that folded into settees and a table, a wardrobe and a cooking space. A perfect mobile home! I loved it.

"How much is it?" I enquired.

"Five thousand dollars." It was way beyond my budget, I knew I had to be careful with how I spent my money, as I had no idea what the future held. I asked Jacqui to ask her guide how much we would get it for if I bargained. "A thousand," came the reply.

The following weekend was a series of visits to the car salesroom. Very soon the young sales assistant could not handle us. He handed us to his boss. I was insisting he was going to sell the van to us for a thousand dollars. The boss, Roger, (we were now on first name terms) insisted he could not sell it to us for that. I was utterly convinced he would. He came down to four thousand then three thousand five hundred. I was having none of it. Jacqui kept saying, "He's been very fair, he's come down a lot."

"Your guide said a thousand," I said, "so I'll get it for a thousand." Roger finally came down to two thousand five hundred. "I can't go lower, I'm making a loss at that," he said. Then Jacqui said, "I wonder if my guide was working in sterling? If so, it would be *two* thousand dollars." At that, after a weekend of bargaining, I finally began to give in. I upped my price to one thousand five hundred dollars. I think Roger was so astounded I had moved, he finally agreed to meet me halfway at two thousand dollars.

Roger then offered me a job. "I'd rather have you working for me than against me!" he said. He even sent me a Christmas card, so I do not think he minded too much. To me it was a lesson in belief. I truly believed that Jacqui's guide was right. So, I created the situation where I could buy the van at a price I could afford.

I took my American driving test; bought insurance and we were set. By taking the test, insurance was cheaper, and I gained an identity card that ended up being very useful. It meant learning the American road code which is quite different from ours. While over there, I heard of an English man who was driving on his international license and had not bothered to check the American rules. A very important one is that when the School Bus displays its Stop sign, traffic must stop in *both* directions completely. Even though he was not on the same side of the road as the bus, he had no idea it meant he had to halt. He carried on, tragically killing the school children who had got off the bus and were crossing the road expecting the traffic to be waiting for them. Since hearing that, I have always acquainted myself with the road rules of the country where I am driving. Unless of course I am driving in Naples, where rules do not seem to apply!

Having made our first contact with Patti and Tom, we then went up to Tuba City where Jacqui had the name of someone she had been told to contact, called Vanessa. Vanessa was the vision of what Anglo people imagine is the typical Native American woman. She was very beautiful and strongly into her heritage. "I'm a real mixture," she would comment, "five Nations rolled into one." Her mother was Dine and Lakota, her grandfather was Iowa, and her father was Iroquois and Lakota. Then her husband had been of the Ojibway Nation of Manitoba in Canada, so her children were an even greater mix. She was proud of all her native ancestry and ensured her children were fully aware of the rich cultural backgrounds they were descended from. As with many indigenous people, she had a very dry sense of humour and ability to laugh over many situations.

First Nations sense of humour is more aligned to British humour than the mainstream American. I remember once we were all in a garage while the van was being repaired. A telly programme was on, about an aerobics class. Jacqui and the rest of us were laughing our heads off; it was like a Monty Python sketch. Then this American guy came in and looked really offended. "That's my favourite programme," he commented. Following that programme, a comedy came on, which we watched in stony silence. It was not funny, yet the American thought it was hilarious. It never ceases to amaze me how people from the same root source can grow to be utterly different.

Both Vanessa and Patti told me I would be very welcome to come back and stay with them after my trip with Jacqui and co. I was beginning to feel as if my adventure was really starting. Having two safe houses to go to felt wonderful. I was very grateful to both my friends-to-be.

After a few days, we decided to take up the Elder's offer and try to find the pow-wow on at the White Mountain Apache res.

A day of driving down there meant we arrived quite late in the evening. Soon we noticed the same cars cruising up and down the road we were on and a few vans parked at the side. Our van was unknown in the area. A strange feeling started to creep up on us, as we drove in the looming darkness along the forested roads with the mountains rearing behind. The charged air was heavy with anticipation, adding to our feelings of unease. Suddenly the storm broke. Rain lashed down in between the dark tree silhouettes then lightening flashed, giving a brief glimpse of intense light. I have never seen lightening like it before or since. It was not just brilliant white flashes; they were green, blue and other colours. We were all picking up a nervous and unwelcome energy, very different from our previous encounters.

Normally we were quite happy to park up on the roadside to camp for the night. We drove into a large layby. The engine was still running when another car sidled in behind us.

"This doesn't feel right," I said.

"We need to go, right now!" countered Jacqui. I had learnt to trust her instinct, so needed no second warning. I spun the van round, regained the highway and set off again. The night was coming on, we could not find anywhere to stop, we had been on the road for hours and I was getting tired and ratty.

"We must stop somewhere soon," I moaned.

"My guide says we will find safety in the clouds," said Jacqui.

"And just what is that supposed to mean," I snapped. "Bloody great! We've to drive up into the sky now!" As usual with messages from guides or the spirit world, it is never what you expect it to be. A few miles down the road we saw a sign-Cloud Nine Motel. "That's it!" said Jacqui.

"It looks really posh, beyond our normal budget," I grumbled, "we'll never be able to afford it." On enquiring, it was quite expensive, but we got a good deal, with us all sharing a room, apart from one, who decided that it was beyond her budget so she would sleep in the van. At least the van was in a safe place for her to do so.

In the daylight, the res did not look quite so threatening. We set off again looking for the pow-wow. "Let's try this way," someone said. Driving down a hill we started to cross a dirt track when the van got well and truly stuck in the mud. The more I tried to drive, the more the wheels dug in. We all piled out. "I don't think we are supposed to go to this pow-wow," was a comment.

Suddenly from nowhere another truck pulled up. Three very tall Apache guys got out and assessed the situation. They had the strength and know-how to release the van from its muddy prison and without further ado, did so. We thanked them very much and wanted to give them something for helping us. They turned to Liverpudlian Steve who had long hair and glasses. "You remind me of John Lennon," one of them said. "Have you any skins?" Steve explained he had asthma and did not smoke cigarettes. All we had were some cans of pop and a few cans of Steve's beer. They were happy with that and then kindly guided us to the edge of the reservation. We decided to give up on the pow-wow.

On the way out we saw a lovely lake. It was very hot and I was desperate to get in the water. Steve and I decided to have a swim. The others were not so keen. Steve set off swimming out into the cool depths. I started to follow, the silky water pleasant on my skin. Not feeling very comfortable in deeper water, I stayed closer to shore. Suddenly I felt something grab my ankle. I yelled out. Immediately Jacqui called out urgently, telling me to get back as fast as I could. I needed no second warning. Dripping and a little shaken, I clambered out. Steve was fine and swam back feeling nothing. It was an odd experience and it remained in Jacqui's mind.

On returning to England, she mentioned the incident to a Lakota friend who lives in England. "Your friend was very lucky," she commented. "The lake monsters do not like women in the lake. Your male friend they would not touch, but she was very fortunate not to have been pulled under. I have known of other cases when the woman was not so lucky." Apparently, the lake monsters are not living creatures that inhabit the lake, but spirit forces. The indigenous people know which lakes are safe and which are not. Whatever it was, it felt like a hand grabbing my ankle and I was more than happy to leave that lake and the whole area.

After calling back to the safety and welcome of Tom and Patti for a brief visit and to relay our adventures, we set off again.

CHAPTER 22

"Don't take life too seriously. No-one gets out alive anyway."
Unknown.

Next stop was California. On the way we got stopped by the police. He said I had been wobbling on the road markings. He wandered round the van and saw the sticker on the back door. Jacqui had seen it in a shop in Flagstaff and I had to have it. It said, "Spirit Guides on Board." His eyebrows raised, he started forward. Twelve-year-old Nazima leaned out of the window. "Oooh, is that a real gun!" she exclaimed in her East End accent. "Can you show it to us?" The policeman could not keep a straight face. Trying to look as severe as possible, he told us to go on our way. Naz saved the day.

To reach California we had to pass through Death Valley. Knowing it would be impossible to drive in the day, we decided that Steve and I would take turns and drive through the night. We were running low on gas, so it was a godsend when a gas station appeared out of the darkness. As we pulled up a sign said, "This station is dry."

"Oh no," I said, "have they run out of gas?"

"I don't think so; I think it just means no alcohol."

Jacqui went in to pay. Women in long dresses and pinafores stood behind the counter. "It was like going back in time," she commented on her return. As a Mormon truck stop, no coffee or tea was available. "Oh great," said Jacqui, "how will we make it with no coffee?" and shoved five cigarettes in her mouth in response to my ban in the van and the lack of other stimulants.

"I need to do my tai chi," I said. "It'll help me stay focussed as we drive." Lots of massive trucks stood around, the drivers resting and taking a break before the long slug through the desert darkness. Totally unaware of their glances, I just got on with the form. Coming to the end, I bowed and returned to the others. Feeling a lot better, I was ready for the next drive. "Did you see the looks on those truckers' faces?" Naz said laughing. "I thought their jaws were going to drop off! I don't think they've ever seen anything like it before."

We set off into the dark night. Finally, as dawn broke, we seemed to be arriving at an alien landscape of barren hills, covered in wind turbines. Their silent whirring wings hovered beside us as we drove through this forest of metal. I had never seen so many together before. It looked very strange. We had reached California.

Jacqui and the other woman had been writing to some indigenous prisoners on Death Row in San Quentin. They had arranged to visit them; the arrangements had had to be made months in advance and permits received. Steve, who was travelling with us, had not been approved and neither had I, so we had a great day driving around the coast, while the others went in to visit. Afterwards they relayed what it had been like. They had to pass through numerous locked doors, then had everything searched, until finally they were allowed to see the guys. Guns were pointing at them in every direction as they sat and talked to the prisoners.

Life on Death Row must be hard to endure. Apparently, there are several levels of cells on different floors. The lower down the level you are, the closer you are to your execution. Charles Manson was imprisoned there. The men said he used to terrify the guards, by making out he was doing black magic. He somehow managed to work his way up from the bottom to the higher levels. Apart from him, the majority on Death Row were from Black or Native American communities. They were poorer, so could not pay for the good lawyers, unlike the richer Anglo community. A good lawyer can really affect the outcome of a trial.

Jacqui had told her prisoner, Ray, about us all. I asked her if he would like me to write to him during my travels. I felt it might help him a bit, maybe bring the outside world to him. Through Jacqui he agreed, and I wrote to him for several years. When Arnold Schwarzenegger came to power as governor of California, he reinstated the death penalty, which had been quietly forgotten. Ray by then was an old man, disabled and already near the end of his life. Schwarzenegger had him killed a few months before he would have died naturally. I believe the crime for which Ray was convicted was far, far less than that of Manson, yet as I write this, I believe the latter still lives.

134

Our next stop was Los Angeles. Here, we stayed in Hollywood Hills. Jacqui looked up another First Nations contact who was an actor in films, married to a film director. She (the director) very kindly put us up for the night. We swam in the pool, chatted to our hosts, and discussed where our next adventure would land us...Disneyland. Naz wanted to go, and I was not going to say no. For years I had had a poster, sent by Priscilla, illustrating this dream of childhood on my wall. It was a map with all the different areas in pictures. I would sit and look at it for hours, deciding where I would go, fostering dreams of being there. By now, it had not the same high priority for me that it had been as a child, but I certainly was not going to turn down a chance to visit.

We all felt like kids again, deciding which ride to go on. Luckily, we were all happy with each other's choices. Opting for the gentler rides whilst avoiding the ones with long queues, we managed to experience quite a few throughout the day. Personally, I found the ghost ride best. In those days, holograms were a very new concept, and as our ghost cart entered different scenes, ethereal misty figures appeared and disappeared around us.

After our visit to Disneyland, we decided to leave California as evening fell. Steve had already returned to England, so I was the only driver. We had to drive through the desert where temperatures rocketed during the day. The air conditioning in the van was dodgy. Travelling through the cooler night we needed to cover the desert stretch in one go. Stopping on the barren road, we would fry once the sun came up. Taking it in turns, the others stayed awake next to me and kept me going. As the night wore on, I began to get more and more tired. Jacqui cheered me up by saying that four o'clock in the morning is the lowest point in the night. Her nursing experience proved to her that is when people often die. She took the shift around then, hopefully to make sure I did not follow the rule. Finally, the long night was over, the desert was behind us, I saw a track in some woods, pulled over and sank into a deep sleep. The others were annoyed that I did not park somewhere they could have entertained themselves, but I could not go another mile.

Whilst we were driving from place to place, we played a variety of different tapes. It felt good, on the long straight roads with no traffic, viewing amazing vast expanses of scenery, the sun powering down out of the enormous sky overhead with the music of Buddy Red Bow,

Floyd Westerman, Buffy St Marie and The Eagles playing. I grew to love the music of all of them. The Grand Canyon was on our tourist route, about seventy miles west of Tuba City. Further north, we visited Monument Valley. Both had been seen so many times on pictures, in films and in magazines, that it seemed slightly unreal to view them in real life. We, also, called in to Walpi on First Mesa, the Hopi village that gives guided tours to tourists.

Sadly, Jacqui's visit was nearing its end. After visiting everyone in Flagstaff again, we set off. I drove them back to Albuquerque where they caught their flights home.

I was finally on my own.

CHAPTER 23

"There are far far better things ahead than ay we leave behind." C. S. Lewis

The next few weeks were taken with settling in and getting to know my new friends. I tried not to stay too long in my van outside anyone's house. They kept inviting me in to sleep in their homes, but I was quite happy to live in my own space at night, sharing time with them during the day. Over time, Patti and Vanessa both introduced me to their friends and relatives, so that I gradually began to feel a part of the place. I tried not to be a burden on anyone, helping with food or energy bills, looking after the children, or buying treats to augment the income of each household.

After a few weeks it was mentioned that the Grandmother Canyon gathering was taking place. The Havasupai tribe, who live in the bottom of the Grand Canyon, were hosting it. Traditionally, the Havasupai would migrate between the Canyon floor and the rim of the Canyon, spending half the year in the bottom and half the year on the rim. The tribe now live mainly at the base, as a helicopter has been purchased to fly goods and people in and out. The reason for the Gathering was that more uranium mines were being planned in the area, this time around the Grand Canyon.

Since my arrival I had met several Dine and Hopi friends who told me how they used to play on the open uranium tailings dumps as children. Tragically, I know that one of those friends has already died at a young age from cancer. Of the others, I have lost touch, so do not know of their fate. I was told of other Dine adults who had built their homes of these rocks and ended up 'burning up' from their inside. There were no warnings on the tailings dump, no signs and no education to stop the children or adults from using these toxic materials.

The gathering was held in the glorious sunshine, on the flat grassy plain near the canyon rim. Numerous people from different tribes in the area attended. There was singing, drumming, dancing, fry bread to eat and a small stage for speakers and performers. The sun was warm, the sky blue, and the atmosphere friendly. It was great to see both my Hopi and Dine friends together in one place.

One of the speakers was Thomas Banyacya Senior. He was the elected spokesman for the Hopi Nation, chosen by the Kikmongwi (the village elders) to speak about the Hopi prophecies to the world. Visiting places all over the planet, he had become a well-respected person in many countries. As part of those journeys, he had been to England. Some years earlier, on the invite of the Archbishop of Canterbury, he had been asked to speak at a Conference which also included Mother Theresa. He travelled on his Hopi passport.

The traditional Hopi do not take any government hand-outs, still farming the desert and living independently, as they have for millennia. As a result, they quite rightly argue that they are an independent nation. To this end, they have created their own passports. Tom showed me them. They are covered in soft deer hide, whilst on the inside it is similar to other passports, with a photo, details and other official information about the owner. A sacred eagle feather gives it authentication. It states that the passport is valid as long as the sun shines, the grass grows and the waters flow on Mother Earth.

When Thomas Banyacya Snr., a highly esteemed person around the world, entered our country on this passport, he was held by officials, like a criminal, even though he was here at the invite of the Archbishop of Canterbury. They eventually contacted Jacqui and he was allowed to stay with her, but he had to have a police escort to and from Canterbury. The reason the officials said they would not accept the passport was because it had no expiry date.

Back in the Gathering, Thomas Banyacya stood on the stage and addressed us all. He spoke many words of wisdom that day but the ones that left the greatest impression, were about 'intention.' He stated that uranium is harmful because the main reason behind its production was to kill. Although it has the capacity to heal, through its use in medicine, the main intention is for weapons. So, it harms. Thomas argued that if its main intention is for medical use then it would not be toxic. This made total sense. There are some land masses of granite which emit natural radiation. Some areas, such as

138

in Cornwall, emit so much radiation, that the levels are too high for American soldiers to be stationed there. Yet the people who live there are fine. I once heard a woman on the radio say she was so addicted to the radiation she had to go on holiday where there was a similar granite land mass because she could not live without it. So why doesn't this make people poorly? Simply because the Earth's natural radiation has no intention of harm behind it. It makes so much sense.

Taking it a step further I then began to consider my intentions. If I truly act with the right intentions towards someone, it cannot be the wrong thing to do. The best way to judge this is if I act from the highest form of universal love. Love in its purest form cannot harm. The tricky bit is making sure of my true motives and intentions in every situation and checking that my ego is not poking its nose in! It is not something that happens overnight, it takes a lot of practice and I certainly do not get it right all the time.

One of the performers was Buddy Red Bow. I could hardly believe I was seeing the man in person whose music we had been listening to on our driving trips around the States. I could not wait to write to Jacqui and tell her. I was even more flattered when I was asked to befriend him and drive him round, as he was extending his stay after the Gathering. We became friends and I took him to visit some of my newly acquired friends in Flagstaff and Tuba City.

Soon after this I took off up to New York State for a break. Mum and Dad were visiting our distant cousin there and I did not want to miss this chance to see them. My cousin Janette lived in a beautiful house built by her ancestors. I instantly took to her and her husband Bob. It was brilliant to see Mum and Dad. We laughed and had such a good time together. Janette was an intelligent Anglo American who had travelled a lot in Europe. Bob had also travelled and had a very interesting past. He had been a test pilot in the U.S. Navy, then a fighter pilot in the Korean War, until a tragic accident had pensioned him out. He told me how he had known some of the men that later went on to be the first astronauts, some of whom went to the Moon. They were both very interesting to talk to, open minded and willing to listen.

One evening, Janette and Bob invited their Mennonite friends to visit and meet us. They were a charming family. The children were so polite and well behaved. I was fascinated to learn about their culture

139

and ways of living. They live with no television, producing all their own food and making their own clothes which all the children in the family are expected to take part in. They farm traditionally, living very simple but real lives, connected to the things they need in a sustainable way. I could see the attraction of that sort of life.

Janette and Bob also took us around, showing us the traditional Anglo culture of America. We saw pumpkin harvests, craft fairs and they gave us a Thanksgiving Dinner. Interestingly, when I visited Sweden, years later, it reminded me very much of the craft orientated lifestyle, with the homes and gardens being very similar to that of New York State. I then discovered that thousands of Swedish people had emigrated to North America, which was probably this influence on the culture there.

One afternoon, Bob informed us he was taking us up in his plane over the Finger Lakes. Flying over the landscape always gives such a different perspective. Suddenly, he told me to take control, so keeping the horizon at a level; I tried to maintain a balance. As he was on dual controls, it was quite safe. I had had a few gliding lessons at the University gliding club, so I felt quite confident taking charge of the joystick.

Recalling those days at Uni, I remembered the feeling of anticipation as we were being winched up, the grinding chain pulling us higher and higher into the air. Then the rather scary thudding jerk as the winch was released, followed by the smooth, quiet glide, floating above the airfield below, watching the levels of the horizon with the wind whistling past. I would have done more sessions, but the instructor, who was rather large and sweaty, asked me out. I did not want to be confined in a small space again with him, so that put paid to my gliding career. In comparison, it was much more fun with Bob. Mum was very impressed he had let me take control.

Soon Mum and Dad had to leave for England. Mum kept worrying about where I was to spend Christmas and whether they would be able to contact me. Before she and Dad left, she got in touch with another distant relation who lived in Key West and arranged for me to go there for the celebration. I was happy to meet these relations and explore another part of the States. My parents left for home, content in the knowledge that at least they would know where I was on Christmas Day.

CHAPTER 24

"To be Human is an Honor..." The opening words of the Mohawk Thanksgiving prayer translated by Chief Jake Swamp.

Whilst I was in the north, I wanted to visit a reservation in New York State, but it was a good hundred miles from where Janette and Bob lived with no public transport. Quite nonplussed, they offered to lend me their car. I could not believe their kindness. They were even shocked when I returned it full of petrol in exchange for using it. To me, it was simple courtesy.

The drive up to Akwesasne was very pleasant. Driving in the country in America is so easy, there is little traffic and the roads are wide and straight. Akwesasne was very different from the large expanses of desert that form the Navajo reservation. It was very small, mainly centred along the highway that ran through it. Instead of being trailer homes or prefabs, many of the houses seemed to be white wooden shutter homes, like the rest of New York State. Balconies and verandas framed some of the homes, with green grass and trees surrounding each plot. Jacqui had told me of a few people with whom I could make contact and they directed me to the Akwesasne Freedom School. The Mohawk people of this reservation had been subjected to European influence much earlier than the tribes in the west.

Again, I was treated with so much kindness. I met the Head of the Freedom School, a young woman about my age and we formed a friendship which has continued. Interestingly, we both married about the same time, and both had a son about the same time. These coincidences have served to forge a further bond between us. On that first visit, she very kindly showed me round the school and then looked after me during my stay.

The reservation is on two sides of the St Lawrence River, being partly in the U.S. and partly in Canada. When the two countries were invented, an imaginary line was drawn between the two, ending up with some Mohawks belonging to the new country of Canada and some to that of the U.S.A. The invisible line may separate them officially, but the Mohawk Nation remains united despite the political boundaries.

The international bridge over the river starts and ends in reservation land on both sides. The Mohawks allow it to co-exist on their lands but will block it when necessary to make a political statement. Even though the tribe here seemed materially better off, they have still had to fight and struggle to maintain their cultural rights and heritage. The bridge has proved to be a strategic weapon in this fight. It is one way the people can stand up for their treaty rights that have frequently been broken or dishonoured. In 1978, during one of these disputes, the Freedom school was established so that the traditional language, beliefs and culture could be maintained. Mohawk is the first language in the school and all the lessons are taught through it. I loved the large mural depicting the Thanksgiving prayer which the children say every morning. To me, the words were so beautiful and meaningful. This is a translation:

"To be a human is an honor, and we offer thanksgiving for all the gifts of life.
Mother Earth, we thank you for giving us everything we need.
Thank you deep blue waters around Mother Earth, for you are the force that takes thirst away from all living things.
We give thanks to green, green grasses that feel so good against our bare feet, for the cool beauty you bring to Mother Earth's floor.
Thank you, good foods from Mother Earth, our life sustainers, for making us happy when we are hungry.
Fruits and berries, we thank you for your color and sweetness.
We are thankful to good medicine herbs, for healing us when we are sick.
Thank you, all the animals of the world, for keeping our precious forests clean.
All the trees of the world, we are thankful for the shade and warmth you give us. Thank you all the birds in the world, for singing your beautiful songs for all to enjoy.
We give thanks to you gentle Four Winds, for bringing clean air for us to breathe from the four directions.
Thank you, Grandfather Thunder Beings, for bringing rains to help all living things grow.
Elder Brother Sun, we send thanks for shining your light and warming Mother Earth.

Thank you Grandmother Moon, for growing full every month to light the darkness for children and sparkling waters.
We give you thanks, twinkling stars, for making the night sky so beautiful and sprinkling morning dew drops on the plants.
Spirit Protectors of our past and present we thank you for showing us ways to live in peace and harmony with one another.
And most of all, thank you Great Spirit, for giving us all these wonderful gifts, so we will be happy and healthy every day and every night."
(Translation by Chief Jake Swamp)

I was amused to hear the children say it in the same repetitive monotone that children in our country would say the Lord's Prayer in assembly. Children are the same all over. Beautiful artwork depicting the traditional legends and the creation story, adorned the walls. I learnt of some of the stories behind the pictures and have been able to teach those in school, confident that I was using the true Mohawk version.

Norma then directed me to the museum where I researched more about the culture. I bought some books telling the traditional stories and some beautiful hand-woven baskets made from a sweet-smelling grass. I could still smell the scent for years afterwards. These baskets are the hallmark of the Mohawk Nation. They are well known for the black ash splint baskets, some of which are wrapped in sweetgrass to strengthen them and increase their aesthetic beauty.

I was beginning to realise that there are many publications and stories that have been published over the years by non-native people, which were not necessarily accurate or true. Feeling that I was beginning to collect information that I might use later to educate others in Britain, I wanted to make sure I was getting the 'right stuff.' Our knowledge over here is so limited and biased from the film portrayals of Native Americans. Overall, at that stage in the eighties, it was still very negative images. Even in America, most of the Anglo population seemed to be woefully ignorant of the culture and true history of their indigenous peoples. An even bigger crime was that the native children were not being taught of their own rich cultural heritage. Unless they were lucky enough to attend a school like the Freedom School. Of course, I am only referring to the education system; there have always been Elders who have passed on their knowledge to the younger ones who were prepared to listen.

Norma contacted some friends who allowed me to stay in their home; even though I was a total stranger to them all. I could not believe the kindness shown to me. She, also, took me to visit her family, who welcomed me warmly, making me feel at ease. Her parents made sure I was looked after and comfortable, whilst her sister, Leah, sat and taught me how to make beaded earrings with porcupine quills. I felt very honoured that she was willing to spend time with me to show me this intricate and delicate task.

Another day, Norma took me to meet Tony Barnes, a respected Elder and medicine person. I was thrilled to meet him and be taught a little bit about the Mohawk traditional medicines. Feeling very privileged to be trusted, I realised how lucky I was to be allowed to share some of this important knowledge.

Another day, I returned to the museum and visited a Longhouse; the traditional building used by the tribe until European influences gradually caused this to be superseded by individual family houses. I imagined how it would have felt to be living with other families and friends, supporting each other, and living closely from the land. A very different but much healthier lifestyle than modern living, I imagined.

Whilst at Akwesasne, I heard of the fearless young Mohawk men who are heavily relied upon in the building of skyscrapers, both in the past and nowadays, in New York City. They have an amazing head for heights and have been involved for many years in the construction of these scarily tall buildings and bridges. I had never heard of their contribution to the building of this vast city before and was quite shocked to think that I was so ignorant of the fact.

It was time to move on again. Thanking my new friend Norma and travelling on from Akwesasne, I ventured into the glorious Adirondacks. It was the Fall. The trees were a vibrant mass of gold, orange, yellow and brown. The air was clear and the sky intensely blue, creating a stunning contrast. I drove through the multi-coloured forests and by beautiful lakes, marvelling at the sheer beauty of our Mother Earth. There I was seeking the home of Ray Fadden, a renowned storyteller and teacher who established the Six Nations Indian Museum.

The Mohawk tribe was one of the Iroquois, a Six Nation Confederacy whose constitution was the inspiration for the American Constitution. This concept of a League of Nations was also the founding idea behind the U.N. Sadly, these facts are rarely acknowledged by the public education system. On my return to Arizona, I told Patti's son, Chris, about it. He was shocked that as a First Nation child in a State school he had not been taught of the importance of his people's influence on the founding principles behind American society. He went into school the next day and challenged his teachers about it. I am not sure even if *they* knew the facts behind the drawing up of the Constitution.

The museum was situated in the middle of the forest, with outside and indoor areas. I was fascinated to read and hear more of the stories and true history. Ray talked to me and explained he was very concerned about the wildlife being decimated by all the real estate which was taking over the Adirondacks. He used to feed the creatures of the forest and he told me how every night he would put out food in his yard (garden to us). As dusk would fall, the creatures of the forest would enter, including bears. He said their territory had become smaller and smaller as people purchased 'real estate' in the forest and fenced off large areas, restricting the bears feeding areas. I was fascinated to hear him tell of the large beasts and how they would amble in to where they knew they were welcome.

I learnt how the Iroquois was a group of Nations who were united by a spiritual being called the Peacemaker and assisted by Aionwatha-named as Hiawatha in the poem by Longfellow. (My mum loved that poem and was always quoting from it when I was a child.) For many years prior to the coming of the Peacemaker, the Onondaga, Cayuga, Mohawk, Seneca, Oneida and Tuscarora had apparently been consumed in blood feuds causing tragedies for families and nations.

At this point I would like to suggest a little theory of mine, which is totally unendorsed by any tribe or historical evidence. Recently I have been teaching about the Vikings in one term, then about different Native American tribes in the next term. When the children learned about the Iroquois League of Nations and how they traditionally lived in longhouses, they commented on how the Vikings also lived in longhouses. As far as I know, only the Northeast Coast has traditional buildings in that style. The Vikings are known to have reached North America from Greenland, Eric the Red's son, Leif

145

Eriksson is supposed to have done so. Further evidence is out on Pine Ridge reservation, where a friend of my husband once showed him an ancient Viking helmet in his possession. How did it get there? Did the helmet travel the distance of hundreds of miles as part of a trading system?

When I heard of the blood feuds, again I was reminded of the Vikings, who were notorious for them. Did some of Leif Eriksson's crew stay and did they marry into the local population, bringing with them some of the ideas from their culture? Or did they take the ideas of a longhouse back to their country? Was there a small connection there that led to these similarities or is it all a coincidence? Or alternatively is there something in all humans that makes us behave the same way in similar environments, leading to the belief that we are all connected?

Returning to the story; over a period of many years, a new way of living was developed, guided by the Peacemaker and assisted by Aionwatha. Twisted minds were healed, and the leaders gathered on the shores of Lake Onondaga to be instructed into making the Great Law of Peace. Women were assigned a lead role, establishing true equality in a time when European women were completely owned and possessed by their husbands or fathers. In fact, 'western' women still do not have equality on parity with the traditional Iroquois or Hopi matriarchal societies.

Families were set up as clans, with a Clan Mother being appointed leader. She would choose, through her wisdom and insight, the Chief, who would be male. Her choice would have to be ratified by the rest of the clan. If the Chief behaved improperly or started to abuse his power, then the Clan Mother would be able to remove him from his position, in consultation with representatives of the people within the tribe.

The Chief or leader must be an exemplary person, full of compassion, free of any crime against a woman or child, believing in the ways of the Longhouse. He has no authority other than the respect he earns from his own behaviour. He needs to lead by example, not be influenced by his family in his judgement, and cannot make anyone obey him through weapons or use of force. He would also end up being the poorest member of the tribe. The reason for this was that if anyone needed anything; clothes, food or weapons, then the chief would give them from his own possessions.

How brilliant is that! What a shame our politicians cannot follow this model. I believe some of them try but it is hard with all the pressures they are under, whilst others do not even start with the right intentions. No matter how good they are, it takes an extremely strong person to withstand the temptations and outside forces that seem to control our politicians.

Another little-known fact is that women's suffrage in the U.S. was inspired by the Iroquois Nation. Interestingly, in a bizarre co-incidence, my cousin Janette was intensely involved in the Women's Hall of Fame in Seneca Falls, which celebrates women who have achieved greatness. It is situated there because the first American women suffragettes lived in Seneca Falls and Rochester. What is less publicised is how they came across their ideas. Near the towns where they lived, was a Seneca Nation village, Ganandogan. (The Seneca Nation is a member of the Iroquois League of Nations). The Anglo women set off to visit, hoping to spread some of their missionary fervour and convert the members of the tribe to Christianity. On arrival at the village, they met the Clan Mothers.

Ironically, the women who had gone to convert became converted in a different way. Observing how much power and authority the Clan mothers had, they started to question their own lack of power in Anglo American society. They saw how the Clan Mothers told the men what to do each day, directing them to fish, hunt or gather wood. They saw how the Seneca women were the Head of their families and how they elected the Chiefs. The women named the babies when they were born and were responsible for ensuring the stories and history were passed down the generations. All this must have made their own situations seem stark in comparison.

A woman at the turn of the nineteenth century was virtually owned by her husband; no rights to vote, to own property, no rights even over her own children. No wonder those first suffragettes started a movement to change, when they saw how different their lives could be. How interesting that these women are now famous throughout North America, yet the Clan Mothers who inspired them are all but forgotten. I wonder how many women in North America realise that

147

the origins of their freedoms and modern rights are directly attributable to the Seneca Clan Mothers.

On my return to Janette and Bob, she was very interested to hear of my experiences and the knowledge I had gained. Until then, Janette had been quite wary of the local indigenous population. She freely admitted that I changed her mind and she started to view them differently. In fact, I became very proud of her.

Several years later, she was working on her local council to try and improve the pollution problems in the Finger Lakes. She realised that the First People in the area wanted to work towards the same end and decided to enlist their help. In a strangely parallel move to her suffragette predecessors, she went to visit the Clan Mothers and was astounded by the love and welcome she received.

Later, she was at a meeting in the capital, with another council member and some officials. The Clan Mother had been invited to attend. Janette was seated at a table with them, in an imposing building. Suddenly the Clan Mother arrived. Janette noticed that the tribal elder looked very overwhelmed, so Janette got up, walked over and hugged her, drawing her to the negotiating table. Janette was echoing the behaviour she had received, on her visit to the tribe.

My cousin paid a great price for this behaviour. The other council member related this show of friendship to others on his return. Janette was shouted at, called names, received death threats and had to have a police escort to and from council meetings. In the end, the stress was so great she had to give up her position on the council, just because she had hugged a Clan Mother. I could not believe this level of racism still existed, until on a subsequent visit to New York State, I saw notices along the roadside 'Indians go home.' No doubt the irony was completely lost on the low intelligence of the perpetrators.

I am sure there are many people who live in that State who are not racist and who would be appalled by the notices; just as many people in this country are appalled by the behaviour and views of supporters of UKIP. Sadly, as is often the case, the racist ones are the most vocal.

I felt bad that through my influence I had endangered her life, but I was very proud of her for listening and changing her views on the indigenous population of her area, against such ingrained bigotry. I

148

do not know how long it will take, but hopefully over time, the Anglo population will gradually evolve into a better appreciation of the rich culture and traditions by which they are surrounded. I keep praying for a better understanding between people.

Back then this was still in the unknown future. All I knew was that I really rated my cousin Janette and Bob. They were a good example of what intelligent and educated Anglo Americans could be like. I loved debating with them and their open-minded approach to life.

CHAPTER 25

"No Hopi , no cry" The Wailers , Kykotsmovi 1988

On returning to Flagstaff and Tuba City, it felt like I was going home. I was not back long when I saw Buddy Red Bow, who was still around. He asked me to drive him up to South Dakota in my van, offering to show me the reservation up there, at Pine Ridge. All for adventure, I was very tempted to go.

At that Patti really laid into me. "You have no idea what it'll be like up there," she said. "Your mother has entrusted us with your welfare, anything could take place, and you will be all on your own, with no friends. How could I face your mother if anything happened to you? Things aren't the same up there as down here, "she continued. "Up on Pine Ridge, it's a patriarchal society, not matriarchal, like we are. Besides, it's Tom's birthday soon and the Wailers are coming to Kykotsmovi and I've tickets for us all. You can't miss that." She continued in this vein, and I began to realise how safe I was and how many friends I had got in Arizona. She was right. I had no idea what I would be going to. Most of all I didn't want to hurt and upset my friend Patti, who had become very dear to me. Reluctantly, I refused to take Buddy. He was alright. He found other people to help him and eventually managed to make his way home.

On several different occasions, Tom and Patti took me to visit the ancient remains in the area. We visited Montezuma Castle, Walnut Canyon and Wuptaki. There they showed me the spectacular remains of stone homes built into cliff faces, canyon walls and the desert landscape. I loved the warmth of the ancient stone, glowing gold against the blue clear sky. There were never very many people there, giving us a sense of freedom as we wandered amongst the ruined walls and through doorways that led to a different world. The National Monument notices declared they were the remains of the Anasazi or Sinagua.

I learnt that the Hopi have never been forcibly moved on to a reservation. They were told by the Great Spirit over a thousand years ago, to leave their existing homes, break their pottery and inscribe their symbols on the walls, then migrate to their new situation on the Mesas. All over Arizona there are sites attributed to the Anazasi- supposedly an ancient people who 'mysteriously' disappeared. Anglo archaeologists have all sorts of reasons as to why; the Anasazi ran out of water, a mysterious plague happened and so on. However, the pottery remains can be identified by the Hopi as their style. The inscriptions on the rocks around the homes can be understood and explained by the Hopi, other remains can be identified and explained, as they are recognisably part of their culture. It all points to the mysterious Anasazi being the ancestors of the Hopi. I realised that the Anglo based culture does not want to admit this, because to do so would be to acknowledge the Hopi have a historical right to these sites where their forbears lived.

After leaving their cliff face dwellings, the Hopi settled on the Mesas to which they were so wisely guided. They have lived there ever since. As no-one else wanted to live in the desert, when the European settlers started taking people's land, the Hopi lands were largely left alone.

The main enemy was the threat to their belief system, but they managed to keep Catholicism at bay, even though they paid a great price to do so. Still Christians continue to try. Today there are a multitude of different denominations competing for the Hopi soul, even though many other people from around the world revere the Hopi way of life and belief system as being highly superior to anything in 'Western' culture.

Interestingly, when the Catholics tried to build a church on Third Mesa, it was struck with lightning every time. Three times it was built and three times it got struck by lightning as soon as it was finished. Finally, the Spanish priests got the message and gave up. The ruined church still stands as a monument to this.

More threats constantly emerge, as western culture infiltrates through the media, particularly getting at the younger generation. Another threat is the interest from outsiders, who know a little but not very much. The longer I lived amongst my Hopi friends, the more I realised how miniscule my knowledge of their culture was. I was gradually trusted to share some of their dances and learn a little of their culture. However, I was very aware of what an enormous privilege it was and was very keen not to abuse this trust.

The attendance of white people at Hopi dances in the villages has been restricted, as people who want to go and watch from just a curiosity factor, affect the power and balance of the ceremonies. Certain dances have been closed for many years. I was very worried about what I could and could not say to others on my return to England. Tom helped me compile a slide show, telling me what would be acceptable to say. I have used that as the basis for what I have related here about the culture, so hopefully I am not betraying anything I should not.

Very quickly, I learnt to ask permission before taking anyone's photo. One time I asked one of Tom and Patti's friends. She said no. I later forgot and ended up taking her picture. The photo came out blank. I felt bad afterwards for not respecting her enough to remember. I have heard of that happening on several occasions, an unsolicited photo of an indigenous person not working.

Up on the mesas, they are very strict. Notices state clearly that photos are not to be taken and film will be removed and destroyed if anyone takes photos up in the villages. They are not idle threats. I am not sure how it works nowadays with digital images and devices, but in those days, I heard of people's film being taken out of their cameras by Hopi villagers, annoyed by tourist's lack of respect. There is a set route in each village that tourists can follow. Around the village are many sacred places and sites, which can be affected by visitors walking over them with no knowledge of what they are doing. This lack of understanding has caused the villagers to limit access or to give conducted tours, as they do in Walpi on First Mesa.

On the reservation and on the Hopi mesas, everyone is identified by their vehicles. Soon my green van was an accepted sight, as I gave people rides and visited people I knew. Once my vehicle was accepted, I became more accepted.

From the summer solstice to the winter solstice, the dances in the villages are all social dances. There are many layers of understanding and meaning connected with each dance, but as an outsider, I would not presume to talk about or even claim to know any of it. If you want to research for yourself, I believe information on the internet that is written or endorsed by the Hopi Cultural Center, is approved of by the tribe.

I felt very privileged to be invited to attend a Hopi Basket Dance with my friends. I was directed to stand on a roof top overlooking the plaza. Only men and teenage boys were in the plaza itself and soon I understood why. The women entered the plaza singing and throwing out gifts from their baskets. A rugby style scrum enveloped around each gift as it flew through the air. Bodies tumbled on top of each other, attempting to grab the object. I began to realise that it was not the gift so much as the catching and the fun of catching it. Laughter rang through the air and good-natured comments were shouted out. As a non-Hopi, reticent English person, I felt it was not my place to grab a flying gift as it landed beside me on the roof, but after a while the people around me urged me to join in the fun. Down on the plaza it was getting rough. Apparently, the local hospital is always full of Hopi men with broken thumbs and fingers when the Basket Dances are on. The ultimate prize is at the end when the hand-woven baskets are thrown out. Then the scramble gets fierce. The atmosphere was electric. We ended up going to quite a few Basket Dances in different villages, over the autumn. There is much more involved in the ceremony than I have relayed, with an important significance to all that takes place. As a non-Hopi I would never presume to talk about any of that. All I have described is some of the atmosphere that I experienced there.

From the Winter Solstice to the Summer Solstice the dances are focussed around the Kachinas. The belief is that the Kachinas reside from mid- summer to mid- winter in the mountains north of Flagstaff, generally known as The San Francisco Peaks. Then from mid-winter to mid-summer they return to the Hopi villages and take part in the dances.

To explain the Kachinas in the slide show, Tom recommended that I should first look at all the elements in the periodic table. They represent the basic chemical elements of existence according to scientists. In those days there were about fifty-four. Now I believe there are a hundred and twelve. Tom pointed out that the Kachinas represent every form of existence on the planet and there are more Kachinas than elements in the periodic table. However, they do not just have a name and number; they have an individual look, a way of behaving, a dance and a personality. Many different Kachinas

153

appear at the dances. A Hopi might never see all of the Kachinas in their lives. I do not want to claim that I know much about them. I do not. Only a Hopi, born and raised can ever know or be an expert on their own culture. I have only had a small glimpse of this wonderful culture by living and being there for a while.

As time went on, I was gradually allowed to share more. Each time there was a Dance we would be based at the home of one of Patti's relatives, who would feed us and make us feel welcome. I gradually began to feel at home in her family villages. I loved driving in along the dry dusty road, parking up and being taken into her aunt's or grandmother's home. Entering the village was like travelling into a timeless zone. Up on the mesas there is no running water or electricity unless it is created without harm to the earth. Solar panels were very innovative then and were only being considered as a possibility. Phones also were not allowed, unless the Kikmongwi had sanctioned their use for people in need. Toilet facilities were on the edge of the mesa and of the compost style. Water was far too precious to be used wastefully in that way. When going to use them, I was always jokingly warned, "Don't fall off the edge!"

Flat roofed, stone houses were dotted around the mesa, with a central focus on the Plaza. Ladders leading down into the sacred underground kivas could be seen jutting out against the vivid blue skyline. Beyond the cliff edge of the mesa, the rocky desert plains expanded into the distance, so vast, so empty of human interference and so peaceful. Different hues of red, brown and orange shimmered in the heat, as the desert rocks gave off their light. Other mesas jutting out of the plain giving off a tangible presence, making the desert feel alive, a large and powerful being.

Over the time I spent in Arizona, the moments when I felt most at peace, most happy and most elated were when I was attending a dance in the village, as a guest of my Hopi friends and their family. On the odd occasions I visited the mesas independently, the feeling was not there in the same way.

As autumn rolled on, Tom's birthday arrived. We piled up to the large community centre in Kykotsmovi. It is like a large gym, purpose built and near the tribal council offices. The administration of the Hopi tribe is run by the progressives, people elected in the U.S. government style, to the tribal council. These guys run the tribal

154

police, hospitals, schools and other government agencies. This is separate from the traditional governance of the villages by the Kikmongwi, who follow the ancient laws and traditions of the Hopi Spiritual path.

The Community centre was heaving. Mainly younger Hopi had come in from the villages, the surrounding towns, like Flagstaff and Tuba City and possibly from further away. Bob Marley had passed on by then, so it was The Wailers, on their own, who were performing. Patti told me that the only place the Wailers would perform in Arizona was on the Hopi lands. The Rastafarian belief and culture has a similar strong link to Nature and the Earth, so they feel very close. The atmosphere was amazing as the Wailers came on stage and started performing. Everyone sang along, called out and took part. Vibrancy and excitement pulsed around the hall and when the Wailers sang "No Hopi, No cry", it felt like the room would explode. I was glad I had listened to Patti's advice and stayed after all.

I did not get to visit any Hopi schools, although I had lots of contact with all the children of my friends. I would happily look after the children, particularly Patti and Tom's little girl. They joked about her having an English nanny because I would help them out by looking after her when they had to go to work and college. She was only a toddler and we would have great fun, going to the local park, reading stories, and playing with her toys and games together. I have always got on well with children because I enjoy their company. They are much closer to the Source, with fewer layers of conditioning to have to work through, to find the true person. Children smile easily and find fun in so many things. I love the way they can make a whole game out of a simple object, like a cardboard box. The best thing is their imagination. I love to run with them in my imagination, creating fantastic worlds together. Those early years are very precious.

The younger the child, the more knowledge they soak up, eager for anything you can impart. It sickens me how people can ignore, reject and harm these little beings. Every action they experience as a small child is a crucial part of the building blocks for their life. There seems little understanding that the love experienced by a small child is what gives a secure and confident basis for that child's future reaction to everyone they will meet in life. Society seems hell bent on separating the young child from their parents (who usually have their

155

best interest at heart) placing them for long hours with relative strangers in nurseries, along with lots of other little ones.

The Hopi, like all First Nation people, value their children. I would only ever look after my little friend for short bursts of time. One time I had taken her to play on the swings in the park and got chatting to an Anglo woman. She asked if I was the child's mother and when I explained, she was very surprised. "You must really be trusted, if your Hopi friends allow you to look after their child," she said. "You never normally see an Anglo person looking after a little one." After that, I felt very honoured to have the confidence and love of my friends.

CHAPTER 26

"Always Walk in Beauty." Traditional Dine

Parallel to my 'Hopi life,' I had a 'Dine life' when I visited my friends in Tuba City. Navajo is the uncomplimentary Spanish name given to the people who have always called themselves Dine (which simply means The People). Vanessa was my main friend but I, also, built friendships with her friends, gradually becoming a recognised face around Tuba. Her friend and neighbour, Leona was a frequent visitor, and she would always come round when I returned after my travels to see what I had been up to. She would laugh so much when I told them about different things I had done.

One time I had been on one of the back roads, which are basically dirt tracks that lead from one place to another. They end up like the old-fashioned wash boards, with ridges running across them. It is not a quick route and can be very bumpy. However, I enjoyed exploring the different routes and finding where they took me. One time I saw a van that had stopped. A man was standing to one side. I stopped my vehicle and shouted out did he want any help, asking if he was stuck. It was only then did I realise he was having a pee! He was very good natured about it, but I decided to move on rather quickly.

I loved the landscape of the Navajo res. with all the canyons, desert and red rocks. A few times I visited Monument Valley. After my first visit with Jacqui, Vanessa took me up there next. She introduced me to a few of the families living there. Other times I went on my own. I loved the approach along the straight, empty road, with the towering cliffs of red, erupting out of the landscape. It was familiar from the movies, yet grander and more beautiful in real life.

Page and Lake Powell was another destination, but it felt very new in comparison. The connection of the land to the people was barren and empty there. When I walked round to Rainbow Bridge, it felt more connected, but I think the lake had changed the energy in that area.

Vanessa was great at teaching me about her culture through experiencing it. "We're off to the pow wow," she said one day, "it's

157

over in the school gym." Entering the hall, it was full of people of all ages milling around. Children ran and played, dressed in traditional outfits, girls stood, hair beautifully and carefully plaited and tied up, a single feather sometimes fixed into their hair. Young men and old, walked around, bells and rattles marking their steps. Young women in jingle dresses walked past, a shimmer of sound trailing in their wake. It was a colourful, energetic and vibrant scene. Vanessa and her daughters and son were all dressed and ready to take part. An announcer came on, the drum group started. The Grand Entry began. First came the Flags of the Dine nation and the U.S., with the anthem of both being played at the beginning of the event. Everyone stood as the Eagle Staff came next, removing their hats as a sign of respect. Tribal dignitaries followed and behind them came the veterans.

I was very impressed by the honour, respect and value placed on the people who had risked their lives to defend the country in the Second World War, the Korean War and the Vietnam War. I met many veterans of the latter War in my stay there, the physical and psychological scars visible from that terrible time. I thought back to our culture or even the wider American culture where often the veterans are marginalised, particularly if they have mental and psychological issues. A banner announcing the Navajo Code Talkers heralded the oldest veterans in the parade. Vanessa had told me that in the Second World War, the Navajo language was used as a code between the Allies. The language was so unlike any other, that the Germans and Japanese found it impossible to break. Obviously, the Navajo were the only ones able to communicate in it, so they formed a vital and important role in the War. I was amazed that in all the stories I had heard about the War, this was never mentioned.

As the dancers entered the circle, the energy levels soared. Colours swirled in front of my eyes, as jingles and gentle swishing of outfits blended with the regular, heartbeat drum. I observed the careful steps, timed to place each foot fall with the downward beat of the drum. A thrill of excitement surged through me, as I felt honoured to be included in this social gathering. I have never been able to hear the drum, with the high singing that accompanies it, without feeling the same rush of anticipation and well-being. It is a very comforting sound. "That's an amazing outfit," I commented to Leona, who was standing next to me.

"Where?"

I knew it is very rude to point, particularly with my index finger, so I indicated with my lips, following the Dine etiquette. When wanting to direct someone's attention to a person or any natural phenomena, like a rainbow, the Dine will use their lips. I learnt to do the same whilst I was there. It feels a bit awkward at first trying to push your lips in the right direction, but I got the hang of it in the end.

Every part of the pow-wow outfit is imbued with significance and meaning. Hours and hours of work goes into making an outfit, from the beadwork to the collection of feathers, then beading and sewing it all together. Often parts of an outfit are inherited and passed down through the generations. The dancing is in different categories. There's traditional dancing which is a steady step following the drum. Fancy dancing is mainly performed by the younger ones with fast, spectacular movements, then there is shawl dancing, where the women must make sure the fringes sway in time with the drum.

Suddenly the drum stopped. Everyone stood still. A shocked silence ran around the hall. I looked to Leona, "An eagle feather has fallen to the ground," she whispered.

"What does that mean?" I asked.

"It is not good," she replied. "The Eagle is very revered as the creature that flies the highest and is therefore the closest to the Creator. If a feather falls from an outfit and touches the floor, then everything must stop. A veteran has to retrieve it, a certain ceremony and prayers have to be followed and no dancing can be done until the feather is returned."

I have attended many pow-wows since then and have learnt to behave with respect and quiet appreciation. I do not always understand the significance behind the actions but recognise that if I am being allowed to share in this great social and cultural event, then I need to respect my hosts and their customs.

When I was staying with Vanessa, she would tell me different things about the culture. We would do beadwork whilst watching the morning T.V. soaps. I could not believe how extreme the situations were in these programmes. People got kidnapped, put in cages and horrendous situations would occur in the brief five minutes of action

159

between the regular ten-minute breaks for adverts. The intensity of the feeling eventually became too much for me and I finally stopped being addicted to them. It was then that I began to analyse what was going on. I realised the programme had to be incredibly intense to keep the audience engaged during the lengthy advert breaks. The emotions and situations were so extreme they were laughable. However, being a gullible non-TV watcher for most of my life, I would get sucked in and feel every emotion, till it made me feel quite ill.

Vanessa taught me how to use colours of nature in my beadwork. She would teach me to look at a flower or plant, observe its colours, and then use that colour combination in my earrings or necklaces. She was great at beadwork, and we would sit for hours, working together. As a way of earning a small supplement to her income, she would go out to the Junction, where the road from Flagstaff joined the turn off to the Grand Canyon. There she would sit with her van and a stall, selling her beadwork. I joined with her a few times but felt the tourists did not want to see a white girl, when they were looking for traditional native sellers. 'Everyone in their place.' However, some of those same tourists would be quite happy to stay in the local motels in Flagstaff, who would turn a native person away, pretending their motel was full, when it was quite clear it was not.

Of course, we visited the Grand Canyon together as well. It was so big, it did not seem real. It is still a stunning backdrop, but because of the high tourist element, it did not feel like other areas on the res.

On the reservation, the colours of the rocks and sands are a vibrant presence. Soon I learnt of how these beautiful elements of the Earth are used to help people who are sick, in Dine traditional medicine. It is not appropriate for me to describe the ceremony. They are very private healing ceremonies for the curing of a range of sicknesses. I did not attend any, as they are too important for casual observers, but I know that they work. I know of people who have been healed through them. An echo of the ceremony can be seen as an art form in tourist shops. There I was able to purchase a carefully crafted sand painting, depicting important elements in Dine life, done in different coloured sands.

As I got to know Leona more, she took me to visit her parents and her extended family, making me feel very welcome. I felt honoured when she invited me to a sacred Yeibichai healing ceremony. One of her

160

relatives had sponsored the ceremony for their family member to be healed. Again, it is not within my rights or knowledge to explain it. All I can say is that I remember the big cedar boughs smelling sweetly, protecting the Yeibichai before they emerged to dance and perform the sacred rituals. I was very appreciative of Leona's kindness and willingness to share this with me.

Feeling a great sense of freedom, I kept coming and going, travelling around the res. My friends warned me not to be driving around too late in the dark on my own. Initially the reason was not apparent, but gradually it came out about Skin Walkers. These are bad medicine people who can turn themselves into goat like creatures and do bad things. They definitely do exist, in fact later on I had proof in more than one way of their existence, but the fact that they were sometimes there on the res, a very real threat to people, was indisputable.

I tried to understand this. Why could this shape changer exist here in Arizona, but not at home in England? I decided it must be something to do with collective belief. A whole community of people believe in shape shifters, so it enables them to exist.

Trying to make sense of it in my own mind, I recalled the old moment in the Peter Pan pantomime, when Tinkerbell is dying. Peter shouts out to the audience to clap if they believe in fairies. Tinkerbell is dying because of the lack of belief in her kind. I know that is 'just a story' but often important messages are disguised in stories. That way they can be accepted into people's consciousness, which would otherwise be resistant.

I recalled my days in Findhorn. Up there everyone believes in the existence of fairies and they are a tangible presence. Many people have seen fairies and nature spirits in and around the woods near Findhorn, because collectively they are believed in. I took the thought further to consider the missionaries going to tribal communities all over the world. They truly believed what they were doing was right, because they were stopping people believing in their spirits and medicine. Of course, the bad medicine and cruel practices are always sited as the justification. In some cases, I can see why, but the good medicine is destroyed as well. So many cultures have had to go underground or have died because of the 'good intentions' of well-meaning people. Sadly, the culture they destroy in the process is very suited to the environment of the people living there. The culture is lost, and then the environment begins to be lost also.

To return to the Skin Walkers, I was initially fascinated and asked my friends to explain more. After discussing these strange beings for a while, my friends told me never to mention them, as even saying the name attracts them. Later that night, after the conversation, the dogs started barking uncontrollably and a figure was glimpsed running up and over the roof of the house. I shivered. I was very careful not to mention them again in the household or to any of my Dine friends.

My favourite canyon was Coalmine Canyon. It is well hidden, on a poorly signed dirt track off a tarmacked road near Tuba. One Dine family lived way down in it, a day's walk from the rim. It is so beautiful, empty and quiet. It is not as vast as the Grand Canyon, so it feels more accessible and real. The rocks tower from the desert floor in a multitude of shades, of cream, brown and orange. Each rock could be a thousand different beings, imagined from the shapes and curves, blown and carved by the Earth's breath. I loved to scramble down into it. The lack of vegetation takes away perspective, so it is difficult to assess size and distance. The dry gullies between the towering rocks, formed passages to explore, leading to yet more magical, still spaces.

There was a local legend about a Hopi woman who had been killed there with her baby. It was said that one of the rocky towers turns into her and her baby at the full moon. Vanessa and some of her friends said we should go there and see the Canyon in the moonlight. I was wearing a long white cardigan and my Dine friends were all dressed in black coats and jackets.

If it was beautiful by day, it was unearthly and surreal by the full moon. I loved it. We parked near the rim and I took off, running around, jumping from rock to rock. The beauty and sense of freedom was intense, the daytime colours were muted, blending into silver and white shadows. The rocks still towered, but what little perspective there was in the day, had totally dissipated. A feeling of unreal space, silence and time surrounded me. Suddenly, the headlights of a truck appeared at a point further along the rim. A large light shone towards us. I froze in the act of jumping, and then raced back to my friends.

162

"What's going on?" I questioned. No-one else knew, but someone suggested it was probably hunters. "Don't worry about them," someone else said. "They'll not bother us." Soon after, they left. We carried on enjoying the moonlight, although try as I might, the Mother and Baby rock tower did not seem to move in my eyes, as the legend said it would. It did not matter though. I was grateful to have had the experience of being out there, amidst such beauty and splendour.

A couple of days later, we heard about the 'hunters.' It was a group of young Dine men who had gone out to Coalmine Canyon and had seen us in the distance. They had been frightened by us. Because I was leaping around all dressed in white, they thought I was an 'unmentionable' and they thought my friends, dressed in black were people into the 'dark side!' That gave Leona another good laugh. We always seemed to be laughing over one thing or another.

Several months later, I decided I would take myself off for an overnight horse ride into Canyon de Chelley. It is something organised for tourists, but I love horse riding and it was my dream to ride into a spectacular canyon, sleep on the valley floor under the stars and ride out again the next day. The night before, I parked up outside the Canyon in a tourist park. Even though I was still on the res, I felt as if I was not there in the same way, as when I was with my friends, because I was being a tourist. Probably because of this, my guard on my tongue dropped a little. In the washrooms, I met an Australian woman and we got chatting. She was very interested to hear about my life out there and somehow or other we got round to talking about the Shape Changers. I mentioned their name, something I had learnt never to do normally. Later that night, in my van, I woke from a troubled sleep. Something was running right over the roof of my van, something that had hooves like a goat. I was petrified. I could not get back to sleep. In the morning there were dusty hoof prints around and on top of my van. I felt I had had a warning and vowed never to mention them again when I was in North America.

Further proof of their existence came to me through my growing friendship with a private investigator. She had been employed to investigate the murder of a nurse, which had all sorts of strange circumstances around it. My friend was an incredibly impressive woman, who was very high powered and willing to focus everything

163

on proving her case. I met her on the res, where she had come to follow the lines of investigation. She eventually managed to prove to an American court that it was a ritualised murder committed by a Skin Walker. Even getting the court to acknowledge that they exist was a testament to her abilities. She had amazing tenacity and grit as an investigator. Some of the things she told me that had happened to her in the process of her investigation were astonishing, scary, and very much out of the ordinary.

She was really kind to me. I would go and visit her when I was in town, where she gave me a taste of Anglo-American culture in Arizona. She kept trying to get me to carry a gun with me when I went on the res. I was highly amused by this. "I couldn't use one if I tried," I responded. "Furthermore, how could I be trusted by people, if I had a gun?" Interestingly, I do not recall ever seeing one on the res.

I hate guns and the last thing I would ever want to do, is own one. It showed me how endemic the gun culture is in America. I was never threatened with a gun; mainly saw them only in Walmart,where there was, incredibly, a whole wall of them, with apparently no restrictions on who could buy them. I compared it with Britain where you must be registered with the police, there are only a few highly regulated specialised shops that deal in them, and numerous checks are done to ensure you are a fit and proper person. I could not believe how different the whole gun thing is over there. My belief is that if you trust people they will respond with trust. If you fear people, they will respond with fear. There are exceptions to this, I would never argue there weren't. However, in general I've found this to be true.

I remember when living in London, I gave up my car in the last few years. Arriving home late, I would have to walk down the street in the dark. I would always ask my guides to come close, so that I walked with confidence, showing no worries. Thankfully, nothing ever happened. Similarly, on the underground and walking round the city, if I looked lost or vulnerable, I knew I would be an instant target. I learnt to always walk with purpose, as if I knew where I was going, even if I did not. I also used this technique when travelling on my own in strange cities. I try to blend in and look as if I live there, or at least as if I know where I am.

Back in Arizona, people kept asking me why I was there. I could not respond, other than to say, "I wanted to be here."

164

I thought it would be good to have some sort of focus, so I decided I would look at different schools on the res and how the children were educated. Visiting the Akwasasne Freedom School gave me a good start, so I decided to ask one of my friends if I could visit her children's school. She made enquiries and I was duly allowed to go. It was a state-run school. This was in the years before the terrible tragedies with gunmen in schools, so it was all quite casual. I just turned up with the children and followed them round in their lessons.

It was a real eye opener. My friend's children were very bright and in the accelerated class. The first thing to astound me was that every morning these Dine children had to stand with their hand on their hearts and swear allegiance to the American flag. Apparently, this happens in all state schools. I imagined trying to enforce something like that in British schools. There would be all-out rebellion. People in this country would see it as daily brainwashing by the government.

Then I found that all the lessons were taught from a book. This was totally frowned upon in England at that time. The teacher opened the book at a certain page, she read out the lesson, and then the children had to do the exercises. Again, I could not believe it. There was no teaching involved. One of the children's friends was really struggling to understand the concept of division that she was supposed to be doing. She asked me for some help, so I showed her how to share, modelling it with a few pencils. "Oh, I get it now," she said, later telling her friends that I was a wonderful teacher. All I did was totally normal, very basic practice in British schools. I was astounded that the children had no apparatus in maths and that the teacher taught purely from a book at a certain page each day.

Imagine my horror when I returned to England to discover that the American system was being espoused and looked at for a model for our education system.

I must qualify this by saying that I understand that I only saw one state school and that I am sure there are masses of wonderful, hardworking and inspirational teachers across the States. In fact, I see some of their work on the internet nowadays which confirms they are. I just was not very impressed by what I saw that day.

The traditional Dine schools I visited gave me much more hope and inspiration. One was Rough Rock School in the north of the reservation. I was thrilled to see that the children were taught in Navajo and English. Interestingly, they were using the Haringey reading scheme (a product of I.L.E.A.) because the teachers there recognised it was of value for their children. The culture was integral to their learning, with visiting Elders coming to impart their wisdom. The community was very much a part of the school and while I was there, a pow-wow with traditional dancing and fry bread was taking place in the gym. The whole attitude was one of high professionalism, care for the children and investment in the future of the children's lives. A very far cry from the state-run school I had visited.

I had been given a name and contact to visit, so that I could be introduced properly to the school. The people I stayed with had been instrumental in the founding and development of it. They lived in a traditional hogan, way out in the res. Fascinated, I listened to how the ideas for the school had grown. They, also, taught me about the hogan and how the door always opens to the east for the morning sun. They showed me how to pray, as the Dine do, in the morning. The prayers start as the first edge of the sun comes over the edge of the horizon and continue until the full orb hangs above the horizon's line. They believe that the prayers get through easily during that window at sunrise. I remember standing in the dusty orange landscape, surrounded by rocky out crops, with the hogan behind me. It was so quiet and peaceful there. I felt privileged to be their guest. Since then, whenever I have a special prayer, I pray during those special sunrise moments.

I loved my excursions out into the reservation in the desert landscape. I always felt so free out there. Wash board roads led off the tarmacked road, taking me and my green van on new adventures. Often, I would see herds of sheep wandering around with just a sheepdog looking after them. I learnt that the Dine have the most amazing sheepdogs.

Apparently, the bitches teach the puppies how to shepherd the sheep and the skill is passed down through the generations. The sheep go out on their own, into the desert, with the dogs herding and guarding them, bringing them back when they are needed. For the Dine, sheep are paramount. The Dine legends tell how Spiderwoman taught them how to weave in an underground room. To maintain their traditional lifestyle, the women spin, card and dye the wool, then weave it into beautiful rugs. Every rug has a song which is woven into the patterns. The finished rugs are then taken to the Trading post where they are traded and sold to art collectors from around the world. A traditionally woven Navajo rug can command a very high price nowadays.

Leona was very good at helping promote the Dine culture. One of the groups she was involved was a co-operative supporting traditional weavers. She introduced me to Nia, who was a beautiful mother, weaver and poet. Nia showed me how she wove. First, she carefully chose the cedar bough for the frame, then smoothed it by hand, with love, care and attention to detail. Then she carded and spun the wool, dyed it and finally wove it into beautiful scenes.

Her home, like many, was a trailer, near Window Rock. This is a spectacular, oval window, in a crest of red rock. Starkly contrasted against the deep blue of the Arizona sky, this beautiful landmark denotes the place of the Navajo tribal government.

I spent several happy afternoons with her, appreciating her kindness. As we clambered around the rocky outcrops and desert with her children, she taught me about her culture. After that, I would call by when I was in the area and we would catch up. She was a very wise person, who had a sensible down to earth approach to life.

One time I called round after a friendship with someone had turned sour. At that point, I was beginning to wonder what was going on. Strange things were starting to happen. I was beginning to feel unwell and worry about silly things. I mentioned all this to Nia and asked her advice. She queried if this person had ever given me anything. I showed her a black stone, which I carried around with me. She picked up on that as being the source of the troubles. She told me to bury it, somewhere far away from the usual areas that I frequented. As I buried it, to ask that any attachments that had been made to it should be returned to the giver. Then I was to ask for protection from any future attacks, reflecting back any energy sent to me.

I drove along a distant road, not on the reservation. The sun was setting. As I pulled over, the evening sky darkened. Digging a small hole in the desert, I planted the black stone, sending any energies back where they came from. After that I felt lighter, happier and free.

After our friendship had gone wrong, the person who had given me the stone, had stayed with other people, where he had been abusive. Soon after I buried the stone, he left the area, and everyone was relieved to see him go. Since then, I have remembered how that worked and used the same technique, sometimes physically, sometimes metaphorically.

If someone has been horrible to you, another way to cope is to imagine mirrors around you. Any energy then directed towards you, gets reflected back. Bad thoughts, jealousy, mockery, wish to do harm, any negative thought form can be sent back to its owner. It does work. I have tried it lots of times and other people have, also, used it to good effect. You are saying on a psychic level, "I don't accept this and won't have this in my life." Ultimately, we are the ones, and the only ones who have power over our lives.

This was sadly brought home to me when I learned of the fate of many of the indigenous children who were shipped away to Carlisle Schools. These were another of America's ways to subdue and control the people from the First Nations. I suppose the thought process was, "If we educate these children in the way of the white man, they will be integrated into our culture, forget theirs and then they will forget their claims to the land we have stolen from them."

It was incredibly cruel and left a lasting legacy which is one of the major causes of the alcoholism and fragmentation of families, visible as part of some reservation life today. Traditionally, First Nation families were always very close. The children were the future, so they were treated with much love and nurturing. They were never hit or harmed. People understood that the way a child is treated, is how that child learns to treat others when they become an adult. Imagine for a moment that you are a child from such a background. You are surrounded by loving parents, aunts, uncles, cousins, part of an integrated family. Suddenly, from nowhere, strangers appear, probably with weapons. You are snatched or rounded up and taken. With many other children you are shipped hundreds of miles from your home. Your hair, which has always been a sacred part of your religious life, is cut. You are scrubbed till your skin is raw and bleeding; your loose comfortable clothes are removed and burnt, then replaced with tight, uncomfortable restricting garments. To complete the picture, when you try to talk to your friends and relations in your own language, you are cruelly beaten.

168

Physical abuse wasn't the only sort of abuse suffered by those little children from the priests and nuns running the schools. These were the Carlisle Schools. Shockingly, the last one only closed in the 1990s, not the 1890s, the 1990s.

Everything had been taken from those little pure souls. Around the schools, both in Canada and the U.S., they are now discovering the graveyards, full of these young children. Some survived the brutality, but the cycle of nurturing had been broken.

The Carlisle schools started the idea but the Mormons continued it, particularly in Tuba City, a Mormon founded town, named after a Hopi man who converted to Mormonism. There I met lots of friends of my age, who had been shipped off to live with the Mormons in the fifties and sixties as children. Their parents had been persuaded to let them go, as it was believed that they would get a better education off the reservation. Some had had good families to live with and been converted to Mormonism, which they practised alongside their Dine beliefs. Others had had a bad experience which had turned them against the religion and reinforced their wish to be part of their own cultural heritage as an adult.

Often the outsider's view of reservation life is that it sounds as if it was a very gloomy place to be, full of sad events, past traumas and upset. As I lived amongst my friends, I learnt about these things, but my experience with my friends was one of joy and laughter for a lot of the time. I remember Ron when we first met him asking us what we thought of the reservation. We said we thought it was awful that people were herded there and expected to live in isolation away from others in the society. He said, "Quite the opposite. To me the reservation is freedom; freedom to be myself, to practice my culture and to live as I want to."

CHAPTER 27

"We'll need more of you young people, who imagine the world as it should be; who knock down walls; who knock down barriers; who imagine something different and have the courage to make it happen. The courage to bring communities together, to make even the small impossibilities a shining example of what is possible." Barack Obama

As well as learning about the culture I was surrounded by, I shared a few things from England with my friends. I discovered that no-one knew about the pudding we call trifle in Britain. They could not believe I would use stale cake and thought it was hilarious when I went into Basha's supermarket and asked the cake counter for their stale cake. Custard is also unknown. You could not buy Bird's custard powder anywhere, so I had to make it fresh from eggs and milk. I piled the layers of cake, tinned fruit, custard and cream on, scattering the top with hundreds and thousands. When I carried the final product from the kitchen, they all loved it. Every time I visited after that, I was often greeted with, "Will you make a trifle?"

In turn, I learnt about fry bread. I love that food so much. Originally, I believe it was the Native American response to commodities. In exchange for the land taken from them, which was their food source and livelihood, the government agencies distributed commodities. These amounted to poor quality flour, dried and tinned foods. With usual resourcefulness, the people used them to turn into their own delicious food called fry bread. It is basically a dough mixture that is fried till it is fluffy and crunchy. Then it is served with anything you like. Savoury dishes include chilli and salad and cheese, whilst sweet dishes can have ice cream, maple syrup or any other sweet delicacy.

My private detective friend came from a wealthy area in southern Arizona. On her visits to the reservation, she sometimes brought her daughter. Her daughter was quite shocked at the material difference between her own lifestyle and that of her Dine friends and wanted to do something about it. Coming up to Christmas, she and her mum decided to organise some gifts for the children. She asked Leona and Vanessa to draw up a wish list. I went round with them, visiting families and asking the children and Elders, what was on their wish list for Christmas. Some were touchingly simple; others were more materially expensive. It was a real testament to my friend, her daughter and her school mates, who managed in a few weeks, to fulfil every wish. Basha lent them a truck and just before Christmas they arrived.

First Nations people do not receive without giving back. The visiting school children were supplied with a massive feast of fry bread and chilli, which I helped my Dine friends to serve up.

To further reciprocate the kindness, a trip to the children's school was organised by a group of dancers and a drum group. Again, I was invited to accompany them. Before we set off, one of the young Dine teenagers, who was a dancer, did a ceremony and prayers with sage and sweet grass. It was to ensure a safe journey and good day. It was great to see the young people involved in the cultural life, as the temptation to be wooed away by the lure of the dominant culture is very great.

Although the school children lived relatively close to the reservation, few of them had experienced the thrill of seeing a dance and drum group live. Hopefully, some prejudices were broken down and the beginning of bridges built on that day.

CHAPTER 28

"Life is a sum of all your choices." Albert Camus

Christmas was fast approaching, so I flew off to Key West to visit my Mum's relations. One of them was married and it was her house we stayed in, the other was visiting with her boyfriend. Touched by their kindness to a virtual stranger, I was happy to join their celebrations.

As there was no space in the house, I slept on the veranda. It was very warm, a lot warmer than Flagstaff, where snow falls in winter because of its altitude. Excited to meet my distant cousins, I enjoyed wandering round Key West with them. The Key was very arty, quite bohemian and felt intense and crowded after the vast openness of the desert landscape in Arizona.

Unlike Britain, the main celebration meal is on Christmas Eve. Our hostess had prepared a wonderful meal and I was feeling very heady and full of myself, enjoying the company of my new-found relatives. I know I can go over the top sometimes, and I was probably quite insufferable, but I was feeling very confident and happy. In doing so, I made a very silly mistake. I was so used to talking about spirits as a reality with my native friends, that I forgot to have respect. I announced I was putting a bowl with some of my food in, for the spirits to share, on the table.

That course had finished, so the two women and the boyfriend disappeared into the kitchen. A few minutes later, my hostess reappeared, snatched the spirit bowl away and informed me I was making several people extremely uncomfortable by my behaviour. I later discovered that the boyfriend was a fundamentalist Christian. I was devastated. Close to tears, I could not trust myself to speak. I had overdone it and made a fool of myself. Making my escape as soon as I could, I still could not cry, as I was sleeping on the veranda and they would hear me. I did not want them to know I was upset.

Christmas morning was not much better. I had a phone call from my Mum, Dad, Jeremy and family who were all in Bramhall. Hearing their lovely voices made me even more homesick. My hostess' mum was doing her best to make me feel happy and welcome, but I was fighting hard to suppress the tears and look as happy as I could for everyone else's sake. We had a short walk near the sea front, then the others returned to cook the meal. I offered to help, but they said it was fine; I should go on the beach for a while.

Finally alone, I wandered round the crowded town. On the reservation, if I felt upset, I would drive off into the desert and deal with my feelings, cry if I wanted to, then come back when I was ready. Here there was nowhere to go. Somehow, when it is Christmas, the feelings are all amplified. If you are feeling joy, it is great, but if you are feeling sad or lonely, it is more intense, as everyone else appears to be happy. I passed a taxi driver and he said, "Cheer up love, it's Christmas!" That did it. I knew if I could cry it would feel better, but where could I go in this crowded island? Then I thought of the beach.

Discovering one that was relatively quiet, I lay on the sand and was finally able to sob into the sand, trying not to let anyone else see. Not wanting to appear tear streaked on my return to the house, I put my face down, trying not to be noticed, and went in the sea to wash. Before returning to the house for the meal, I managed to regain my composure and got through the rest of my stay uneventfully. I was much quieter than when I had arrived and left having learnt a valuable lesson.

It all helped me understand how others feel, particularly at Christmas. It's a day which many people try to make special. Lots of people are invited to visit others, who would normally be on their own. Going back to my understanding of the spirits from the trance work I used to do, there are fewer sad humans around on that day for the confused souls to express themselves through. As a result, if anyone is upset, they get more than the usual amount of 'free-riders' wanting to express themselves, so the feeling of sadness intensifies more than ever.

The taxi driver made me realise never to say to anyone, "Cheer up it's Christmas." That is the worst thing you can do. It has also made me sensitive to people being left out and feeling alone. Since then, I have tried to make sure that no-one I know is in that situation.

173

CHAPTER 29

"The best and most beautiful things in the world cannot be seen or even touched. They must be felt with the heart." Helen Keller

With a sense of relief, I arrived back in Arizona. My green van was so welcoming, as were all my friends. It felt like I was home again.

In January, my six-month visa was due to expire. I started thinking about moving on to the next stage of my trip. Patti persuaded me not to. "You can't go yet," she said. "You have to stay for the Bean Dance." Earlier in my stay, my friends in Tuba, had introduced me to a Hopi guy who was a solicitor. He knew me from my various visits, so he could vouch for me and helped me do all the paperwork. Soon my visa was extended till the fourth of April.

The winter solstice had been and gone, so the Kachinas were back from their summer and autumn home in the San Francisco Peaks, performing ceremonies in the Hopi villages. Rustling cornstalks from the summer and autumn were being replaced in the fields by the seeds to create new life. The Kachinas were there to assist in this life-giving act. I seemed to be spending more and more time with Tom and Patti, the Hopi life drawing me closer. It had taken a while for their friends and family to trust me, but once I had been accepted, they were very warm and caring towards me. I was incredibly touched by several deep and meaningful gestures of that friendship, showing me how much I had been included in their lives.

Finally, the long-awaited Bean Dance arrived. I do not think I should say too much about the Bean Dance and my experiences there, other than it was one of the most special and moving days of my life. Etched on my memory like it was yesterday, I felt extremely honoured to be included to the extent I was. I know how private the Hopi are about their ceremonies and it would feel as if I was betraying the very treasured trust of my friends, if I were to reveal any details about it. Suffice it to be known, it was well worth staying for and I was so glad that I listened to Patti again.

Apart from having seen my Mum and Dad, the only other friends I saw whilst out there, were my friends Helen and Jonathan, with whom I had shared a flat in London. They happened to be on tour as part of a singing group and were near enough to come and visit me. It was great to see some friends from home and share some of my experiences with them. I introduced them to Tom and Patti in Flagstaff and then Vanessa up in Tuba. I asked Tom if it was okay to take them up onto the mesas and he suggested I took them up to Walpi for the guided tour.

They could not believe they were still in America. For them, the Hopi mesas had a similar feel to the timeless buildings in Israel. (Interestingly, I heard that the Israelis had visited the Hopi to learn about their techniques for farming in the desert.) Helen and Jonathan loved wandering around the old stone houses, seeing the stout wooden ladders peeking out above the kivas. Viewing the rocky, burnt orange desert, they gazed down at the cornfields far below the precipitous cliffs, which marked the edges of the village. I warned them about the strict rules that the Hopi adhere to for tourists in their villages. They totally sympathised. Apparently, the Anglo-American population did not appear to have the same regard for personal space that we are afforded in Britain. My friend said that she was often in her dressing room and fans would just walk in, with no respect for her privacy. She found it very intrusive.

I had become so absorbed with my life in Arizona, which was utterly different from my life in England, that it felt very special to share a fraction of it with my friends. It was hard to think how I would relate to others who had not shared my experiences on my return to home. On reflection, it must be even harder for people who have been away to extreme situations like war zones. The worlds they have encountered are so vastly different from the world their families are left behind in, I can really understand how they feel bonded to their colleagues and set apart from others who have not experienced the same things.

Waving goodbye to my friends from home as they left to resume their tour, I knew my own time to leave was fast approaching. It was incredibly hard to leave everyone, particularly my closest friends and their children, of whom I had grown very fond. I said my farewells in stages, leaving everyone in Tuba City first, and then Flagstaff. I promised Vanessa that I would write. "I'll look forward to your letters," she said as I left. I could not imagine never seeing them again, but I knew it would be a long time before I did. As I hugged them all goodbye, a wave of sadness threatened to overwhelm me. In the eight months of visiting and getting to know Vanessa, Leona and their families, I had grown to feel very close to them all.

Down in Flagstaff, Tom and Patti organised a big cook out in a local nature park, inviting their friends whom I had got to know. Patti was very worried about me travelling on my own. She was very motherly towards me and we were like sisters to each other. She kept warning me about the perils of Mexico and how dangerous it would be to be travelling on my own. I promised to keep writing and let her know how I was. It was very hard leaving her, but I knew I would keep in touch, no matter what.

As I took my final leave of them all, I hugged their little daughter in my arms. Tears started rolling down my cheeks. Tom very quickly took his little girl back into his arms and made light of the parting for her. Later, I realised he was trying to protect her from my emotion. I had been very selfish, indulging in my feelings, whilst holding the little girl that I was going to miss so much. I suppose I wanted her to remember me, like I would always remember her. Tom realised it was not fair on the child to be engulfed in my emotion and quickly moved to protect her from it. Chris was older, a teenager, so he was less vulnerable to my emotions and could understand my hugs and tears in context.

I knew I would miss them all so much and they would always have a special place in my heart.

I stayed with my friend's father in Phoenix, whilst I sold my van, making a small profit, although I had spent quite a lot on repairing it and keeping it in good shape. Some Australian women who were travelling to the east coast bought it. I then lived and travelled on the proceeds of that sale for the next four months. Finally, I was embarking on the next stage of my great adventure.

CHAPTER 30

"We live in a wonderful world that is full of beauty, charm and adventure. There is no end to the adventures we can have if only we seek them with our eyes open." Jawaharlal Nehru

Knowing I should not stay in the border town, as they are very dodgy places for a woman on her own, I took the first bus out to a small northern town, called Nuevo Casa Grandes. Near to the town were some ancient ruins called Paquime that I wanted to visit. Falling asleep on the bus, I woke with a shock to realise the five-hour bus trip was over. It was dusk and I was in a strange town. The Spanish I had hurriedly learnt in evening classes before I left London was rather rusty and minimal. Picking the name of a hotel from my traveller's guide to make it look as if I knew where I was going, I tried to ask the driver of the bus where it was.

His English was on a par with my Spanish. He could see we were getting nowhere between us. He leaned out of the bus and called to a group of men standing by what looked like a taxi rank. One man came on the bus, who could speak English a bit better. He explained where the hotel was, but said I should not go alone, he would accompany me. Thinking of all the fear from my friends in Arizona, I shook my head, declining his offer. The bus driver, who was incredibly kind, then decided he would take me in his bus (a large coach) round to the hotel. The man followed in his car. Then he insisted on coming in with me, carrying my bags and helping me to register with the woman on the desk. In the back of my mind, I kept thinking, "Oh no, I'm going to have to fight him off." Despite my protests, he carried my bags upstairs to the room, where he deposited them outside the door, shook my hand and left. I was astounded. Touched by the kindness of everyone involved, who looked for nothing in return apart from having helped a stranger, I felt very humbled and sad to think I had misread his motives so quickly.

From then on, I felt safe travelling in Mexico, more so than I did in America. At least everyone here did not own their own guns.

I loved that village. The ancient ruins of Paquime, felt linked to the Hopi migration stories. I felt a strange bond with the people that once lived there, knowing what I did from the Hopi. It looked like quite an advanced civilisation, with channels for running water visible, amongst the ruined streets and adobe buildings. Key-hole shaped doorways led from one maze of rooms, open to the sky, into another. No-one else was about; it was free to wander round. Seemingly the local town did not think to exploit the ruins in anyway. It was a privilege to spend time there, totally alone, apart from the odd crowing of a distant cockerel and the dusty heat of ancient memories.

Travelling on I took the bus through the state of Chihuahua, to a catch a train. In my mind, I felt this would take me to more living links with the Hopi, the Taramuhara Indians. Like the Hopi, this tribe has been historically reticent to interact and talk to others about their cultural secrets. They still lived in cliff cave dwellings, like the Hopi ancestors did. The dwellings are situated in the ravines and canyons of the largest Grand Canyon in America, Barranca del Cobre or Copper Canyon. Planting corn and beans, weaving from the plants around them and living from the animals that survive there, the Raramuri, as they call themselves, quietly get on with their lives. They wanted no interference and lived a quality of life that many in our crazy modern world are beginning to see has much value. The Raramuri are the most amazing long-distance runners. If any Taramuhara were to enter the Olympics, no-one else would stand a chance. Traditionally they run barefoot, over large distances, to visit each other, for races and for survival. A two hundred mile run over two days is commonplace for all members of the tribe.

Since the early nineties, the existence of this amazing people is under threat. Apparently, the drug cartels and logging companies have moved into their remote region. Their crops are sprayed with herbicides to prevent them from growing their own food, so that the drug barons can force them to grow their illegal substances. Torture and life threats subdue these gentle people into an awful existence. I look back to the time when I visited, just prior to this terrorism of their culture. I feel so sad and angry for the wasted lives of people who just wanted to live a peaceful, gentle life. It is so short sighted. Can't these apologies-for-humans see how much the Raramuri should be valued? A day will come soon when we need the survival knowledge of peoples like the Raramuri. I wonder if the greedy drug barons will ever finally understand. How many more lifetimes will it take for their souls to evolve into better human beings? If only they realised what they are condemning themselves to, with their greed and avarice.

Back in the late eighties, the Raramuri were very reticent and quite rightly, reluctant to have much contact with the surrounding culture and the growing tourist trade in the area. In the eighteenth century, a mission post had been established at Creel in the Barrancas del Cobre, where the train would stop. I took the spectacular train ride from Chihuahua and landed in Creel.

As we pulled away from Chihuahua, I was shocked to see people living in railway trucks alongside the line. Even in difficult conditions, people were still trying to make the best out of it, with bright red geraniums splashing colour onto the steps of the old trucks. As the countryside began to stretch out, cowboys herded cattle across the dusty flat plains, the large, blue sky stretching overhead. Eventually, the plains gave way to the beginning of the Sierra Madre, hills clothed in cacti and dry rocky outcrops. The train travelled on, gradually climbing through spectacular gorges and passes, tunnels and alongside ravines. I wished Dad could have been with me. He would have loved the trip. I did the next best thing and took lots of photos of the bridges and curves in the line, as the front of the train looped its way ahead of us.

Arriving at the dusty station in Creel, we discovered a town under construction. Everything seemed to be half built or in the process. On the station I met a woman about my age and discovered she was from Leeds. I love that side of travelling alone. It is easy to meet others and link together for a while, till our roads split. We became friends and travelling companions.

It was great to chat in English again. Sue was travelling to Nicaragua to do voluntary work. She had learnt Spanish and was much more fluent than I was. I felt a bit frivolous, travelling purely for pleasure, but it did not feel as if that was my path. Nowadays it seems very different; the next generation are more like Sue. I am impressed by young relatives and friends who travel to help others, work in shanty towns or to raise awareness of people's plight. Travelling seems to be more focussed on helping others instead of just pleasure and voyeurism, as it used to be. I see that as a very positive move forward.

179

Together, Sue and I explored the local area, hitching rides on the local's trucks. One day we visited a beautiful, tranquil lake, nestling in pine woods and then on another day, we went to the local Cusare waterfall. We had to walk along a white dusty track, which meandered amongst the pine woods, dotted with grey rocks, weather worn into amazing shapes. After quite a trek, we arrived at the falls. Several streams combined to fall over a large rock escarpment, tumbling ninety feet to massive rocks at the base.

On arrival we heard laughter and shouting. A group of glamorous looking young Mexican men and women were taking the opportunity to turn life into a party. They were dressed in shorts and tee-shirts, getting soaked under the cascading streams, drinking beer, and screaming with the laughter we had heard. Beckoning us to join them, their friendly warmth quickly enveloped us. Soon we were clambering around the massive rocks together, drinking beers and cooling down, with the silky water rinsing away the dust. They were on a day out from work and were making the most of it.

Again, I reflected on the people that I had been warned about before I left the States. The Mexicans I had encountered could not have been further from the truth. I had received nothing but warmth, care, friendliness and kindness. I am sure there were unkind people out there, but I have learnt to treat everyone as I find them. If I treat people with kindness, more often than not, I receive kindness back. If I approach someone with an aggressive attitude, I generally get aggression back.

The sun was setting as we left the valley, our new friends kindly giving us a lift in the back of their pickup truck, back to Creel. Nothing beats the feeling of sitting in the back of a pick-up. The warm wind was blowing my hair, as the moon came out over the silhouettes of the tall pines growing amongst rocky outcrops. Their shadowy forms were outlined against the darkening blue depths of the sky as we sped past, feeling tired but happy after our long day out.

Another day we decided to do the long trek into the base of the Copper Canyon. The hostel, where we were staying, organised a tour there. We joined it, walking down through the winding paths amongst the trees and rocks till we finally arrived at the river in the base of the canyon. Swimming in the natural rocky pools, was very welcome after our sticky climb down.

My Hopi friends were foremost in my thoughts, and I kept feeling drawn to the Raramuri. I felt in a very special place, having been included so much by my Hopi and Dine friends and I suppose I wanted that indescribable feeling to continue. Aware that the Raramuri lived in caves in the cliff sides, as the Hopi ancestors had done, I wondered if they were linked. Their traditional lifestyles were similar, farming beans and corn on difficult and dry terrain. Despite wanting contact, I was very aware of respecting their privacy and not intruding on them. The only connection I had was when I bought the tourist gifts, a tiny wooden doll, a carved figure and a beautifully woven basket from pine needles. The smell of pine lasted for years, reminding me of the pungent resin abounding in the remote canyons. I bought some slides of the Taramuhara, which showed their homes, as I did not want to photograph them without their consent. The slides had been taken by a local priest. I was assured they were taken with permission and that some of the proceeds would go to the Raramuri people.

Obviously, I was not going to have the same connection I had had in Arizona. I did not speak the same language, the Taramuhara were less integrated into the surrounding culture, I was only there for a few days, not months, and I had no opening introduction. Irrationally, I still felt a little sad at not having made any links. I do not know what I was expecting. Maybe my time there was to mark the transition between living amongst my friends and experiencing their lives, to becoming a tourist, viewing from afar and not fully understanding. Whatever it was, I felt as I mounted the train to leave Creel that I was beginning to put away the special feelings and sensitivity I had built in Arizona into a carefully guarded box. As a result, I could then harden myself to a more distanced approach, observing, but not being a part of, my surroundings.

If I had thought the train ride to Creel was good, I was in for an amazing treat. From Creel down to Los Mochis, the railway wound itself down mountain sides, through tunnels which curved into the sheer three-thousand-foot slopes, then emerged lower down, curving back on itself. Suddenly we would find ourselves crossing a terrifically high bridge, spanning a deep gorge, with no protective railings, and then plunging into a dark tunnel to come out hugging another steep cliff face. Consistently spectacular, it is an amazing feat of engineering, travelling through a total of thirty-seven bridges and eighty-six tunnels through the Sierra Madre.

At the end of this spectacular journey, we had to catch another train to get to the seaside. If the last train was heavenly, this was the train from Hell! To say it was late was an understatement. British Rail was as efficient as the Swiss trains in comparison with this one. We sat on the platform for *ten hours* waiting for it to arrive. As we sat, different vendors wandered onto the platform tempting us to buy snacks. We dare not leave the station as it could have arrived at any time. None of the Mexicans seemed bothered. No-one got angry or hot-under-the-collar starting to threaten this and that, as they would have in England. They just shrugged their shoulders and sat there in the sunshine. We ended up feeling the same in the end. "It will get here when it gets here," we kept saying.

Sue decided to buy some banana chips from the vendors. She was vegetarian and there was a limit to what she could get to eat for the journey. I bought some raisins. Finally, the train arrived. Settling into our seats, we opened our snacks. Eagerly we shared the raisins and the banana chips. Suddenly Sue gasped. "Oh no!" she exclaimed, "I don't believe it." Wriggling amongst the dried fruit were banana-coloured maggots. The bananas had not been dried properly giving rise to dampness which had allowed the maggots to breed. We decided to go hungry.

As dusk fell, we tried to settle as best we could into a sleeping position on the hard seats. Wriggling around, using our bags as pillows, we gradually started to doze fitfully. Darkness descended and the train rattled on through the night. We drifted in and out of consciousness, aware of our fellow travellers around us. Suddenly I was jerked out of an uncomfortable dream. "Pam," Sue whispered, "Something's dripping on me."

"Is it raining? Is the roof leaking?" I queried.

"I don't think so; I can't see any rain on the windows."

"It must be coming from somewhere. Are you sure you're not dreaming?"

"I think it's coming from the suitcase above me in the luggage rack."

"Oh my God. What colour is it?" I replied.

"I can't see. It's dark. Oh yuck, it dripped again. I can't stand this." The middle of the night gives rise to many crazy ideas. All sorts of horrific scenarios started going through our heads, the most extreme being that the suitcase had a severed body part inside it. Sue tried to move herself to stop the periodic dripping. This was not easy as the train was very full. The long night ended, we arrived at our destination and the owner of the suitcase claimed it. On mentioning the dripping, we discovered that the water torture had been occasioned by a defrosting fish.

Guyamas seemed like a good seaside town to experience the Pacific Coast, so rather than risking another train, we took a coach to get us there. We stayed in Hotel Mysterioso. It looked quite posh from the outside. A different view was to be had on entering the place. I do not know if it still exists. Looking at Guyamas on the internet, it looks as if it has become a resort town catering for tourists, so I am sure it will have disappeared under a swathe of redevelopment by now.

At that time, Guyamas was a quiet seaside town, with palm fronded huts along the front and driftwood marking trails on the sandy beach. The sea was a brownish colour, more like a northern English seaside resort, with frigate birds swooping and diving across our heads as we walked along the sand, scuffing our toes. Our hotel was the epitome of decayed splendour and had obviously been quite special once, but the gardens were the only area that reminded us of its past glory. An empty pool in the middle of the stately palm trees emphasised there was no-one to maintain it, whilst we were housed in a concrete room which was intact. Wandering round the rest of the building, we discovered other rooms that were not being rented out because they were not secure. It felt very bizarre. Our room was basic but sound. We had a window, a door that we could shut and lock, with a shower room down the corridor. Walking along the corridor, one side was open to the garden, where we could see the palms waving and beyond that the beach. On the other side were doorways. Some led into rooms like ours, whilst others were derelict rooms with birds nesting and holes in the ceiling. Wandering on to the next floor, we found a room that had a spectacular view and would have been a beautiful restaurant or dance hall, but it was just the basic space with the concrete walls and plastic tables looking very bare and barren. We loved it. Sue had the same way of looking at things. We romanticised on how it used to be, what went where and who would be there. The cheap cost was an added bonus. We had a splendid position, right on the beach, with a room that was safe to sleep in yet easily affordable on a backpacker's budget.

After a few more visits to different Pacific coastal resorts, we decided to hit Mexico City. The efficient and quick coach system was great to travel on after the vagaries of the trains.

By this time, we had linked up with another woman. For economy, we all shared a room. Mexico City was great, so much to see and learn about; the Aztec ruins and wall murals, the museums, the National Palace and the Cathedral, purposely built by the Spanish on the site of the main Aztec temple. Above all, I loved going in the park to see the Voladores. They are amazing. Five men climb up a pole that is thirty metres high. At the top is a square frame. On reaching the top, four of the men tie themselves to the pole with a rope and wrap it around their waist. The fifth stays on the top and plays a flute. Simultaneously, the others launch themselves off the top, one on each side of the square frame, then 'fly' upside down, spinning round, the rope lengthening with each turn of the square. Finally, they reach the ground. The flute player then descends with the help of his fellow Voladores. I would be petrified launching myself off such a height but apparently the men believe it is a great honour and work hard to become one.

Whilst in Mexico we visited one of my favourite ancient ruins, Teotichuacan. Outside the mayhem and polluted air of the city, the ruins rise in peaceful grandeur. The pyramid of the Sun is at one end and the pyramid of the Moon at the other, with a large road or channel leading down the middle. It was already in existence when the Aztecs arrived. They believed it had been created by the Gods. I once read a theory in a book called the 'Fingerprints of the Gods' by Graham Hancock. It states that the monument is a giant seismograph, to register earthquakes around the world or at least it could, if it had water in the channels and modern-day people knew how to understand it. The book argued a fascinating theory that if a civilization wanted to leave a record of how advanced their culture was, they would leave that record in a form that went beyond the written word. This symbolism would have to be understood by a society who had an equally advanced scientific knowledge, to show the people of the future that earlier times, also, held this knowledge.

184

The intervening peoples of a maybe lesser developed civilisation would marvel and wonder at them, but not decode their meaning (like us). I really like this theory.

In present day Mexico, the ruins echoed to the sound of clay flutes, touted to the tourists. People wandered amongst the remains of ancient buildings that line the broad walkway, whilst guidebooks tried to explain the mysteries of the place. No explanation was as satisfactory in my mind, as the one I was later to read in 'Fingerprints of the Gods.'

CHAPTER 31.

"You may be deceived if you trust too much, but you will live in torment if you don't trust enough." Frank Crane

Back in Mexico City a young Mexican man, let us call him Carlos, had started chatting to us in the park one day. I showed some interest in him and we started seeing each other. The others were not bothered, but I suppose I was looking for a connection to local people. I wanted to be more than a voyeur, touring and watching life as I sailed past. I wanted to know what it was really like to live in Mexico.

Looking back, I was utterly naïve and stupid. At the time I got caught up in it all. After a few days, my travelling companions and I were all heading off south to Palenque. I told Carlos. He then told me a tale of how his mother had suddenly been taken ill, he could not afford the hospital fees and he did not know what he was going to do. Part of me knew it was a con, but there was enough of a question in me to think, well what if it is not? Could I in all conscience, not give him the money in case it was true? After all, I was travelling in a country with massive poverty as well as wealth, I was fortunate enough to have enough to share and if it were true, I could never forgive myself. Even though I was still suspicious, I gave him the money, giving him the benefit of the doubt. He thanked me, and then left me with a phone number to ring him on my return to Mexico City.

Palenque was beautiful. I loved the waterfalls and the ruined Mayan temples. The carving was so different from the Eastern carvings I had seen in Asia or the western carvings in Europe. What I enjoyed about these sights was the lack of commercialism around them. I do not know if it is still like that, but back then, it was all very casual. Very few people were visiting, and we could climb down into the temples, wander around the ruins and go where we liked. Different sorts of birds screeched and sang in the trees, lush vegetation grew all around us and the warm sticky heat slowed down the speed of exploration.

186

As usual, our accommodation was cheap and basic with rather rickety plumbing. I was sitting on the loo, early one morning, when the whole toilet shook. Searching for a logical explanation, I thought it must be a cleaner being a bit vigorous with the loo brush in an adjacent facility, which then had a knock-on effect on my loosely fixed bathroom wear. I thought no more of it. Later that day, I heard there had been a big earthquake in Mexico City, over a hundred miles away. Then I realised what the wobbly toilet meant.

On returning to Mexico City, I was worried about what we would see and if there would be casualties from the earthquake. The Mexicans seemed unbothered. The only people that were traumatised were other travellers. One bloke told me he had been in bed asleep and without even knowing it, he found himself standing in the doorway. Apparently, his subconscious got him to the safest place. He, and others we talked to, said how unnerving it was to feel the earth shifting under them. We are programmed into thinking it is solid and unmoving, so when it does the exact opposite it's very traumatic. All of them told us it had affected the way they looked at life.

Thinking of my Mexican friend, I wanted to check he had been okay. I rang him. It seemed a bit strange. I tried in my broken Spanish to explain who I was trying to speak to, as a variety of different people came on the phone. Eventually, Carlos came on and arranged to meet me. When we met up, he was fine. I asked how his mother was. He seemed to gloss over it and said she was getting better. I explained I was going on to the Yucatan next and would be leaving in the next few days. He then started talking about joining me in a few days...but he would have to borrow some money to be able to get there. He swore he would pay me back. At this point I really did feel he was a con man, but again there was the element of doubt. I decided that if I trusted him, I would find out if the whole thing was a con. I gave in and gave him some more money. We arranged a time and place. Unsurprisingly, he never turned up.

Sue and I were taking our leave of each other. She was going on to Nicaragua hoping to work on projects helping local people. I was carrying on as a tourist. We exchanged addresses and moved our separate ways.

CHAPTER 32

"No snowflake in an avalanche ever feels responsible." Voltaire

The Yucatan was beautiful. In Merida I bought a hammock, on the recommendation of other travellers, who told me I would need it for sleeping in on the beaches. Avoiding Cancun like the plague, it was already a built-up tourist town, I headed to Playa del Carmen.

It was like arriving in a building site. One main road led into the place from the highway and that was the only tarmacked one. On either side, buildings were being constructed. It was very dusty on the main street. Turning off to the left, I found a beach camp for back packers. It was fab. There were little huts where I could sling my hammock at night, palm trees rustled above, their dry leaves crackling together. In the middle of the area was a communal washing place. Everyone lived in bikinis and sarong style clothing. The day was spent swimming in the warm blue sea, sunbathing and dozing in our hammocks in the shade. I relished experiencing the silky waters of the Caribbean, the hot sun and the relaxed lifestyle after all my travelling.

After a day or two's rest, I was eager to explore again. Just a short walk down the road was a lovely lagoon called Xcaret. Walking down the dusty track, I noticed some palm-thatched wooden framed homes off to the side. They looked in a bit of disrepair. At the end, was a lovely collection of rock pools. We wandered across the rocks marvelling at the tropical fish swimming in them, caught by the tide. Walking further round we came across the lagoon. A massive overhang of rock shaded the pool, which was calm, deep and dark. Slipping into the cool water, we could swim in this wonderful place. I cannot remember if we had to pay a small entrance fee to get into the area, but I do not think we did. I am sure we just walked round.

Only six years later I returned to the same place. Playa del Carmen was a fully built commercial resort, I could not recognise it. Saddened, I went round to see the little lagoon in the rocks. Gone was the dusty track, gone were the locals' wooden homes, instead was a massively guarded 'Swim with the dolphins' resort village at a hundred dollars a day entry. Fancy air-conditioned coaches were lined up in the drive to deliver the tourists, cushioned from the environment they had come to see. Their only contact with the local people was when they tipped the maid who cleaned their room or the waiter who served them. I could not believe it, such a vast change in so short a time. We could not afford to go in and I am glad we did not. I am sure it would have been a massive disappointment. That beautiful untouched piece of nature was utterly commercialised.

With hindsight, sadly I was probably part of the movement that caused it to happen. Backpackers like myself, saw the beauty, visited, and showed an interest in a place. Local or foreign entrepreneurs, recognised the potential and saw an opportunity to make money, based on our enjoyment. It does not take long before the masses invade with their cushioned TV view through glass coach windows and their separation from local life. For that sort of tourism people will pay European or US prices, in an economy which operates on much less. Wanting home comforts, they are willing to pay to get it, rather than experience what it is like to sleep and eat like the local people do, at a fraction of the cost. I prefer the other way. I only enjoy going to Mexico when I can spend a lengthy time there, a month or two, seeing the place properly and meeting people. Two months of my travelling style cost less than one week on a package tour.

Whilst at Playa, I took a local bus and visited the amazing temples in the area. Rising out of the forests, they tower like hills. Chichen Itza sprawled across acres of closely cropped grass. Warmth and security oozed from the stones, as I followed well-trodden tourist routes around the site. The perimeter walls of the ball court towered above me, covered in geometrical carvings; the peace and calm belying what must have happened there in the past. Following a shady path, I discovered the Cenote; a large circular hole in the earth, about sixty metres across, holding an invitingly cool looking pool way below. The rings upon rings of chalky white limestone formed steep walls leading down to the water, only navigable by rope. I shuddered, thinking of how hard it would be to get out of the water if one fell in.

Moving back into the scorching sunlight, I walked over to explore 'El Castillo' the most spectacular pyramid, believed to be built as a temple to the Mayan God Kukulkan. Climbing the ninety-one very steep steps, I panted to the platform and was rewarded with a spectacular view over the forested landscape, stretching for miles in every direction. I had not realised how flat the surrounding area was. A soft breeze helped to cool me down. After edging round the steps on the platform, (which combined with the ninety-one steps on each side total three-hundred-and-sixty-five steps altogether) I decided to brave the descent into the interior.

Deep in the centre of the pyramid was a softly lit room holding the jaguar statue with its jewel bedecked eyes. It was protected behind a set of bars, presumably to stop people pinching its wealth. The weight of stone above and around me felt oppressive. Emerging back into the sunshine was a relief.

Whilst I was standing on the flat land near the four-sided temple, one of the guides clapped his hands. The acoustics were amazing. A zing zing sound ricocheted back from the temple steps. I have no idea how that sound was created from the clapping, but it was. Apparently, the sound imitates the precious quetzal bird, considered sacred to the ancient Mayan peoples. To be there at the spring or autumn equinox when the shadow of a snake appears on the steps of the temple, would have been amazing, but I could not wait for four months. Humbled by the achievements of past cultures, I continued on.

Discovering a guy who was going the same way as me, we teamed up to hitch lifts down the long coastal road. Still eager to see more temples, I marvelled at Tulum, another ancient Mayan collection of buildings. The guide told us it was a study place for Mayan priests, where they trained in astronomy and developed their understanding of the heavens. The rectangular structures, again covered in ancient symbols and carvings, are situated in one of the most stunning situations they could be. Green trees dotted around the site contrasted with the deep blue sky. An azure sea lapped against the cliffs, at the foot of the temple. Very few people were there. Again, we had the freedom to go wherever we wanted, in and out of the buildings. It took up much less area than Chichen Itza, so our tour was completed quite quickly. As we climbed down the cliff path, I felt a sense of peace and beauty. Paddling in the sea from the white sandy beach was blissful.

Leaving Tulum, an American couple gave us a lift and they asked us if we would like to join them in a stop-off at a nature reserve. We wandered along paths crossing beautiful lagoon, after beautiful lagoon, the succession of lakes following one on from the other.

After that stop-off, we hitched another ride. This time it was with a local car driver. As we drove along the forest road, suddenly the air was filled with clouds of butterflies. I have never seen so many. Beautiful orange and black winged creatures fluttered in every space around the car. I was devastated. The driver did not slow down. Hundreds of the tiny bodies were battered by unforgiving steel as it progressed through them. I could not say anything. My Spanish was not good enough to explain what I felt, whilst feeling obliged to be polite to the person who was giving us a lift. The cloud seemed to go on for ages.

Later, I discovered that they were Monarch butterflies. They migrate in huge swarms every winter, travelling two-thousand-five-hundred miles, ending up on the same fir trees every year, even though they are the next generation each time. Sadly, as the coastline is becoming more and more developed, the precious trees are being cut down for houses and resort developments. Some people are working to protect them, but as with everything, until the overall human mind-set changes, money and profit will destroy any form of nature that impedes its psycho-pathway to greed.

CHAPTER 33

"As a child I loved visiting my grandparent's house in Goole. It was called Belize House." Joan Colbran

As we reached the border of Mexico, my travelling companion took my leave as he had no papers to get into Belize. After crossing, I decided to take the bus, as a safer option when travelling on my own. I later discovered that my family had connections with the country from the last century. As ship merchants in Goole, my great grandmother's house was called Belize House because of their trading links. My mum said that visiting that house as a child was like a dream. It was full of treasures to a little girl. Toys tucked in attics, strange things in jars and always something new to be discovered. She, in turn, created a home full of treasures and toys. Our home was noted for being a wonderful place to visit, particularly if you were a child.

Belize City was reputed to be a dangerous place. It seemed okay to me in the daylight, but people had warned me to get a boat to the Cayes, rather than staying the night. I would be safer there. Following the advice, within an hour of arriving in the small city, built around the mouth of an estuary, I was speeding out to Caye Caulker. Leaving behind the wooden houses on stilts and muddy waterfronts, the small motor launch carried several backpackers into the blue sea. As we approached the tiny island, I could make out a few wooden huts where travellers could sling a hammock at night, with decent showers. On my first day, I had explored the whole place from one end to the other in less than twenty minutes. With no cars and only bicycles as traffic, I loved the sign that stated, 'Slow Down,' painted on an old board.

The Rastafarians that lived there encouraged this 'slow down and take life easy attitude,' so that strangely, over the days I stayed there, the island appeared to become bigger. Everyone was motivated to walk slower. It gradually became more of an effort to get from one end to the other and I began to be aware of the details between places. The longer I was there, the more I began to identify the different zones on the island, who lived where and what I could do in different places. It is something I have never forgotten. As I have lived in other places, I have become aware of the same effect. The longer I live somewhere, the bigger it gets, as I learn the details and nuances of life around me. Remembering the Rastafarian links with the Hopi, I was interested in their views on life. In Britain, the impression one got was that Rastafarians were only linked with reggae music and the culture of marijuana smoking.

After a few chats with people, I discovered that contrary to my preconceptions, Rastafarians were not all about smoking weed. Keen on nature and living in balance with their environment is very important to them, which was reflected in my experiences on the island.

One of the Rastafarian guys had a boat and charged the visitors to go out for the day. He made it a whole experience, taking us into what looked like the middle of the sea, dropping anchor, and then letting us swim from the boat amongst the amazing coral and fish. I love snorkelling. The flat surface of the smooth blue sea appears endlessly the same, stretching away to meet the deep blue sky. Donning the snorkel and mask, a vast scene from another world is revealed. It is like looking at a plain façade of a dolls house, only to open it and discover detailed and intricate worlds. It is better than a doll's house because it is alive and you become a part of it, swimming amongst fish, which glide past you in ever swirling shoals, swaying with the currents. The living colours assault the senses, feasting your eyes with beauty. I love the sensation of floating, suspended above this other, hidden world.

We would keep returning to the boat, resting a while on the deck in the sun, and then swimming off again. Meanwhile, he caught some fish. Gutting, skinning and cleaning them, he then cooked them, providing a delicious fish lunch. I did find it rather sad to be eating some of the beautiful fish we had seen, but he assured us, they were very common on the reef and he never caught any that were not plentiful. As the day wore on, he began to tell us his story. Growing up on the Cayes, he decided to make a living from the gradually developing tourist trade. He worked hard to raise enough cash, got himself a flight to Florida, walked into a fishmonger's shop and asked for a job. They looked at him sceptically, but when he showed them how quickly and efficiently, he could clean a fish, they took him on in a breath.

After a couple of years hard graft, he had saved up enough money to return home and buy a boat. Now he an idyllic lifestyle, out on the boat all day, doing what he loved, in a setting most would regard as paradise. He was a real inspiration. He showed me that if you want something, decide how to achieve it. Then follow the path till it all happens. No matter how hard or difficult it may seem, you will get there.

On Caye Caulker, I met up with a couple of guys called Mark and Chris, who were going the same route as me. After several days of laid-back bliss, we decided to leave and travel together. Catching a bus from Belize City, we wound our way through lush countryside, which gradually turned from farms into rainforest.

CHAPTER 34

"We are not myths of the past, ruins in the jungle, or zoos. We are people and we want to be respected, not to be victims of intolerance and racism." Rigoberta Menchu Tum (Guatemalan Indigenous Rights Activist 1992 Nobel Peace prize winner)

Our destination was Guatemala and after crossing the border, we stayed in a hostel in Flores, near the ancient ruins of Tikal. As in Chichen Itza, these towering pyramids rose out of the jungle, with rectangular rooms atop the steep steps. Brilliant birds flashed among the trees, butterflies flitted around our heads and monkeys chattered at us, as we wandered amongst the ruins. The site was quite big and there were mounds still to be uncovered, looking like small hills, amongst the other temples. One was partially uncovered, soil and trees still clinging to half of it, whilst scaffolding was erected around the steps, which protected and supported the workers, who were cleaning the vegetation away. In this climate everything grows so rapidly that it does not take long for the earth to disguise man-made edifices.

Tikal has one particularly high temple. Looking up from the bottom it presented a challenge to climb. The steps were steep and treacherous, particularly as there was nothing to hold on to. I used both hands to support me as I pulled myself up the daunting staircase. It was well worth the effort. The view from the top was amazing; jungle floated like a sea of green around us, the treetops stretching as far as the eye could see. Having walked amongst the green filtered light of the trees below, it was surprising to be up in the canopy and see how far the tree covered area extended. I tried to imagine being an ancient Mayan priest seeing both above and below. It must have seemed a very privileged position to be in, to have such a different physical perspective on their world from most of the Mayan citizens. As I left Tikal, I thought with admiration of a culture which so many years ago, had recognised the power of height on the human psyche.

Flores is situated on a lake. Other travellers told us about a waterslide we should go and visit. Taking a ferry, we found ourselves on an island in the middle of the lake. At the top was a concrete slide that travelled the complete height of the island until it shot people out into the lake at the base. As the only people there, we wondered if it was safe. It did look very high and very fast. We found a tap to turn on the water so that it was running down the concrete to ease the passage. There was no-one there to say do not do it, so several of the guys decided they would have a go. The speed they reached seemed to be very fast, as I watched from the top. Scrambling back up the hill, they were full of how exhilarating it was, urging me to have a go. I decided I was not going to be left out and took off down the chute in my swimsuit.

The concrete was made smooth by the water and the angle of the slide was steep, so I found the speed building very fast. I thought back to England and all the health and safety regulations. This slide would have been condemned in a breath there. I dare not put my hands out to slow myself down, because they would have been ripped to shreds on the concrete. After a short while, I found myself flying through the air, as the slide had seemed to end about ten foot above the water. With a slapping crack, the base of my spine hit the water. The breath was knocked out of me. It took all my energy to swim back to the shore. Gradually, the pain started to invade every sense and I realised I must have bruised my coccyx. Worse was to come.

The next day we set off for our next destination. Chris was a regular visitor to Guatemala and suggested this town. The bus ride was excruciating. As usual, the bus was full and I could only find a seat at the back, which of course is the bumpiest. The roads were very rough and full of potholes, with the bus seeming to hit each one. It was the most painful ride I have ever taken. I tried to distract myself by observing the other passengers. Women would climb on with their babies strapped to their bodies, wrapped in colourful woven cloth. I noticed that on the crowded bus, the baby would be moved from their backs to their front, so there was less chance of their precious bundle being knocked. Men clambered on, carrying many different packages, bundles of wood, sometimes hens. The rocking and swaying of the bus jolted everyone against each other as we wound our way through the mountainous roads and passes. Finally, the torture ended. We had arrived at our destination, Panajachel on the shores of Lake Atitlan.

I was to end up staying about ten days in this town. Blown out in a volcanic eruption many years ago, the massive caldera filled up with

196

water, creating the spectacular lake of today. Ringed by dark brooding younger volcanoes, some still occasionally smoking, small Mayan villages cling to the sides of these mountains, fringing the edges. A small jetty struck out into the water from where, I later learnt, we could take a boat to visit other villages around the shores.

It had a part wild feel about it, with an undercurrent of strangeness, alien to our normal understanding of village life. As always, I wanted to find out about the local Mayan people. They, as in other parts of native Central America, had had Catholicism forced upon them, yet had uniquely adapted it into their own culture. I went to watch a parade through the town one day. A blue plaster Virgin Mary was carried on high, whilst around her, marimba players, dancers with masks on and people dressed in the traditional colourful woven blankets and embroidered tops, wandered along. It felt like the Virgin Mary was a token gesture. The heart of the event was something else, hidden deeper, repressed and only allowed to surface in little hints, the secret essence of the ceremony. All the Catholic imagery seemed for show, but the real stuff, which I could not quite see or put my finger on, had to be hidden so well, that it was almost lost. I wished I could speak their language to understand more. Instead, I had to watch and glean what I could. At least I learnt that all the beautifully embroidered tops, worn by the women, were different for each village. You could tell which village they came from depending on the design and colours used.

Panajachel catered for 'gringo' tourism, with lots of restaurants, bars and cafes where we could meet up with fellow back packers and hang out, drinking beers or coffee and eating yoghurts and fruit. They also catered for our entertainment in the evenings. One vivid memory is of going to watch a film in the local hall. It was called El Norte. I have never forgotten that film. It portrayed two young Guatemalans, a brother and sister, escaping the persecutions in their country, trying to get to America. Anyone who complains about immigrants should watch that film. It shows the tremendous risks, courage and sacrifice that people undertake to try to find a safer life. It is very sad in places, but the girl eventually finds work as a maid in a rich white household in California. The woman of the household is very disturbed to find that the main character is washing clothes by hand, not using the machine, then hanging them all over the bushes outside to dry. With the best intentions, she tries to make the girl wash their clothes in the machine. She did not get it. The girl from Guatemala found much solace in washing clothes like she used to at home.

Seeing her pride in hanging out the washing has changed my attitude towards it in my own life. I now enjoy hanging it out, pleased to transform dirty, unwearable garments into fresh new clothes again. Wandering round the countryside in much of Central and South America, I would constantly see spotless whites, lying on grass or bushes, drying in the sun, so I could understand where she was coming from. The film brought home to me the massive gulf in understanding that there can sometimes be between people, even when they are well intentioned towards each other. It gave me a new understanding of people who are forced to leave their homeland, for whatever reason, and live in an alien culture.

I cannot remember where it was, but I do remember visiting a museum somewhere. I was interested in the information and exhibits so I chatted to the girl behind the desk. She was kind and helpful, answering my questions. As I was about to leave, she hurriedly looked around, saw there was no-one else there and asked in a brief whispered conversation if I would sign a petition to help her. She explained that lots of men and boys were being taken from their villages and had disappeared. Their wives and daughters and sisters had no idea what had happened to them, but they knew it was not good. I had heard this from other sources, so I was more than willing to sign and help her. I realised how very dangerous it was for her to be even asking me for a signature. The furtive glances she kept throwing over my shoulder showed that she was terrified of anyone seeing her, particularly her boss. I felt extremely humbled that my signature might help in this tragic situation. More evidence of indigenous people being persecuted and harmed, just for being who they were. The vision of the brother and sister escaping came back to me. I understood that the reason people risk so much 'to go north,' is often because of very awful circumstances.

* * *

One day, Mark and I went over the lake to visit another village which had an interesting custom. In Santiago del Lago, there is a statue of a local saint called Maximon. In some places he is referred to as a Mayan God, in others as a Catholic priest. I tried to find out more about him. He is moved from house to house within the town. He

198

wears traditional garments, draped around his body, a cowboy hat, smokes a cigar and is fed alcohol, cigarettes and money by locals and visitors, in exchange for prayers for good health, good crops and marriage counselling. Arriving in the village, local children escorted us to the house, where we placed our gifts. It did seem strange, coming from a very Methodist upbringing, to be plying a statue with these sorts of offerings, which are classed in our culture as bad, and certainly not something to be promoted through religion. Another example of how we humans need to bridge our thinking to understand each other.

On another day, Chris took me up to visit one of the remoter villages. He had visited Panajachel many times and was familiar with the area and people. He took me to see a family he knew. The woman of the household showed me how to use the long, woven cloth to wrap up a baby and carry it. I was fascinated to learn how it was done. His Spanish was fluent and he chatted away to her. Suddenly he turned to me and asked if I wanted to buy the cloth. I said I was happy to do so but I felt a bit bad because it was obviously her own baby's cloth that she had used. I asked him to check with her that she did not need it, but she passed it over with smiles.

Afterwards I realised that she was probably grateful for the money, but I felt I had something very special and treasured. The cloth was softened from use and felt very comfortable. Years later, when I had my own child, I tried to remember how to use it and managed to wrap him in it a few times. However, I was never as confident as Guatemalan women with their baby sling techniques.

We lodged in the village that night. The next morning, with sun filtering through the shutters, I woke to the sound of cockerels. Wandering out into the village, I asked where I could wash some clothes. I was shown the washing place on the river, where the women were slapping clothes on large rocks, chatting and making a social occasion out of their work. I felt quite shy and reticent to join in, but they encouraged me with friendly gestures. I was a very feeble washer in comparison, brought up with machines doing my arms' jobs. I was conscious of their looks, watching to see how this 'gringo' woman performed. My washing wasn't perfect, but it felt a lot better for having some dust free clothes to wear.

Another house Chris took me to, was in Panajachel. He took me to visit a friend of his who carved coffee wood roots. There are many coffee plantations in the area and there was quite a settlement of gringo 'ex-pats' farming it. I began to make the distinctions between the long-term gringos (there to make a living in this idyllic setting) and the visiting gringos, travelling the area. Chris was part of the former group. He explained that the coffee wood root is incredibly hard and difficult to carve. The man he took me to visit, carved the root into beautiful, distinctive and polished Mayan statues, with the remainder of the raw roots sprouting from the top like hair. I bought one of his skilfully carved statues, persuaded that it was good to support the local people, as well as having an unusual and beautiful reminder of these villagers by the crater lake. By this time, I was acquiring quite a few treasures to send home, so I did one of my regular parcels to England, to limit what I needed to carry on my onward journey.

After ten days of staying in Panajachel and chatting to other travellers, I had defined my next steps. Chris and Mark had both gone their separate ways and I decided it was time to find my next adventure.

Before he had left, Chris warned me of the dangers in Columbia. He had been travelling on a bus there when it had broken down. Offering to help, he bent over, revealing his money belt, normally secreted under his clothes. As they stood around, waiting for the bus to be repaired, one of the other passengers offered him a biscuit. The next thing he remembered was waking, all alone and naked in a ditch. Luckily for him, he was found by a local man who took him to some nuns to be nursed. He had completely lost his memory. Somehow, they managed to piece together, through various clues, which country he came from. Then they contacted his embassy, who went through all the people who had recently entered the country, until they eventually identified him. After he was repatriated, he went through treatment till most of his memory returned. He warned me never to take food from a stranger, as he believed that the biscuit had been drugged.

Aware of these warnings, I decided to follow a route suggested by other travellers. I was told that the best way to go from Central to South America is to fly to an island in the Caribbean, owned by a South American country. That way, the flight south is cheaper

200

because it is an internal flight. The island I was told to use was called San Andres, owned by Columbia. What hardship! Having to go and stay on a Caribbean island, with white sandy beaches, turquoise blue sea and rustling palm trees. I intended to spend a few days relaxing there, before heading into Columbia, then Ecuador, finally finishing my journey in Peru from where I had a ticket home.

CHAPTER 35

"The light which shines in the eye is really the light of the heart."
Rumi

The island was reasonably compact, so the airport was right next to the sea. As the plane flew down over the expanse of shaded turquoise, it looked like we were going to land on the water. Suddenly, at the last minute, the runway appeared and we landed on solid ground.

Leaving the plane, a wall of heat hit my face. I immediately slowed my pace and started to relax. As soon as I had found somewhere to stay, I was straight onto the beach and into the divine looking sea. My first day was spent acclimatising to the place, visiting the town, beach, and sampling delicious drinks at the palm fronded beach bars.

On my second day I was eating in one of the fish restaurants, when one of the local guys came and sat with me. We started chatting and I discovered I enjoyed his company. We ended up talking till quite late and going out onto the jetty to watch the moon, hanging in the rich dark sky, a silver glow over the sea. After arranging to meet up again, we started to go out with each other. He told me later that he had had a bet with himself, that we would end up together and he was determined to make sure we did.

After a couple more days of sunbathing and swimming on the beach, then seeing Sonny in the evening, I came down with a bit of a fever. Sonny was worried about me and took me to see his doctor. It was something I had picked up on my travels and unfortunately it was not long before he had, also, come down with it. He told me I could not stay on my own in the hostel, so I went to stay with him and his mum in their home. She was a lovely woman, versed in old Caribbean remedies, which she fed to us both. A few days later, I was back on my feet and feeling better. I began to feel very lucky that it had come on me there, rather than when I was travelling alone, in some dingy hotel room. My original plans of staying only three days on San Andres were changing. Sonny did not want me to travel on till I was feeling a lot better, so I settled into life with him and his mum.

During the day I would occupy myself with cycling round the island and visiting different beaches, although none matched the one by town. Other days I would sunbathe on the beach and watch all the traffic of people. The airport was fascinating. It was tiny, with one runway and one terminal building, yet people had to register two hours before the flight. Seeing washing machines, fridges, driers and all manner of bulky white goods being transported to the plane, I understood why the check-in was so long. San Andres was a duty-free island, so lots of Costa Ricans would fly over to buy their white goods at a fraction of the price.

On the beaches were many rich Columbians. One of them was a middle-aged bronzed male, who wore a lot of gold (mainly medallions) even on the beach. He sat down next to me and started chatting me up. His eyes were so cold. I do not think I have ever seen anyone's eyes that were harder and colder. There was absolutely no compassion anywhere, even in a fleck. I reluctantly engaged in conversation, not wanting to appear rude, but equally not wanting to talk to this man. I gathered that he was a very rich and owned coffee plantations and lots of land. As we spoke, we got onto the subject of his employees. He then announced, in a very matter of fact tone of voice, that if they did not do as he wanted, he had them shot, as if it was the most normal thing in the world to say. I was speechless. This monster beside me was a murderer and admitting it, as if it were normal. If I had been trying to get away before, I was determined to move away now. Never have I met anyone so purely evil and repulsive. I made some excuse and almost ran off the beach to get away. After that, I kept an eye out for him and made sure I avoided him at all costs. The beautiful surroundings felt tainted by the awful energy of the man on the beach. I felt so relieved to see Sonny, a decent example of humanity, at the end of the day.

On his day off, Sonny took me to visit the island's interior. After wandering through the grassy shrub-covered terrain, we came upon a magnificent tree. We wandered under its massive branches, which were dripping with fruit. The fruit was oval, green and some of them had juice, oozing from the stem, where it was attached to the branch. "That is when it is ripe and ready to eat," Sonny told me. He picked the luscious mango and handed it to me. I have never tasted a mango like it. Its sweet, soft orange flesh was running with liquid nectar. I thought of the mangoes we get in England, after they have been

203

chilled and transported halfway across the world. No wonder the taste is nothing like the same.

Another day, I was out on the bike and a storm started to blow in. I could not believe the ferocity of the wind. The tall palm trees were bending right over with its power. The sky darkened and rain started to lash down. Luckily, I was near a restaurant at the northern part of the island. I hurried in, dreading seeing that monstrous man, but luckily, he was not there. Sipping a drink, I watched the power of the storm as it roared across the island, glad to be in shelter. As quickly as it had blown up, it passed over and soon I was out and heading back to the town.

The longer I was there, the more I began to piece together the hidden stories behind the island. Sonny did not tell me, I gradually picked it up from chatting to different people. Some of the big fancy mansions lining the coastal road that ringed the island were owned by drug barons. The island was used as a stopping off place to transport cocaine from Columbia to the East coast of America. Apparently, one drug cartel controlled the West coast of America and one the East. Florida was the entry port from this island, while other islands were used for the California route. I wondered if that monster was one of them. I could not understand the women who would be with such men. He had a wife because I had seen him with her; did she not know what he did? Is money so important to some people that they put other people's lives below their own creature comforts? That way of looking at the world is so hard to comprehend. I know it is a legacy from our country, where many of the stately homes were built on the slave trade, but I thought we had evolved as a human race since then. Obviously, I was sadly wrong.

One day, I hope all humans will begin to see each other as being linked, as a part of the same wonderful manifestation of that beautiful spirit that flows through life. We are all connected, none of us are separate. If we do separate ourselves with acts of grossness towards another living being, then we cut ourselves off from the beauty we could achieve. There is nothing more amazing than the feeling of being a part of every living thing around you. That monster on the beach had done so much he would never begin to see what he was missing. Maybe he is dead himself now and having to deal with all the horrors he committed in life. I will never know. Out of all the humans I have ever met, no-one came near his isolation from life. Thankfully, most people are not like him and so there is hope.

Time was ticking on. My ticket home from Peru was booked to be used before the end of July, so I needed to go. Sadly, Sonny and I parted, with a half promise I might return. I took an internal flight to Cali. On the plane, I recalled the story told to me by Chris, my travelling companion in Guatemala. Some Columbian women whom I had met on the beach in San Andres, had also warned me. They reinforced his message of not taking any food offered to me, even if it is in a packet.

The trip from Bogota to the border by bus was a good two days. On San Andres people had advised me to get a flight straight to Cali, as it would be nearer. I followed their advice. So full of dread was I, that on arrival I checked in to a cheap hotel room, locked the door and stayed there, not emerging until the morning. In the light of day, nothing seems so fearsome. I booked my bus ride south and set off to Ecuador. I did not want to spend another night in Columbia, so I opted for the ten-hour journey to get me over the border in one day.

Initially on the bus, a young lad was sitting next to me. His energy was good and we chatted together. I enjoyed his company. At the next rest stop, I noticed an older man go up to him and talk to him. As we got back on the bus, I discovered this unpleasant man was now sitting next to me. I wanted to move but could not. Very soon after setting off, he tried to engage me in conversation, and then offered me a biscuit in a pack. By now every internal alarm bell was screaming at me. I declined his offer politely, studiously ignoring his advances. The trouble was, I was right in front of the inevitable film screen, mandatory on all long-distance buses. It was playing an awful film about a hitchhiker. It was a horror movie, the worst sort of film in my opinion. I hate them. I tried to ignore him and the terrible images on the screen. It was the longest journey ever.

At the next rest stop, I was so relieved to get away from him. I got chatting to a lovely Columbian woman. With her help, I managed to move seats, so I did not have to sit next to him anymore. She changed my whole view of Columbia and the journey. Now, when I looked out of the window, I could admire the stunning scenery and appreciate that not all the people of this country were to be feared. This young woman was so full of life and the joy of living, it was infectious. We swopped addresses and we wrote to each other for several years afterwards. She told me what was said about her country, "God created paradise and called it Columbia. Then the people came and turned it to Hell." However, she did explain that most of the people were lovely, kind and good fun to be with.

As everywhere, there are bad people and good people. As everywhere, there are those who prey on tourists and those who welcome them. She certainly changed my mind about the people and what I saw of Columbia confirmed that it is a stunningly beautiful landscape.

CHAPTER 36

"Life is either a daring adventure or nothing." Helen Keller

As dusk was falling, we arrived at the border. For the first time in months, I was cold. I was almost on the equator, yet I needed a jumper. It is so high up. I bought a beautifully soft alpaca wool jumper, cuddled into it and went through the border crossing.

My guidebook suggested visiting the graveyard in Vulcan to see the amazing topiary in the grounds. Sculpted figures repose in green vegetation all around the cemetery. The figures are very stylised, squat, rounded with Mayan-like features and totally breath-taking. Added to the fact that I was now three thousand metres above sea level, (about three times higher than the tallest mountain in the U.K.) I was quite justified in being short of breath. The rest of the graveyard was equally fascinating. I discovered that the people's ashes were housed in mini multi-storey blocks of carved stone and plaster. A façade of white, open-fronted boxes, each with a curved arch framing it, stood alongside the pathways. Inside each, were pictures, flowers, tokens and memories of loved ones. It was the most colourful graveyard I have ever visited and certainly the most unusual.

Travelling south, I stopped off at Quito. It was a beautiful city, high in the mountains with winding streets and dark doorways leading into cafes. As I sat in one, waiting for my meal, a man walked into the restaurant carrying some guinea pigs, upside down. One was pregnant. I was horrified to discover that they were on the menu. Luckily, I had ordered something vegetarian. I know it is normal for people to eat a range of different animals in different parts of the world. I also appreciate that the meat will be a lot more sustainable than the corned beef created from destroyed Amazonian rainforest, which we receive sanitised in supermarket tins. However, having come from the world that divorces us from our food sources, I find it disturbing to see the live animal before the meat is produced. I think the fact that the guinea pig was pregnant upset me most. I feel that all pregnant females should be treated with respect and care.

Studying my guidebook, I made my way south to where I could organise a trip into the Ecuadorian rainforest. At that time there were just a handful of backpackers and some resident gringos who had settled in this beautiful place under the towering slopes of a volcanic mountain. Sadly, I never got to experience the thermal springs in the town.

I located a guide who agreed to include me on a tour. It all happened very quickly, he told me the next tour was tomorrow or else I would have to wait a week. I was running out of time. My return ticket to England was only valid for a year, so I felt the need to book and go.

On arriving at the travel office where he operated from, I was surprised to find no other tourists. Expecting other people to arrive, I waited while my guide was making last minute preparations. We got on a minibus, no-one else was collected from anywhere and I eventually realised this trip was just him and me. I knew nothing about him. I was going to have to trust a lot.

Over the next few days, I gradually pieced together his story. Vince was an indigenous tribal member who had grown up in the rainforest. He had gone north and worked in the American army, where he learnt English. On returning home, he saw an opportunity to link this with his tribal knowledge. Now he shared his amazing and beautiful homeland with tourists. His second language was Spanish, so we communicated in a mixture of broken Spanish and English.

After careering round some steep hairpin bends and swerving round recent landslides from heavy rainfall, we were finally deposited at a local person's home, to gather ourselves before setting off into the rainforest. The roof was thatched with leaves over a wooden frame. I will never forget the young woman of the house taking me quietly on one side and asking in hurried tones and gestures if I had any pills. I soon realised she was asking for contraceptive pills. I could not oblige her. As we set off again, I worried about her situation that she would feel so desperate not to have a child. In comparison, I was reaching a stage when I was conscious of the biological clock ticking and was beginning to desire the opposite.

Vince had told me to wear wellingtons so that we could wade in water and to protect my legs. The humidity was intense as we set off into the dense vegetation. Moisture abounded everywhere, with no relief. No path was visible; the only indication of a route was the odd nick out of a tree trunk. I would never have noticed it, but Vince pointed it out. His machete forged an opening in the undergrowth through which we passed, knowing that it would very quickly re‑grow. A dull green light permeated through from the towering leaf cover, making it relatively dark on the forest floor. A beautiful, faded flower lay at my feet and Vince explained it was from the treetops. Few flowers flourished on the floor level, with most of the colours and vibrancy being in the canopy.

Vince suddenly bent down, picked up a shell and handed it to me. It was about twenty centimetres long and ten centimetres wide. I could not begin to imagine the size of snail that once inhabited it. As we chopped our way through the undergrowth, I began to acclimatise to the constant damp and heat. It was uncomfortable at first but once I decided there was nothing I could do about it, I accepted the feeling and got used to it. After about four hours tramping through vines and stepping across tree trunks, we finally came across a shelter that Vince had previously made. A wooden frame formed the main structure, with leaves plaited to create the roof. Hot and tired, we ate a quick meal then unrolled the sleeping bags for a night's rest. As I tried to settle down, I could not believe how noisy it was. Birds still sang in the canopy, monkeys screeched in a cacophony above us and a multitude of rustlings from the forest floor rose around us. I do not think I have ever tried to sleep in a louder place. Eventually I must have nodded off, because before long, dawn had arrived. Soon the smoke of a fire, that Vince lit for a morning drink, was wafting in clouds, drifting through the shafts of sunlight filtering through the upper canopy.

After breakfast we set off again. Being in the Andes, the terrain was hard going; up and down hill, forging our way through dense undergrowth and over whatever obstacles lay in our path. Vince said the first day was the hardest, we would take it easier on each successive day. Soon we arrived at a riverbank. A full flood of brown surging water tumbled and crashed in front of us. Vince looked a bit worried. "The river is flooding, which is preventing us crossing here," he explained, "we will need to take a detour."

209

Further on, after more scrambling up slopes and down, between vines and tree roots, we finally found some machete cuts on trees, indicating we were back on a path. Relaxing a bit, I started to enjoy the adventure. I was getting accustomed to the weight of my backpack and my lungs were adjusting to the high altitude because I felt less breathy. We came across a massive bamboo. The trunk must have been a good thirty centimetres in diameter. It towered upwards, so tall that its leafy top was out of sight. "Do you want to drink the purest water on the planet?" asked Vince. Game for anything I acquiesced. Taking his machete, he sliced a section from the trunk, then showed me how to lean into the stem and suck the water from its tube. I have never tasted such delicious water. A purity and clarity surged through my body, as the smooth liquid flowed down my neck.

Encouraged by this experience, I asked Vince if I could try some rainforest food. We had brought our own supplies in with us; rice with some canned food but I fancied eating fresh food from my surroundings. At first, I really enjoyed the tasting. He found different fruits for me to try, which were delicious and unusual in flavour. After a while we came across a rotten palm oil tree trunk. "This is good food," Vince explained, chopping away at the trunk with his machete. He then lifted a creamy yellow grub out of the trunk. I looked at him in horror. He then shook his head. "No good," he said, "too small." I prayed with everything to my guides, "Please don't let him find bigger grubs."

Eventually I picked up the courage to ask if we would have to eat them raw. "Oh no," he said, "we cook them." In that second, I relaxed my intensity of praying and he immediately found a large grub. I succumbed to the inevitable. "Here," he thrust a large leaf at me, "put them on this." More and more were placed on the leaf. It was very large and waxy, but they started to crawl off it. I let out a small scream and nearly dropped them. The frustration of having to deal with this pathetic white woman could be seen on Vince's face. He picked up the leaf, then gently stunned each grub behind its shiny brown head, so they would not crawl off. The leaf was tied up with a vine and placed in Vince's backpack.

We set off again. The promise of the first day being the hardest was turning on itself. We had now been walking for five hours. We had not seen any machete cuts on the trees for a long while and Vince admitted we were lost. Eventually, we came across a clearing with a hut in it. "We're in luck," he said, walking into it, "a hunter's lodge. We can stay here tonight."

The first thing he did was to cut down all the long grass around the clearing, "To remove places for snakes to hide," he cheerfully informed me. It was still light, so he said he would go off and see if he could find any landmarks, to ascertain where we were. The rainforest is negotiated by rivers. The growth is so dense, that the only way to find a route in or out is by a river. Vince told me he was looking for the big river, because that was a clear way to show us the way back.

Whilst he was gone, I decided to try and wash some clothes in the little stream nearby. I paddled happily in my wellies, enjoying the peace and solitude. I soon found that drying the clothes was a joke in the steamy atmosphere, but I hung them over some sticks and hoped for the best. Vince had not returned yet, so I decided I would have a go at lighting a fire to cook tea. I picked up the driest looking leaves I could find and tried to use them as kindling. What seemed like an hour later, the sky was beginning to darken, there was no sign of Vince and my attempts to light a fire were a complete failure. I began to start worrying. "What if something had happened to him?"

I suddenly realised how utterly vulnerable I was. I had no knowledge of the plants, as to which were poisonous or not. Vince had advised me not to touch any plant unless he had identified it as safe. I had absolutely no idea where I was or how to get back if he did not turn up. I could not even light a fire to cook my food. Nothing in the pack could be eaten raw. I began to start planning what I could do. I reasoned that my saving grace was the little stream. A small stream will lead to a big stream, which will eventually lead to a river. The river is the main highway in the rainforest. People live near the rivers and once there, I was sure I would find someone to help. I decided that if he did not return, I would spend the night in the hunter's lodge, and then follow the stream till I found other people.

Finally, as the dark started to descend, he appeared. I was never so relieved to see someone. He said he had climbed a very tall tree, but he still could not see the big river. I told him how worried I had been and my plan if he had disappeared on me. He had had the same idea, to follow the smaller stream and see if it led us to the river. He laughed at my attempts to light a fire. "Those leaves won't burn," he said, "this sort of wood is what you need." Within a breath a fire was lit, water was boiling, and grubs were on the menu. "They are a real delicacy, the heads are the best bit-nice and crunchy," he grinned. "They live in rotten palm oil trees, so they are just pure palm oil." They were not so bad after all. The heads *were* crunchy, although I only managed one. The rest of the body was pure palm oil and not unpleasant. I did not ask to eat the local food again.

In the night we heard a roar. "Sounds like a tigre," said Vince. I was not sure what tigre translated as other than it was a big cat of some sort. Surprisingly, I managed to get some sleep. I was so tired; my body gave me no choice. In the morning we set off slightly refreshed. Suddenly we heard the roar of a big cat again. We were walking down a slope, with a small stream at the bottom. A few minutes later we heard a crashing on the opposite slope. A tapir was tumbling down the undergrowth with no regard for noise or camouflage. "That tapir is being chased by a tigre, "Vince informed me, "the tigre's lost his prey now and he will be angry."

Suddenly our vulnerability hit me. The undergrowth in the rainforest is very luxuriant and dense. Visibility is restricted to no more than a few yards. The 'tigre' could be no more than a few yards away and we would not see it till the last moment. Admiring the beauty of these creatures in a zoo or game park is very different. I felt a shiver of fear, there was no protective barrier and we were easy prey. As if he was reading my thoughts Vince said, "Don't feel fear. A tigre can sense fear from a mile away and will track you." Even though I was proverbially 'bricking it,' I had to deal with it, for my safety and that of Vince.

I took a deep breath. Recalling mediation in the Thai monastery, my tai chi training and my learning about healing, I focussed on my breath. As it flowed in, I breathed calm through my body, visualising peace and balance. I could not think of the tigre, if I did, the fear would return. Knowing how important it was, lent power and concentration to my intent. There is nothing like mortal fear to focus one's mind on survival, in whatever form it takes. Previously, I had been quite a long way behind Vince when we walked. He was fitter and more acclimatised to climbing up and down mountain slopes, at high altitude, in the rainforest, in his wellies. Acclimatised or not, I was inches behind him as we waded along the stream. "It's safer in the stream," he advised, "the tigre can't get us so easily." After wading for what seemed like an hour, we noticed the tigre's roars hadn't been heard for a while. "I think he's gone away," my guide informed me.

My eyes were beginning to adjust to all the varying shades of green around us and to distinguish details or changes. "Oh look," I motioned to a branch overhanging the stream, "what a beautiful snake." It was small, yellow orange stripes and was draped amongst the leaves. "Well spotted," replied Vince, "but don't get too close," as I pointed my camera, "it's highly dangerous."

I did not linger and stayed close behind him. We were still following the stream, where we could. Sometimes it was not possible, so we cut our way through vegetation on the banks, but mainly we stuck to the water. The sun was rising higher. A timepiece is useless in the rainforest. Time has a completely different meaning. It was merely the space between dawn and dusk. Suddenly Vince stiffened. "Look," he whispered. Ahead, walking towards us in the stream was another tapir. I got out my camera, as silently as I could. I poised the lens, then as it clicked, the creature abruptly turned and disappeared into the undergrowth.

"It's a good thing it didn't charge," said my ever-cheerful companion, "they can break your legs when they charge." I imagined being left all alone in the middle of this rainforest with a broken leg, while Vince went for help. No. Better not to imagine. The day was wearing on and still no sign of the big river. By now we had been walking again for about five or six hours. Vince kept calling me a 'mujer fuerte,' a strong woman, because I kept up with him and would not give in. I was not likely to, given the circumstances. I thought back to my clever plan last night. If Vince had not returned, even if I had spent all day walking, I still would not have seen anyone or found help. With hindsight, part of me wondered whether he was winding me up half the time, to make the experience more thrilling. Or were there very real dangers? It was probably a combination of both. Whatever, it was soon going to get dark and we had nowhere to sleep.

"I'll make a shelter," he told me. I could not believe how quickly his machete cut lots of massive palm-fronded leaves. Then he cut some poles, found the right sort of vine and expertly bound together the poles into a frame. Before long, the leaves were woven and laid over the framework to create a shelter. He cut some more logs to create a raised platform, "To keep us above the ants." In a breath, he lit a fire and soon we were eating supper as the light began to fade. In the space of about an hour or so, he had built us somewhere to sleep, cooked our food and I had done nothing but stand by helplessly, showing what sort of society I come from. It brought home to me how de-skilled we have become in our cushioned lives. As I snuggled down into my sleeping bag, I wondered if we would ever find the big river.

Dawn broke and the night cacophony diminished. As I rolled over, I noticed a line of the biggest ants I had ever seen carrying little green flags from the leaves they had cut out. Suddenly I noticed one of the flags was not green. The cutting ants had removed a small section of my blue rucksack, which was not on the platform of logs, and were marching off with it to their nest. I hope it did not cause them problems. Vince was quite amused. I felt intrigued that a little bit of my property was to remain in the rainforest.

Abandoning the temporary shelter to return to the environment from which it was made, we continued. I was beginning to feel a bit despondent of ever getting out of the rainforest.

I silently asked my guides, "When will we find the big river?"

"When you have lost hope," came the clear reply. The sun seemed to be around midday, so Vince decided to climb another tree to see where we were. It was unbelievable how quickly and easily he shinned up that seventy-foot tree in his wellies. One minute he was ahead of me climbing the slope, the next, I had arrived at the tree and he was already a small dot near the top. He came down and shook his head. "I can't see a river," he said. I sat down. I felt utter defeat. "Right," I said. "I can't go any further without more rest. We have walked solidly for three days now, in our wellies, tramping and cutting our way through thick undergrowth, scrambling up and down steep slopes or else wading through streams, all in hot, humid temperatures. It has not been a stroll in the park. Let's get to the bottom of this hill. Then please can we make a shelter and I can rest for a day. I'm physically at my limit." He agreed.

We made our way to the bottom of the slope, then Vince let out a cry, "It's the river!" There before us, in full flooding flow, were the brown swirling waters of the big river. I have never been so relieved to see a river before. The feeling of hopelessness left. I instantly felt renewed. "Why didn't you see it from the tree?" I questioned.

"It was at the bottom of this slope, so the tree canopy hid it from me," he replied. Happily, we made our way along the river's edge. Soon we came to a house, more substantial than any we had stayed in. An older woman, a young couple and a small boy came out to greet us. Vince talked to them, then informed me we could stay there that night.

The heart of the home was the fire pit. Four logs were laid in a cross shape, with the ends of the logs forming the burning fire. As they burnt, I watched, fascinated, as the older woman pushed the logs in, so their burning ends were always touching. I had never seen a fire that worked in that way before. As the day went on, the elder and her grandson disappeared. They had not returned by dusk. As we prepared to sleep, I realised that Vince and I had been given their places on the sleeping platform. I wondered if Vince had compensated them for our bed space. As I could not speak the language, I had to rely on him and trust that he had been fair with them.

The next morning, the grandma and boy returned, we made our farewells and set off. Soon we hit the 'main road' of the forest. To the untrained eye, it would have looked like a vague pathway, frequently blocked by fallen tree trunks. After chopping our route out for several days, it did feel like a major route way, as there was a faintly defined path to follow. Gradually we began to emerge from the green, lush, vibrant forest. As we did so, we came to a devastated area. Burnt tree stumps littered the dull open spaces. Emptiness and silence abounded. After the constant noise and chatter of the living forest, I was shocked to see the barren landscape. Soon the reason was apparent. We had finally arrived at the tarmac road.

Although I was exhausted and hot, I have never felt fitter and in better shape than when I emerged from the rainforest that day. Getting on a bus to return to Banos, felt very strange and alien. I had lived with no money, clocks or interference from the outside world for five days, but because I had lived in the moment for much of that time, it was very vivid. I could not wait to send Mum and Dad the letter I had written, in the hope they could share as much of the experience as possible. I was relieved it was not a posthumous letter.

My last day in Banos brought me across another young woman traveller. She had just arrived from Peru. As that was my destination, I got chatting to her. I had already been warned about the Sanderos (Shining Light terrorist group) who were targeting tourists. Her tale confirmed my fears. She had been in a bus station in Lima suffering from Montezuma's revenge (the gringo name for a bad belly) when a tear gas attack took place. The bus station filled with the painful gas, making her eyes hurt but she could not move because of the stomach upset. She was in a bad way. She told me that she could not wait to get out of Peru, and when the first bus going to Ecuador arrived, she was on it. Other traveller's tales told of the horrors of the Sanderos killing and capturing tourists. I only had a few weeks left and although I wanted to see Macchu Pichu, I decided that could wait for another time. It was not worth risking my life.

Having made that decision, I needed to get to Quito to change my return ticket from Lima to Bogota. It took a couple of days waiting for all the formalities, so I went to a library where I could research films about the country. Two young Ecuadorian men were there, watching Laurel and Hardy. I have never heard anyone laugh so much. They were giggling away, thoroughly enjoying every moment. I reflected on how wonderful it was that two men, from another culture and another time, could infect others with so much laughter.

My last visit in Ecuador was to a community of villages in the north, who created cloth. Each village specialised in a different part of the process, some dyeing, some carding, and some weaving. Tourists could go on tours into people's homes to observe the process.

On arriving there, it was the nearest I felt to being at home in England, in my whole trip. The temperature was cool, the grass green and sheep grazed the hillsides. Of course, there were differences; the inevitable white washing drying over the bushes, streams were used for washing the wool and the people were quiet, gentle and getting on with a hard life in beautiful surroundings. I enjoyed meeting them, as we were guided through the villages and admired their skill at preparing and creating the colourful, beautiful garments from scratch. One day, I hired a horse with a guide. We had a fabulous day riding through the hills and by deep blue lakes. It felt so good to be somewhere like home.

I was ready to return after my year of adventures.

CHAPTER 37

"No-one realises how beautiful it is to travel until he comes home and rests his head on his old familiar pillow." Lin Yutang.

There was about a week before my flight was due to leave, so I decided to re-enter Columbia, then fly from the nearest airport to San Andres, for a few days with Sonny again. I wanted to be with people who cared for me and knew me, rather than strangers. Sonny was thrilled to see me. His mum cooked a special meal for us. Everyone on the island treated me differently because I had returned. There was the feeling of familiarity with the place and the shopkeepers which was very comforting. It was great to see Sonny again and we had a lovely time together.

Those days flew past and soon our time was coming to an end. At the airport we cried and held on to each other. I said I would come back, Sonny replied, "Don't promise anything, I feel deep inside that you won't." At that moment, I was convinced I would return. I walked across the steaming tarmac, past washing machines lining up to go on planes, then boarded the plane to Bogota. The last I remember of him was his smile and wave.

In Bogota, I had a day before my flight, so I visited the gold museum. Massively reinforced doors, several inches thick, with every lock imaginable, were open to reveal treasures from the lost Mayan civilisation. Intricate carvings, amazing figurines and beautiful pendants, all in the purest gold, shone from behind the glass cases. I felt sad that such beauty had to be hidden and held behind this formidable security, because of man's greed for this shining metal.

Not wishing to be out after dark as a woman on my own, I had a meal and retreated to my hotel room. I was more than ready to return home.

* * *

My homecoming was brilliant. To enjoy the comforts of the house where I was born, the loving company of my family and friends and familiarity with the landscape and temperature was bliss. Travelling has taught me how very deeply I love my homeland. I feel for people who are forced to leave their mother country, there is nothing like the feeling of the place where your roots are.

After a short time settling back in, I knew I had to start sorting out my future. Initially, I was all for flying back out to San Andres to see Sonny again. Mum came into my room, as I sat with a letter from him. "I know you care for him, but what future would it be?" she queried. I could see the pain in her eyes, "We've just got you back, we've missed you so much and now you're thinking of high tailing back over there to see a man you've only just met." She tried every argument she could think of.

As usual with my mum, I made out she was not going to change my mind and that I would make my own decisions, but deep down inside, I knew she was right. I realised I was beginning to put my feelings for Sonny into a special place in my heart. I would always remember him, but it was a long-term relationship that would never be.

I decided I had better focus on the practicalities of moving back home. The first thing I did was buy a car, then I needed to start looking for somewhere to live.

CHAPTER 38

"I count myself in nothing else so happy, as in a soul rememb'ring my good friends." William Shakespeare

As soon as I had settled back home, I toured the country visiting all my friends and catching up. The first trip was to Ireland for my friend Lu's wedding. I timed my return to make sure I did not miss it.

As I waited for the plane, I reflected on my previous visits to Ireland. Ever since my first trip there with Aiden on a horse drawn caravan in the seventies, I have loved the country. After I met Lu, she invited me to her homeland, and I gained a deeper insight into the land of legend and myth. I was shocked that I knew so little of its history.

She explained why the field system is so different in the west from the east. In the west they are tiny fields all boxed in with stone walls. In the east they are much larger. The Irish were pushed west by English land owners, who claimed the fertile rich green lands in the east. The English owned large estates, which were farmed by labourers whilst the Irish were forced onto the poorer land in the west. A family would own a section of land. As the children grew, the father would divide the land between them, sectioning it into smaller areas. Stones littered the earth, so building walls with them helped to clear the land and mark the ever-increasing boundaries. As a result, the poor Irish had a very difficult time trying to scrape a living in their tiny fields. I found it amazing that the landscape could tell me so much about the history.

Through my friends in Ireland, I began to understand a little of the past conflicts and how it must have felt to be Irish. Being Irish was very complex. A bit like the Mayans I had met in Guatemala, the Irish were conquered by an alien race, who did not value their culture. Elements of the old Celtic heritage would find a place in the new Catholic religion like the old Celtic Goddess of Bridie becoming St Bridget, just as the marimba players had become a part of the Catholic processions in Guatemala. Lu explained to me that the reason the Irish gained the reputation for being stupid by the English, was part of a strategy to deal with their unwelcome landlords. If they made themselves out to be thick, the English lowered their guard, then the Irish could get away with all sorts 'because they didn't understand.' Brilliant tactic!

There are many beautiful and ancient places in Ireland and Lu was a great guide to them all. As we toured the west and visited the North, I grew to feel very warm towards the people we encountered and the rich variety of landscapes we explored together. I fell in love with the west coast. The Burren, with its unique limestone plateau, rare and unusual plants clinging to its crevices, sits atop spectacular cliffs, with the Atlantic crashing at their base. Having produced 'Riders to the Sea' at college, it was like a dream come true when Lu asked if I'd like to visit the Aran Islands. Gaelic was still spoken as the main language. Lu had learnt it at school, so we could communicate with the older residents. It was such a gentle way of being.

Every pub we went in someone would pick up a fiddle, someone else would get the spoons and others would sing. The spontaneity gave a freshness and vibrancy to the music. One time we were on the west coast with another friend who was desperate to go to a cultural fair. It was in the mid-eighties, and she particularly wanted to meet a writer called Maeve Binchy who was giving a talk. I was not very interested, as I had never heard of her. Since then, I have grown to love her books, because she captures the Ireland I was introduced to by Lu.

The only time Lu and I visited the North was during the eighties when the British army were still the occupying force. As we drove up to the border, soldiers were lying in the grass on either side of the road, guns trained on the cars and people. We were in Lu's car which had number plates identifying us as coming from the Republic.

"Identity please," barked a young soldier brandishing a gun.

"Oh dear, I haven't any identity cards," I replied, "Oh wait a minute, will my passport do?" On seeing the British passport, the soldier immediately changed his tune. The guns were lowered; he grinned at us and waved us on. Lu and I looked at each other. "We make a good combination, one from each camp, united as friends," we laughed. On returning over the border after our visit, I could not help noticing the

220

extreme opposites. The soldiers were tense, focussed and militarily efficient with us on the Northern Ireland part. As soon as we crossed into the Republic of Ireland, the atmosphere changed. The border guard barely looked up from his paper, casually waving us on with a grin. Talk about laid back, it was almost comatose!

One site that I loved to visit was Newgrange, just north of Dublin. Built five thousand years ago, it is older than Stonehenge. The two monuments are complimentary, opposites in more ways than one. I remember approaching Newgrange across short green turf, echoed on the domed roof that encloses the stones. The outer walls below the roof glowed white, creating a stunning contrast. Above the ancient doorway, a small window could be seen. Through this space, the winter solstice sun slips through, gradually lighting up the passageways, till it finally reaches the inner sanctum. Around the temple, smaller stones stand, etched with ancient, curved lines, reminding me of the Hopi migration symbol.

I ran through the comparisons in my mind. Stonehenge is an open circle of stones, whereas Newgrange is sealed with a roof. Stonehenge is famous for the sun rise at mid-summer Solstice; Newgrange is lit up in the mid-winter Solstice. Stonehenge is on a plain, Newgrange is in a gentle valley. Stonehenge is masculine, protruding out of a landscape, Newgrange is rounded as a womb, enclosing inner secrets like a female. They both have their own beauty, but I would choose to live near Newgrange rather than Stonehenge any day.

* * *

All this had happened on previous visits. This time I was there for my dear friend's wedding. As Lu had met her husband-to-be a short while before I was leaving to go travelling, I had not met him yet. Imagine my surprise when I got chatting and discovered that his mum and dad had been taught by my uncle at the grammar school in New Mills. Small world! Lu looked beautiful and 'a grand time was had by all.'

My next visit was over to Wales to see Helen and Pat. My friend John was also there, with all Helen's family, so it felt like returning to my spiritual family.

Something very important happened there. Pat helped me a lot with my decisions over Sonny. I was determined to meet my soulmate. I was convinced that he was out there. Pat worked with me and asked Guidance for help. I always find it harder to ask for things for myself, than for others. They told her that Sonny was not my soulmate, but I could make him into one. However, there was a soulmate out there for me still. I confided in Pat that I was a bit worried, my period was late. I explained to her how in the rainforest, I had had to fight Vince off every night, but on the last night I had had no strength left and could not resist him.

Pat put her hand on my tummy, closed her eyes and felt the energy. She told me that there was a soul there, but it was only holding on very tenuously. If I did not want it, it would not stay. "If you really don't want the baby, you must go and sit quietly, and tell the baby to return to the forest. You must not feel any love for it, for if you do, it will stay." That was one of the hardest things I have ever done. I sat on a big rock, over-looking the river and valley far below. It was a sunny day, as I asked the baby to leave, willing myself to feel nothing for this tiny soul. I desperately wanted a baby, but not this way. I did not want a child from a situation that had been forced on me; I wanted it from a loving supporting relationship. I felt terrible for this little soul and wished the being well but told it that it was not to be with me.

Later that day, we went swimming in a beautiful mountain stream and waterfall, a bit of a drive away. We were all jumping in and having a great time. Suddenly I knew. I got out of the water and felt a massive sense of relief. My period had started. It was unusually heavy.

That night I had a dream. I was in a plane with a small boy. We were flying over the rainforest. As we flew over the canopy, the boy suddenly leapt from the plane. He floated down and as he reached the trees, it was as if they opened their arms and embraced him, returning him to his source. When I woke and relayed the dream to Pat, she agreed with me that it was my baby and that he had returned to the forest to be born to someone else. As soon as he had gone, I felt safe enough to send him all the love I had wanted to give him but could not allow myself to feel. I have never forgotten that little boy and kept him in my heart. It is something I have never really talked about.

Twenty-five years later, another friend, Rachel, who knew absolutely nothing about this, read my aura in the psychic development group I go to. Hesitantly, she told me the following. "I don't know if this means anything to you, but I saw a tree in the rainforest with a yellow ribbon tied around it. A young native man, dressed in traditional dress, who lived in the rainforest, was standing there. You went up to him. He said, "Remember me," as he embraced you with respect."

I was amazed. To me, here was further confirmation of the whole event. I was very happy to hear that the little soul had been born safely and was hopefully living a good life. As soon as Rachel mentioned it, I instantly knew who the young man was. She was relieved to realise the message meant something to me, as she had not a clue how to interpret it. Instinct told me that this is the soul I asked to leave. Later, I thought about the sort of a life he would have had here. It would have been very hard for him, not knowing his dad and being so far removed from the culture of the rainforest he was attached to. I do not know how it all works, but I believe it happened for a reason.

CHAPTER 39

"If you love somebody, let them go, for if they return they were always yours. If they don't, they never were." Kahlil Gabrain

Whilst I was away, my dear dad had collected up newspaper articles he thought I would be interested in. One was about house prices around the country. I had my lump sum still, having only used the interest in my year of travels. Now I needed to find a house. I wanted one with some land, preferably with out-houses, or maybe a barn in which I could potentially run courses. I was not bothered where, as long as there was enough supply teaching, and it was in the country. Dad's article pointed out where there was property within my price range. I toured the country. Soon I found somewhere on the Scottish borders. Being in the Scottish system I had to put in a bid. If my bid were accepted, it would form the contract. I had taken Mum and Dad to view it and was very keen on it. I lay in bed at home, thinking it through. "Guidance," I said, "if getting this house means I will meet my soulmate, then please let me get it. If not, I don't want to win it."

I did not get it.

As always in life, when I get disappointed, I remember that it means something better is around the corner. Inevitably it is.

Next, I nearly got a place on the borders of Wales, near Ludlow. It still was not quite right. I went back a couple of times, again taking Mum and Dad, but I was not convinced. Meanwhile Pat and another friend were laughing with me about it all. "We should all sell our houses and buy a mansion between us, or several houses that form a hamlet," we joked. One day, Jacqui was writing a letter to Pat, when suddenly her guide took over and did automatic writing. He had never done that before and she was a bit surprised. He initially wrote, "Eastwick." On hearing this we laughed some more and said, "The three witches of Eastwick!" Then he changed it and wrote, "Eastwood, West Yorkshire."

I had never heard of the place. Pat and I got out the map and discovered a tiny hamlet called Eastwood lies between Hebden Bridge and Todmorden. I had not even considered that area because Hebden Bridge was out of my price range. I started looking into it. Supply teachers seemed to be in demand, the Todmorden house market was more reasonable than Hebden Bridge and it was in the countryside. It was looking hopeful.

I decided to visit my old friends Ric and Lin from teenage years who lived in Hebden. They had moved out there in the seventies with the hippie influx, who brought new ideas, health food and hippie clothing shops to the mill town that was in decline. I remember half the place being derelict, with abandoned mills and a general feeling of being run down. The incomers began to re-energise the shops, occupy derelict farms on the tops and create a new culture of music and alternative lifestyles. By the end of the eighties, Hebden was marketed on the London property market. Prices went up and another wave of different incomers were adding to the diversity and quirky nature of the town. In and amongst, I picked up the feeling that the original inhabitants felt rather side-lined by the successive waves of new faces.

My friends took me to visit Eastwood. It was a steep, heavily potholed road leading to a tiny hamlet. No houses were for sale. "It's got to be here, Jacqui's guide said so," I insisted. "He said I would find it easily."

"Don't worry," Lin said, "I'll keep an eye on the paper and let you know if anything suitable crops up."

In the meantime, I went off round the country again visiting friends and relatives. Whilst I was in London, Lin rang me. "I've found your house," she said. She read out the details to me. "It sounds perfect," I replied. The only trouble was it was five thousand more than I could afford. I rang the agent and asked if they were accepting offers. No. The house had only just gone on the market and they were expecting to get the asking price. I informed the agent I would ring back in a month when they were ready to accept offers.

A month later, they were willing. The vendors had a house lined up and were worried they would lose it. I was a gift, a cash buyer with no chain. I decided I would go and see it. I had not wanted to see it before, as I did not want to fall into the trap of liking a house and doing anything to get it, going beyond my means.

Unusually, the agent's photo had not done it justice. As I walked up the cobbled path between the white painted cottages covered in roses, I fell in love with the Fold. The minute I entered the cottage I knew this was it. It felt right instantly. I made an offer of five thousand less than the asking price. It was accepted.

Even though I was a cash buyer and had no mortgage lenders to placate, I was not going to avoid having a survey. The survey indicated that the roof needed doing. I got some estimates and realised I could only afford it if I knocked another five thousand off the price. I duly made the revised offer. By this time, I was in Somerset, visiting my cousin. A phone call came through from the agent. "My, you're difficult to track down," she said, "I've been phoning all-round the country!" I held my breath. Had they accepted my final offer? They had. I jumped round the room and hugged my cousin and all her family. I was ecstatic.

A month later I moved in. As Jacqui's spirit guide had said, I found it easily and everything flowed well, so it was meant to be. It was less than two months after first hearing of the property.

A transit van which was just able to squeeze between the stone walls on either side of the track leading to the Fold, was the method of transport. Dad and one of my parent's neighbours, Robin, who was like family, helped me move in. I always remember Robin leaning out of one window, while I leaned out of the other, to make sure I did not scrape the hire van. It did not take long to unload, as I had very few possessions.

After they had left, I was all on my own in a new house. I got into bed and lay, listening to all the unfamiliar sounds. Normally, it would take me a while to drift off. As I snuggled down, it felt like the house was wrapping its arms around me and comforting me.

As well as saving cuttings from the newspapers about house prices, my lovely dad had also saved different articles he thought I would be interested in. Coming back from my travels, I felt I had grown and changed so much, yet nothing at home seemed to be different. I was itching to follow a new path in life. My supply teaching would pay the bills for now, but I needed to find a new direction.

One article Dad had kept was about a new movement called Permaculture. It fitted with my views on life, caring for and living in harmony with, not against, nature, as I had learnt in my time with my First Nation friends. It was, also, no effort gardening (I liked that bit) and people care (I liked that bit as well). In short it ticked all my boxes and I wanted to do it. In those days, the only courses were in Devon or in Scotland. The Devon course fitted the bill, so I enrolled on it. It was one weekend a month, over eight months.

Soon I slotted into a pattern. Supply work was beginning to trickle in, although not with any Todmorden schools, mainly in Hebden Bridge. Every month I would take off down to Devon, stopping with my brother in Bristol, and on the way back at Stourbridge.

* * *

Rewinding to the summer of my return, Pat and I had gone to visit Jacqui, who then lived on the South Coast. We had quite a strange experience there. I took Pat to see Beachy Head, which I used to love going to when I lived in London. Driving through the early hours to avoid London traffic, we arrived at the grassy headland about six o'clock in the morning. A faint ground mist was swirling around. We parked up and were going to walk to the cliff edge to have a look at the view, when Pat suddenly said, "Oh my God, can you see it? What do you think it is?" She pointed to an upright stone in the grass about a hundred feet away. I glimpsed something dart behind it. She later described it as a small malevolent creature that emanated pure evil. She immediately said, "We need to get out of here." I needed no second bidding, I felt her panic and sensed it was not wise to linger. We later thought about it and wondered what it was and why it was there. Beachy Head, for all its spectacular beauty, is also renowned for suicides, the high cliff promising no possibility of survival. I wondered if the poor souls, so desperate, attracted some sort of malevolent energy that delighted in their torment and that this was what we had seen.

Whilst at Jacqui's we all had a few more strange experiences. The presence of spirits was very strong. Jacqui, her daughter, Naz and Pat are all very psychic. I am less so, but even I physically felt the touches of spirits and sensed presences.

During one day there, the phone rang and I knew it was 'him.' Whilst I had been staying with Tom and Patti, Patti had kept telling me, "When you get back to England you must meet Peter. He speaks like this." Then she would proceed to imitate a person speaking very precisely and carefully. This impression did not serve to enamour me towards him, but as I had sent him a parcel that he had left at Tom and Patti's, I thought that at least I should meet him. I discovered he lived in Stourbridge, which amazingly, was where both Pat and Helen lived. When visiting Pat earlier in the summer, I tried to call and see him, but there had been no-one in.

I knew that Jacqui knew Peter and I could tell from her end of the phone call that she was consoling the caller over something. "I'll send Pat and Pam round to sort you out when they get back to Stourbridge," she said. Coming off the phone, she confirmed to me that it *was* Peter, and he needed cheering up. "Thanks a bundle," I thought, "I'm feeling free as a bird, I don't really want to be encumbered with someone else's problems."

Nevertheless, on returning to Stourbridge, I decided to go and see him. Pat opted to stay at home, so I ventured round to his house alone. I knocked on the door. After a short while, it flew open and a gorgeous looking Native American man asked, "What do you want?" in a strong Yorkshire accent. Quite taken aback, I told him who I was, and I was duly invited in. Against all expectations, I had a really good time. It was wonderful to talk to someone who had shared the same experiences that I had and knew the people I knew. Quite early on he established that he was going back to America and was going to marry an indigenous woman. I discovered he had not met her yet, but that was his intention. As I saw him only as a friend and not as a potential boyfriend, we got on well. I did not feel shy or embarrassed, as I would have if I fancied him, and we talked easily and happily together.

After that first meeting, I would call and see Peter whenever I was in Stourbridge to visit my friends.

In the autumn, my permaculture course in Devon started. Peter was a landscape gardener and loved his plants, being very knowledgeable about them. He showed a lot of interest in the concept of permaculture, so I got into the habit of visiting him on the way back from Devon, unloading all the course information, which helped me to retain it, and gave him an understanding of it. Alongside it our friendship grew.

228

In February, I was staying with Pat as usual, and Peter asked me if I would like to visit a Native American exhibition in Birmingham. I agreed. In the exhibition hall, a class of children were visiting and doing activities with their teacher. I was horrified. The museum was getting the children to make headbands with garishly coloured feathers in. There was no indication that the children were being told of any of the reasons behind the use of feathers or that different tribes all have very different ceremonial head dress. Neither was there any indication that modern Native Americans do not go around wearing feathered headdresses. Nor was there any information explaining that the feathered band they were making out of dyed chicken feathers was a Hollywood invention and is highly offensive to First Nations of America. There was no explanation that Hollywood re-wrote history to portray the Native people in the worst light possible, as a massive brainwashing propaganda exercise.

After all I been through in America, to see people in this country still focussed on reinforcing false stereotypes in this way utterly shocked me. I had moved so far on; I was unaware that others were still stuck in the dark ages of the Hollywood myth. To add insult to injury, I noticed the teacher was trying to strategically place children to ostensibly photograph them whilst making sure Peter was in the background. She did not ask his permission and I felt angry on his behalf. I knew how people felt about having their picture taken without permission. It would have been different if she had asked, but she was doing it sneakily.

Holding back the tears, I asked Peter if we could go. As we left the building, the floodgates opened. I wept with anger. Peter put his arm round me to comfort me, but as I calmed down, he kept it there. I was amazed. I suddenly understood that he liked me as more than a friend. I realised that I liked him rather a lot too. I put two and two together and recognised the gorgeous man I had seen outside the American Embassy, several years earlier. I had found my soulmate at last.

From then on, my visits to Stourbridge became even more frequent. All sorts of amazing co-incidences started to happen. I took him to meet Pat, of course, and to see John and Marilyn. When we walked into John and Marilyn's garden, Peter said, "I built this garden." Apparently, the previous owners were the parents of a good friend and he had created the garden. In turn, he introduced me to his

229

friends, many of them bikers. I recalled my younger teenage years when I had hung out with bikers. I felt our two worlds were becoming intertwined.

After a spring and summer of bliss, the cloud hanging over me loomed dark and thundery. Still determined to go to America, Peter had a leaving party. It ended up being quite a bizarre night. He arranged to hold it in the caves in Kinver Edge, near Stourbridge, as there were too many people to entertain in his house (surrounded by neighbours who would not appreciate an all-night rowdy party). Lots of his biker friends, as well as his other friends, turned up. As the night grew darker, drinks were flowing and the party was underway. About seventy people were gathered in the shelter of the caves. Suddenly, above the laughter, shouts and party atmosphere, there came the sound of dogs barking.

Emerging out of the surrounding woodland, we were confronted by a group of police and MOD men with large and fierce looking Alsatians on leads. "You can't stay here lads," they ordered, "this is MOD land, off limits." A long and prolonged argument then ensued between several well inebriated bikers who quite rightly protested that they had been drinking and should not ride their bikes to a different section of the woods which was not MOD land. The police argued back that they were not allowed to stay on this land and in the caves. The bikers protested that if they then got on their bikes, the police would arrest them for drink driving...and so it went on. Eventually a compromise was reached. The police agreed not to arrest anyone for drink driving, as long as they could escort us all to an 'allowable' area of the woods, where we could party all night.

The police left us to it; we settled down again and got back into party mood. Several people decided to wander off into the woods. They came back reporting something strange. Others joined them, hiding in and behind trees, to observe the phenomena. In the middle of the night, the woods were full of people in medieval costume, with bows and arrows, playing a make-believe game. Some of the party goers could not believe their eyes, thinking that things they had consumed were having a strange effect. It was very odd to see shadowy figures from another era flitting in and out of the trees. I am sure they found it equally bizarre stumbling on a load of drunken bikers...each to his own.

The summer of fun and farewells was turning into autumn; Peter was determined to go and settle in America, and I knew that if I loved him, I would have to let him go. If I tried to stop him, it would break our relationship and he would always resent me. As with everything in my life, I knew I had to go with the flow and trust. It was one of the hardest things I have ever done. The pain of parting at the airport was beyond anything, but I knew it had to happen.

That winter was long and hard. My phone bill was enormous as we had long transatlantic conversations; this was still pre-email, Facebook, video links, webcams, texting and mobile phone days. Letters and phone calls were the only means of communication. It was good in one way though, because I felt that he was missing me and hopefully realising how much we meant to each other.

Finally, in the following January, due to family reasons, he had to make a hurried return to England. Apparently, he had to drive through a blizzard on the Plains to get back. The road was indistinguishable from the roadsides. Thickly falling snow was creating a massive white out. His friends and relatives had urged him not to go, telling him it was too dangerous in these conditions, but he insisted. The reservation is a hundred miles from the airport. He had to battle against the driving snow to get there. Suddenly two eagles appeared, flying on either side of the van. They flew, just ahead of him, guiding him to keep on the road. His fears turned to calm, as he followed them. For a hundred miles they guided him, the only creatures he saw in that treacherous journey. Finally, as he reached his destination, they flew off.

On arriving at the airport, the authorities said it was getting too dangerous to fly. Only one small passenger flight was willing to make the journey to a bigger international airport and it was the last one to leave before the airport shut down. He managed to get on it. Twenty-four hours after deciding to return he finally landed. I was there to meet him.

He moved in with me and changed my life.

CHAPTER 40

"Permaculture is the use of ecological design to create self-maintaining agricultural and social systems modelled on natural ecosystems. Others say it is "revolution disguised as gardening." Mike Feingold.

Over time, I began to understand how perfectly placed our new home was. It was fifty minutes to my parents and fifty minutes in the other direction to Peter's relatives. The house is on a south facing slope, we are in the countryside, yet only twenty minutes' walk from the centre of town with good rail and bus connections. It is situated at the end of a terrace, so we have the freedom of having no neighbours at one side, yet we have a small community at the other. Living at the end of a bumpy track, I have learnt that life is much easier if we all look after each other and work together. Jacqui's spirit guide had done us proud.

Peter himself started to change my interactions with everyone. Initially, I was still living in the London mode of not communicating very much with people. Peter's Yorkshire upbringing soon broke down those barriers. He chatted to everyone who walked up and down. Outside the house is a public footpath. Soon we not only knew all the neighbours but all the dog walkers and any other passer-by. He even invited some people in for tea and scones. Before long, my northern friendliness was re-awakened and I lost my reticence to chat.

The land behind the house had only been cultivated on the level patch at the bottom. The hillside above was brambles and bracken with a few silver birch trees. With his landscaping skills, he soon had the whole triangle of our part of the hillside sculpted into a beautifully terraced garden based on permaculture principles. Water flowing through the garden was transformed into pools and streams for wildlife, edges were planted with a variety of fruiting and useful shrubs and trees. Inside the garden, we planted as big a variety of perennials as we could, that were useful for either food or medicine.

Around this time, I had a dream of visiting a permaculture site in France. It was stunningly beautiful, full of flowers as well as vegetables and fruit. In the dream I clearly heard a voice saying, "We need the food and medicines for the body, but we need flowers for the soul." That dream has stayed with me and when I am tempted to the practical, I remember we need beauty as well to lift our spirits.

We put the garden in a booklet called The Permaculture Plot. Soon we began to have visitors from all over the country and Europe. One day, Peter was just in the middle of replacing a beam in the kitchen ceiling when the phone rang. His friend was left holding up the ceiling, while Peter answered it. It was the BBC. They wanted to do a programme about our garden hosted by David Stafford. Being a permaculture garden, it was easy to maintain. The concept is that you plant with a great diversity to create a system that looks after itself with bugs on one plant being food for bugs on another. Companion planting is important and perennials a must. There is no point replanting every year, it is too much effort. The idea is to set up a system then go round collecting the food as you wander. The annual plants self-seed and it is always exciting to see where they will end up. (An angelica plant has moved around the garden over the years, we keep finding it in all sorts of spots.) After the BBC interest and an article in the paper, more local people began to come round the garden as well. A decade or so later, Incredible Edible was founded in Todmorden. Maybe a seed was planted in our garden...who knows. It would be wonderful to think that we might have helped others in their aspirations and dreams.

As the garden grew, people began to comment on the magical feel it had. Peter had built it with love and I loved the plants. I used to take photos of details in the garden. One time I took a photo of a spider's web near the entrance. I was going to throw it away, as it looked a bit blurry, when Peter stopped me. "Can't you see it?" he demanded. I looked at the photo again. Behind the indistinct web was a misty form. Once I had identified it, I could see a face, with a mouth and out of the mouth was pouring a smoky substance. It had very strong male looking features. It looked similar to images of Pan. To us, it is the Spirit of the garden breathing life and energy into the place.

Gradually more objects found their way into the garden. One day our good friends Iestyn and Bev came up to stay. Bev and I sat and chatted in the house as I banned from the garden for several days, which was no hardship as I love Bev's company. As the garden is up the hill behind the house, the mysterious goings on were hidden from view. Eventually, I was blindfolded and led in. Taking the blindfold off, an amazing concrete frog was revealed. I stood in awe at the sight of the Indonesian style frog as it stood, ten feet tall, on its hind legs by the pond. A wire mesh umbrella formed a canopy above, which in years to come would hold two sorts of clematis, one early, one late. Peter had organised it to surprise me. Iestyn is a very talented sculptor (normally in glass) but I do not think he had ever had to put up with so much pain when making one of his creations. I really felt for him. He worked by the midge-ridden pond for several days, winding concrete bandages around the chicken wire frame. To ward off the biters, Peter plied him with copious amounts of lavender essence. Now Iestyn can't bear the smell of it. He is a great storyteller, so hopefully he's had some mileage from the tale.

I love the frog and it has become a landmark in the area. Once a year, hundreds of fell runners run down the path beside it, on a race from Howarth to Stoodley Pike and back. We frequently hear comments such as, "Oh my God what's that?"

"It's a frog!"

"Wow!"

Our friend Robert Hart, who conceptualised the idea of the Forest Garden in this country, told us about the Peace Forest that was being planted in 1991. The local garden centre kindly gifted some trees and we planted them around our garden, on the surrounding hillside and in a local quarry. Twenty-five years on and I cannot believe what a difference those trees have made to the hillside. What was a bleak slope covered in bracken and brambles that baked in the sun, is now a living landscape, full of life and birdsong. Deer often wander through our garden, we occasionally hear foxes, pheasants chuck, woodpeckers sing their exotic song and many other creatures visit. The tree canopy provides shelter from the baking sun and the driving rain. Some butter nuts that Peter was given by my cousin one Christmas (to eat), were planted and have grown to splendid trees, forming a beautiful 'room' where I do my tai chi. Green filtered light in the summer and a golden glow in autumn pervades the space.

234

I often recall a beautiful little book that Peter introduced to me called 'The man who planted trees.' In the story the main protagonist changed a dead and sad landscape purely by planting hundreds of acorns over a barren wasteland. I like to feel that we have transformed our landscape, in a similar way. Once the trees come, other life comes, people feel happier and the forest gives back to them. The land is more stable and the water flows clearer and cleaner. Trees are very important to me. I hope eventually everyone around the world will recognise the importance of these wonderful beings. When we do, humankind will have evolved a step further towards achieving the potential that we could be.

Part of our garden was inspired by Robert Hart. I first met him on the permaculture course when we went to visit his amazing garden. Later I took Peter to meet him, and we developed a good friendship. He reminded me of my dad, a true gentleman, very unassuming whilst being very intelligent and thoughtful. His garden in Shropshire was beautiful. Like Peter he believed in planting with love. He had every sort of fruit you could imagine, introducing us to Japanese wine berries, which have finally got a hold in our garden. I love that fruit. He modelled his ideas on the forest gardens in the rainforests of Indonesia and his concepts were based on Ghandi's philosophy.

He felt that there should be seven layers in a garden with no digging. The forest creates the soil structure which is very delicately balanced and to dig destroys it all. To keep the weeds down we have to keep mulching the surface, which in turn helps to build the soil. The seven layers are a root layer, a ground cover layer, a herb layer, a bush layer, a dwarf tree layer, a standard tree layer and vines growing up them. He managed it beautifully and people came from all over to learn from him. Sadly, he passed over at the turn of the millennium, but his ideas live on. Although some people now do not know where the concept came from, many more people are talking about forest gardens and adopting his ideas.

As we got to know him and he trusted us, he explained what had happened. His mother had bought the beautiful farmhouse with land around it to house himself and his disabled brother. As time went on, his mother and brother died, leaving Robert. He decided to open his home to others, following his Ghandi ideals, to set up a community where all were equal. Initially all went well but after a while, the community started to disintegrate. Unfortunately, others were not so pure minded and lovely as Robert. As far as I am aware, one couple decided to keep possession of the main part of the house. They were now living there in comparative luxury, with the main bathroom, kitchen and living quarters, whilst Robert, who owned the house, was living in two rooms with a tiny bathroom, which led out onto the garden. They had separated his part off, blocked up his access to his original home and basically taken possession of his house. Unfortunately, when he died, he had to leave the battle to a friend to fight for him. I am not sure what all the ins and outs were, I was busy with a small baby at that point and had my own battles where I was living and could not help much. I know that after a few years she wrote to me and said she could not fight any longer, I think it was too big for her. On Google maps it still appears to be there and intact, but I do not know what has happened to it now. Photos of the beautiful garden and people's experiences live on in various forms on the internet. His beauty and work have not been forgotten and he has inspired many, many people to a different lifestyle and way of planting. I feel very privileged to have been his friend.

I have not bought a certain brand of yoghurt for years because of another inspirational person I met on my permaculture course. He was called Arthur Hollins and pioneered a new way of farming in Shropshire. I loved his farm. It was teeming with life and the dawn chorus was unbelievably loud and intense. Unlike normal farmers he loved mole hills, as they provide beautifully prepared soil for seeding new grasses. In line with permaculture principles, he was into creating a natural system for his cattle. He did away with silage or dry winter fodder, as he kept them outdoors all the time. As a result, they did not suffer from moving between internal and external living every year, or with any of the other conditions that cattle are prone to when living indoors. To achieve winter feeding, he set aside an area of his farm where he grew 'foggage' which was their grazing in winter. In the mole hills he kept planting greater varieties of grass seed every year, so his farm grew in diversity. The soil also grew in fertility, the moles helped, as did all the other creatures he encouraged, particularly the worms, and the cows fertilised their own food supply. As the grass was not cut for any hay or silage, the matted grass layer became thicker. Poaching of the earth (where it becomes mud) was reduced and the soil kept on building in fertility allowing more cattle to gradually be able to use the land over the years.

Down from Arthur Hollins's beautiful farm, was a yoghurt factory which was trying to reclaim the tenancy of the farm. Sadly, he died with the stress of fighting them, but his children did not give up and have now created a new model for farming, a community owned farm. Their story is incredible and worth looking up on the internet. Since visiting his farm, I have voted with my pocket and refused to buy the products of that company.

I do the same with another multi-national company. I couldn't bear how they ran the campaign to persuade mothers in African countries that their own breast milk was inferior to this company's powdered milk. They haven't improved. In more recent years they have lowered the fragile water table in California from their water bottling plants.

The women in Ireland who started the inspirational supermarket campaign to avoid purchasing South African brands during apartheid, showed me how powerful our purses and buying power can be. It does not matter to me that hundreds of others do not listen or care, what does matter is that I am doing what *I* can against these companies, they are not getting my hard-earned cash. Many people are beginning to feel that sense of empowerment which is wonderful. The more we work together, the more we can change things for the better. The Fairtrade movement is one example. Do not ever feel you are powerless. We all have so much power to change things. We just have to believe in it and follow our hearts.

* * *

Having completed the permaculture course, I tried to implement the principles in my life.

At home, Peter and I designed and planted the garden, I joined the local economic trading scheme (bartering with favours) and when I heard about a potential credit union being formed, I went along on an exploratory visit to one in North Halifax. In 1995, I joined the training course and became a founder member of our local Credit Union. Many years later, many experiences later and hopefully a little bit wiser, I am still involved. We amalgamated with Calderdale (we were unsustainable on our own) and I have been on the Board of Directors ever since. The establishment is finally starting to be interested in our work, particularly with all the payday loan companies these days. Successive governments have recognised that we tick a lot of their boxes, and we have had a lot of support over the years to grow and develop. In recent years, the endorsement by the Archbishop of Canterbury has helped to 'spread the word.'

There is nothing better than to see the change in someone when we help them out of a terrible debt trap. On top of that, it feels good that we are contributing to keeping money in the local economy which benefits everyone. Again, as with everything, I work quietly with my guides on issues to do with the Credit Union, although I do not 'come out' much about it to other Board members. In fact, since I arrived and settled down in Todmorden, I have been more circumspect about my spirituality.

Early in the 1990s I visited the newly established Ragman's Lane Farm in the Forest of Dean to attend a course run by Bill Mollinson, one of the founders of Permaculture. Like me, he had visited the Hopi, but also many other native cultures around the world. Their approach to nature and understanding of how the world worked, deeply influenced his ideas.

He explained how each native culture specialises in different skills. One culture that he visited in the Pacific specialised in negotiation of the ocean. The women were trained in women's roles, the men in their roles. Like the Hopi, there is no chance of choosing a different role, it is just how it is. End of. The women would lie in a box in darkness inside the boat and listen to the refraction of the waves against the sides of the boat. From their highly tuned and developed knowledge, passed on through secret women's societies, they could then navigate, depending on the sounds the waves would make, over thousands of miles. The men meanwhile would oversee the steering of the vessel to the women's instructions. Both roles were vital and created a social situation of stability and interdependence.

Similarly, the Hopi women owned the land and houses, but they needed the men to work it for them. The women ground the corn; the men grew it. Each had their clearly and precisely defined roles in society, both spiritually and socially. Essentially though, it was a matriarchal system. Traditionally, if the women had had enough of the men, their shoes were placed outside the door to show they had been divorced. Hopi women are a force to be reckoned with.

I think we have got confused over the years with how to achieve equality with men. In our society, the roles that we had were unfairly balanced towards the male element. Since the sixties, women (and some men) have worked very hard to redress the balance, but the way I see it, it has been by trying to adapt to a patriarchal society. The result seems to have ended up stressing women out, trying to do so many roles at once; career woman, mother, wife, running a home, charity work and volunteer in society, as well as pursuing their own interests in any odd moment. The men meanwhile are gradually feeling a sense of disempowerment. Massive guilt is often felt by women for not fulfilling all their roles adequately, particularly the mother role (which is a full-time job in itself) and then stress levels grow, and with it, illnesses linked to stress, such as cancer.

I think we need to take a step back and begin to change the value systems. Instead of seeing mother and fatherhood as a side-line to all our other jobs, it should be revered by society and given the status it deserves. A good parent creates a stable and balanced future for society with reduced healthcare costs, reduced crime costs, reduced social costs and a happier healthier environment for us all. An incapable parent, for whatever reasons, escalates those costs to society and furthermore teaches successive generations the same inadequacies, so it becomes self-perpetuating. I know our politicians are short term and therefore do not focus on the future in the same way, but we are already reaping the rewards of dysfunctional homes. We will continue to do so, until they finally realise how vital Sure Start and all the other agencies that support young families really are. Nothing is more important to a society than getting it right with their babies and little ones. When this culture finally gets that, then I believe we will truly have hope for the future.

Returning to Bill Mollinson, he then went on to explain how the aborigines specialise in the manipulation of time and space. He told us how he had been working with some Aborigine lads and that they were annoyed that he, as a white man, had knowledge about their local plants and their uses that they didn't have. The next day they returned. Not only did they know all the names of the plants, but they could also identify them easily and knew all their uses. Bill naturally asked how they had learnt so much overnight. "We went to our Elders," they told him. "We complained about our lack of knowledge. The Elders told us that we did know. How? We asked.

They replied that we have all that knowledge from childhood. It is in the songs. We queried as to why we did not know the key. The Elders' response was that we had never asked for it till now."

Apparently, this started the lads off and they were eager to learn more. A while later they then went to Bill and told him they were learning to become invisible.

"Meet us in the Bush at such and such a time," they said. Bill took a friend and they sat in the cab of their truck, scanning the landscape around them. They could see for miles. Nowhere could the big aboriginal lads hide from them. Suddenly a wasp got into the cab. Bill and his friend were busy trying to get it out. When it flew off, they looked up and surrounding them were all their aborigine friends. "Give us a lift home in the truck, will you," they grinned.

These tales have stuck with me and served as further examples of how we, as a western society think we know it all, yet we know so little. For some bizarre reason, we have a sense of superiority over our fellow humans, yet we have little or no reason to back it up. We value appearances above all, particularly in the visual culture of TV, social media and YouTube, without looking and listening beyond the image.

Bill also told us how his life experience taught him how to make two problems come together to create a solution. This principle has helped me look at situations creatively in my life.

In the early 90s I was invited to do a stand at Ilkley Healing Fair, talking to people about Permaculture. Nearby, on another stand, were a couple whom I started chatting to. The woman in the couple was called Jan and I instantly took a liking to her. I discovered they lived in Todmorden, so we arranged to meet up. This was the beginning of another important friendship in my life.

CHAPTER 41

"The bird a nest, the spider a web, man friendship." William Blake

It was good to start connecting with a few people in Todmorden who were on my wavelength. Jan believed in Spirit Guides and the afterlife, as well as living a 'green lifestyle' as far as possible. During this time, I was keeping my spirituality under wraps unless I was chatting to someone who understood. No-one at school knew about it, although I would occasionally drop snippets and allow them to brand me as a bit loony. In doing so, it meant people who were on my wavelength could identify me. It, also, gave people permission to unload about strange or unexplained phenomena in their lives. I have lost count of the number of times that I heard, "I don't normally tell people about this, but you will understand."

Sometimes people have told me of how they are trying to help others but are feeling overwhelmed by the burden of taking on their friends' problems. Years ago, Pat told me of a dream she had. I repeat this to help them. Pat told me that in the dream she was walking along a causeway towards a beautiful island. She wanted to reach the island, but the causeway led through a sea of souls. The souls were calling out to her, asking for help. She wanted to help but knew if she got off the path amongst them, she would end up in the same position, incapacitated by emotion. By swelling their numbers, it would not solve anything. She realised the only way, was to continue on her way to the island, sending love and compassion. By staying on her path, she was showing them an alternative way of being, which would give them a chance to crawl out of the pits of despair and hopelessness.

* * *

As I lived here, friends from the past started to emerge and move into the area. One was my friend Ian. I knew him when I was very young, then his family left Bramhall. His parents and my parents had kept in touch over the years, but we had lost contact. One day in his twenties, when he was walking from one end of the country to the other, Ian walked into Mum and Dad's garden. Amazingly we discovered that I was living very close to him in London, so we met up and became friends. When I moved here, I discovered he was living in Rochdale with his partner, so we rekindled our friendship again. After a couple of years, they then moved to Tod. It is very comforting knowing people who have come from the same place, who know where you are coming from. I am still in touch with five of my friends from the road in which I grew up. We see each other and keep in touch on the phone. Again, it feels like talking to family when I am with them. We share so much history. As the years have passed, I have discovered more people who grew up in the Stockport area who are now living here.

For a few years, there were even three of us who went to the same school, living on the same contour line, all within ten minutes' walk of each other. This would not be very astounding if it was the local High School. It is not. It is a school in Cheadle Hulme, on the other side of Manchester, which was a direct grant school when I went there and a private school when my neighbours went there. I went there in the seventies, one neighbour attended there in the nineties and the other in the noughties. Three generations from the same school all living so close. I could not believe it when I discovered it.

After the turn of the century, Jacqui, Hassan and family also, moved up to Calderdale, in an amazing co-incidence of fate.

Gradually we found new friends who understood where we were coming from. One day Peter was walking along the road and this guy came up to him and started talking about his back. Peter's back has caused him many problems over the years. This man, Graham, was the only one who could fix it properly. As we got to know him, I began to realise he was an earth angel. As usual, angel packaging is not what we expect.

Many people passing him on the street would have dismissed him as an 'old hippie' with his straggly grey hair, jeans and an aura of patchouli oil. Incredibly selfless and kind, he always put the needs of others above those of himself. He had a real gift in healing people, helping everyone whose lives he touched. One time I could not get out of the bath. I had slipped a disc and was in absolute agony. Peter rang Graham, and although he himself was not very well, he dropped everything and came to my rescue. Within five minutes he had sorted me out, popped the disc back in place and the searing agony had

242

gone. He had no paperwork to back up his skills, but he could cure people in a way I have never come across before or since. Although he achieved miracles that even hospitals said were impossible, he would only charge a minimal amount, as he knew the people he helped often could not afford much. He trusted that the Universe would provide. Through Graham we met a few more people who were on our wavelength.

In recent years I heard a wonderful story from him, which seemed like a fairy tale. Many years previously, a young man called Steve, had just come out of the army and had been in a bad way with nowhere to go and no-one to care for him. Graham had found him, taken him in, let him sleep on his sofa for a year and gently nurtured him. Grasping the chance Graham had given him, Steve moved on with his life, ending up being a very successful businessman.

Several years later, Graham had been going through some difficult times, was ill and on the point of dying. Arriving providentially, Steve managed to extricate Graham from the terrible situation he was in. Putting Graham up in a hotel for twelve months, he then enabled him to recover as much of his health as he could; before giving him a job, a house to live in and a car. It was a truly beautiful story of karma. Sadly, Graham's health did not hold out for ever and he has now returned to his angelic role on the other side.

Over those early years of the nineties, several schools offered me permanent jobs, but each time I refused, knowing that I wanted to be free to travel again. Like Graham, I liked the life where I trusted my guides to provide for me. Sometimes it got a bit close to the bone, but they have always managed it.

CHAPTER 42

"We are all travellers in the wilderness of this world and the best we can find is an honest friend." R. L. Stevenson

Peter and I decided that we were both ready for another visit to the States. He wanted to share his friends and relations with me. I wanted to do the same for him. I was looking forward to travelling with Peter. We saved up, rented the house out, left Mum and Dad in charge of our affairs and set off. We were not sure how long we were going for, so we got an open-ended ticket. We flew to Chicago, and then had more connecting flights to catch before reaching our destination.

As we passed through immigration and customs we were stopped. That had never happened to me before and I felt nervous. Why had they stopped us? We were doing nothing wrong. They questioned us separately for ages about why we were there, what we intended doing and so on. Searching our bags with a tooth comb, they found my teaching certificates in my bag. I had brought them in case of any opportunity to teach during our travels, to supplement our income. I was told in no uncertain terms that it was totally illegal for me to do that in the USA and our visas were stamped with 'no work permitted' on them.

We were finally released with minutes to catch our connecting flight. I was shaking and upset. Peter told me that he always gets treated like that. It is because of his Indigenous American looks. They are paranoid about anyone with Native connections. It was my first taste of institutionalised racism from his viewpoint. It was not very pleasant.

We arrived in Rapid City to be met by David, a very good friend of Peter's. He drove us the hundred miles or so home and lent us his house to stay in for the summer. The kindness and generosity of him and his family made up for all the bad treatment we had received. One good thing I have learnt about many Americans, is that once you are in the country, whatever their ethnic background, kindness and hospitality are paramount.

David's house was in a tiny hamlet, a few yards from his mum and dad's house, which was also the post office. The hamlet was situated at a crossroads of dirt tracks. The signpost did not indicate the next towns, but the names of people who lived down each track. I had never been anywhere as vast as the prairies. The nearest settlement, a 'city' of a thousand inhabitants, was half an hour's drive down the dirt tracks, then another ten minutes or so on the main road.

One evening when we were driving back from the town and away from any light source, Peter pulled over, stopped the vehicle and turned off the lights. I wondered at first what he was doing; aware we were totally alone under this vast sky. As we stepped out of the van, he indicated that I should look up. The sky was ablaze with stars. I have never seen so many. Every space of dark blue had a light shining in it. A swathe of misty looking cloud depicted the Milky Way. I was breathless with the wonder of it all. The sky seemed all at once close, yet far away.

As I gazed at this wonderful living sky, I recalled the nights when I was a little girl. Walking home from Brownies, we had to go along a road which had very big gardens, separating pedestrians from the reassuring lights in the windows. Even though I was with my dad, I used to be frightened. My imagination has always been vivid, and I created all manner of things lurking in the shadows. My dad, understanding my fears, used to hold my hand and tell me to look up at the stars. I did so and instantly my earthly fears dissipated. I am very grateful to my dad for giving me that gift. All through my life, whenever I have felt nervous in the dark, I look up and the stars help me.

This night sky, however, peaked them all. I never understood how many billions of stars there must be out there until then. The whole sky felt like my friend, glowing with a million sparkles of pure beautiful light. Only on the prairies have I ever been far enough away from lights, with a big expanse of sky, to see those stars like that. As with all special moments, I tucked it away in my heart's memory to access when I have need of it.

Back in Tuthill, I was growing very fond of David and his parents Lillian and Roy. They were amazing. Coming out to the Prairies as children at the turn of the nineteenth century, they were one of the earlier settlers. Arriving with their respective families in horse drawn covered waggons, Roy and Lillian would have lived in a similar way to the children in Laura Ingalls Wilder's stories.

Whilst we were there, they celebrated their seventy-fifth wedding anniversary. Well into their nineties, Roy still wore dungarees and was never happier than when he was driving his tractor and looking out for his pigs. Lillian was one of the kindest people you could meet. She had brought up her children to always remember the debt they owed to the native people around them. Those early pioneers would have died of cold and starvation, if it had not been for their Lakota neighbours who fed them and kept them warm. In turn, when David became postmaster, he went to the local college to learn Lakota, to ensure he could properly serve *all* his customers.

Sadly, later immigrants had not maintained the same attitude. We learnt of shocking levels of racism towards both their Lakota neighbours and towards anyone who was not white. Even people who were part Lakota themselves could be very racist, trying to distance themselves and fit in with the ruling culture. David told us how the local community had run the vicar out of town because he was married to a black woman. I could hardly believe this attitude could still exist at the end of the twentieth century. Although attitudes in England are not perfect, at least views have generally improved since the fifties, with more understanding and acceptance. Not so in South Dakota.

Hanging out my washing in the garden between David's house and the post office, it felt timeless. The sky expanded blue above me, vegetables and flowers waved in the breeze and the sun beat down remorselessly. It was a constant reminder that we were in high summer at the centre of a very large of continent.

A favourite occupation was to sit on the bench outside the post office and cloud watch. As tiny humans, we watched the massive cloud forms shape and billow across the vast blue. Sometimes they were white and fluffy, sometimes streaky and at others menacing and dark, gathering their forces together. On days when life is hectic, I unlock this memory, taking comfort from that time, when we all we did was sit and watch the sky. It had an important purpose behind it. We were looking for grey, dark clouds mounded together with a tail coming down. If the tail was ever to touch the ground, then it was time to get indoors and into the tornado shelter fast. Luckily, this did not happen to us, but we heard plenty of tales to convince us of its terrors.

Being so far from everything, Tuthill had its own volunteer fire brigade. From Peter's last visit, he was enrolled as an able-bodied male, so on our first day there when the fire alarm went off, so did he, racing off to deal with a prairie fire in his jetlagged state. I had no clue where they had gone. In my imagination the fire was raging out of control, as Peter, David, Roy and the others used the fire engine and beaters to fight it. Lillian did her best to reassure my nerves. I was nevertheless relieved when the men returned, the fire engine was rehoused, and normal life resumed.

We had a lovely summer in Tuthill. Peter took me to visit his friends and relatives who lived in different tribal housing sites. Mom Alice and Sage and the family were very warm and welcoming, making me feel accepted and a part of everyone. Mom Alice is a beautiful person, so loving and giving to all around her. Peter introduced me to his sisters and brothers and all their families whilst I tried to keep track of who was who, working out how everyone was related. All through the summer, we kept on popping back to visit them and spend time together. It felt good to finally meet everyone after Peter had told me about them all. Over the years since our first meeting, I have grown closer to all the family; appreciating their love and care. Even though we are so far away physically, it somehow never seems to matter.

At Wanble, he introduced me to his friend Larry, who explained to me about how the Reservation is organised. I began to understand how it is divided into different districts or Chapters. Each district has its own governance with all the districts coming together under the main rule of the tribal council in Pine Ridge. Things like hospitals and the police force are organised by the main council in Pine Ridge, whilst more local issues are dealt with in the Round House in each district.

Peter took me to the Badlands where I marvelled at the shapes and forms created by the ancient mud hills. He told me how fossils are found there from creatures that lived many years ago under the sea. I was amazed to imagine that the centre of this enormous land mass was once under water. We visited Wooden Knife's café and sampled his delicious fry bread made with timpsula, a wild turnip plant that grows on the prairie.

On other days we went to the pow-wow at Pine Ridge (seventy miles west) or Rosebud (seventy miles east). At Rosebud an amazing thing happened. We were wandering round the pow-wow and as we passed a tribal cop, we noticed his name badge. His surname was the same as a Lakota friend we had both known in Arizona. Peter went up to him and said, "Do you know anyone called Greg?"

"He's my brother," the cop replied.

"Can you let us know how we can get in touch with him?"

"He's the Eagle Staff Carrier and dancing in the pow-wow. His face is fully painted that's why you won't have recognised him. I'll tell him you're here."

We were amazed and even happier when we met up with him again. We had both known him separately on our different visits to Arizona. He was a friend of Patti's and she had got him to take us round the area to see the sights. We were now together and seeing him in a different State, five years later and one thousand miles away. I think we were all blown away by the encounter. Greg invited us to visit him. A few days later we did so. We had a great time catching up on our lives.

One little old Lakota lady who we both fell in love with was Myrtle. She was tiny, her bright eyes shining with life. We met her a few times and she asked if we could stow her in our suitcases to take her home to England with us! On another occasion she said she had packed her son off to the Sun Dance to find a nice white girl to marry. It seemed a bit of an anachronism. The Sun Dance is a very sacred ceremony, supposedly closed to non-Lakota people. Maybe she was hoping he would meet a white woman who was sympathetic to indigenous people there.

People who have contact with First Nations people generally seem to be divided into two extremes. At one end of the spectrum are the white 'wannabee' Indians who romanticise the life of First Nation people, idolising the culture, ideals and beliefs. At at the other end are the white racists who tend to live in towns close to Native

248

American reservations and who ghettoise Lakota people, treating them with fear and suspicion. In between, there is the range of everything else. Personally, I admire and respect the culture and feel very angry as to how indigenous people have been treated over the years.

On an individual level, I tend to treat each person as I find them, no matter what race or belief system they come from. I have learnt that most First Nations people will look at you and read you in your eyes. If your intentions are good, you will be accepted. If your intentions are not good, you will be ignored. Most people I have met have been kind, generous and very caring towards me. As in all peoples, I have, also, met those who wished to take advantage or use me. If I act stupidly, then I will be used. It is the same with all people. Unless I am known as family or a friend, then every stranger is game, whatever the culture. I learnt that a long time ago in that shebeen in Manchester's Moss Side.

On one trip back from Pine Ridge, we gave a hitchhiker a lift. She was an Inuit from Alaska and had come down for the Sun Dance. We took her to the site in Rosebud. It was an open Sun Dance run by a Lakota man. In other words, people from all over the world would come to it, pay for the privilege, and camp for the duration in the wooded valley where it took place. Perhaps this was the Sun Dance Myrtle was referring to. The hitchhiker was a lovely person, very genuine, but we felt a bit bad because we knew from our relatives and friends how it is thought of by many other Lakota people.

A lot of Lakota feel betrayed by those who are poisoned by western greed and sell their sacred ceremonies to outsiders. One of Peter's friends had explained to us that he was going to take part in the proper tribal Sun Dance that summer. To do so, he would have to prepare for weeks, fasting, abstaining from alcohol, praying. When he took part, his family and friends would all be there, supporting him and praying for him to get him through. His sacrifice would be for the good of all, not just an experience for him to tick off. The Sun Dance is a very powerful and sacred ceremony. It is not something people should pay to take part in nor is it a one-off occasion. You do not participate only once. It is a very serious commitment for several years. Sadly, this rush to make money, even out of the spiritual side is yet another abuse of the First Nations, some of it done by their own.

249

The original people of America have been treated abominably over the years. As more and more European settlers arrived on the continent, more land was needed for people to live on and to grow food on. The rich fertile prairies were a prize to be wrenched from the indigenous population. After many battles and skirmishes between the US Cavalry; the First Nations were 'persuaded' to accept an 'agreement' assigning a territory (or reservation) to the Lakota. This included the Black Hills. These are regarded by the Lakota as the sacred heart of all their land. The treaty was signed by the government and nothing was supposed to break it. The treaty covered ninety thousand square miles.

Imagine the government's chagrin when gold was discovered there. On the face of it, the government had to be seen trying to uphold the treaty. Why then did they allow Custer to lead an expeditionary force into the Hills? Why was he allowed to take a reporter with him? Illegally, against the treaty, the discovery of gold was mentioned in the papers. The greed of a nation could not be held back. Within a space of a few years the pristine beauty of the Black Hills was devastated as the gold rush took over. The original promises of the treaty were broken, leading to further reduction of the reservation and the desecration of their sacred heart land in the Black Hills.

The revenge on Custer for this illegal betrayal was sweet but came at a great cost. The Battle of Little Bighorn was a short-lived triumph. Soon the tragedy of Wounded Knee unfolded, where women, children and old people were shot down in cold blood when they were walking to Pine Ridge Agency for help in the deep winter, when it is cold beyond belief. This and other less well-known acts of cruelty and betrayal finally broke the resistance to the invaders.

The next stage of attack was not so obvious. It was bureaucratic, institutionalised land grab. In the nineteen-thirties the Allotment Act was introduced. Instead of all the reservation being owned communally by the tribe, the head of each Lakota family was given a certain acreage of land on the reservation. Soon after that, a tax on land was introduced. Anyone not being able to pay the tax had their land confiscated and given to incoming farmers. Lakota people were not farmers, they had traditionally hunted the buffalo, using this revered creature for everything they needed-food, shelter and living. As a result, the heads of families could not pay the taxes, the land was quickly taken off them and soon the reservation had been reduced in size yet again. Unsurprisingly, the tax was rescinded very shortly after the land had left Lakota hands.

Subsidies and grants were then introduced in reward for growing the wheat, which turned into an ecological disaster for the Plains. The rich and deep soil, created over centuries by millions of buffalo roaming and fertilising it, has all been lost. Once protected from the erosive sun or wind by a permanent layer of grass, the plough ripped away this cover and exposed the soil. The wind blew layers away and the repeated crop growth denuded it of minerals, until the once fertile plains are now a sadly denuded memory of what they once were. Only a few carefully preserved pockets of true prairie land still exist. Finally, in the last hour, people are waking up to the wonder and necessity of these ancient grasslands with their finely tuned ecosystem. There is a movement that recognises what has been lost and there are now some people working to restore a fraction of the Prairie. It is sad to think that no-one can now experience the shoulder-high summer grasses of earlier days with the wind rippling through, like waves on the sea.

Alongside the land grab, the Carlisle Schools were operating, shipping children hundreds of miles from their homes, as I mentioned earlier.

Combined with the very powerful Hollywood machine effectively making Native Americans out to be the 'baddies' for many years; plus the replacement of their traditional diet with Government Issue commodities (poor quality supplies of flour, milk powder, dried eggs and so on); it is amazing how Lakota people have managed to survive at all. However, they have and retain a sense of humour, honour and a generosity which would humble anyone. No matter how little food there is, people will always share it. It comes from a very different outlook on life.

At a pow-wow there is often an honouring of someone, during which a give-away takes place. Traditionally, the wealthier you were in the tribe, the more you gave away. The give-away would show your wealth, even out your possessions with others and ensure that the weaker (and less able to hunt and procure hides for shelter and clothing) were provided for. What an amazing system! The complete opposite from the one we live in, where the richest (not always, but often) tend to be the meanest, clutching on to their wealth, whilst the poorest tend to be the most generous, sharing what little they have. My son's paper round has shown him that. The little old lady who lives in a tiny home will be there to give him a tip, whereas the people who live in the larger houses are often rude and dismissive of him, take him for granted and never tip.

Opposite Mom Alice there lived a tribal cop. He was a lovely guy. He had been the tribal President the year before and was very well respected in the Housing. We met up with him and went for lunch together. He understood where we were coming from, appreciating our ideas about permaculture. He wanted us to stay and set up a food growing programme. It was very tempting, but there were the stamps on our passports to consider, plus there was Mum and Dad in England. I could not leave them for too long. We had taken a copy of Bill Mollinson's Permaculture Manual with us and felt he was the person to have it. Twenty years later, I have seen on the internet that there is now a permaculture programme on the reservation. It gives me hope.

In 1986 there was the first Chief Big Foot Memorial Ride to commemorate the hundred years since Wounded Knee. People rode a hundred and ninety-one miles on their horses in the bitter temperature of mid-winter. It was to remember, and to start the process of mending the sacred Hoop of Life, broken with the tragedy of 1890. The ride has continued annually as a spiritual time for reflection and an educational chance for the younger generation to gain a better understanding of their history.

Since then, the white buffalo have been born, another sign of renewal. Lakota people are working hard, with some support from sympathetic outsiders, to build a future for their children that is not as bleak as the past. I have just seen a very inspirational video about the young indigenous people who are working through music to inspire and change the lives for other vulnerable youngsters on the rez. They are not the only ones. There are many people around the world, working to make the earth a better place for each other. They are never sung about or newsworthy, but they are inspirational. As individuals we cannot do everything, but we can do a little. Each little bit counts when it builds to make a whole. The old Roman 'divide and rule' is a very powerful weapon, but there are many people who are united in all sorts of ways. We are all playing important roles in creating a better future together, a very positive future. It is sometimes hard to remember this when the media makes it appear that the giants of politics and business control our lives.

The summer in South Dakota seemed to slip by slowly. David taught us how to paint ceramics. I discovered the joy and creativity of turning a blank white biscuit fired piece of clay into a living object with detailed features. As we worked, he told us many things. One of them was about his terrible car accident. We could not believe how much the medical costs were. As a government postal worker, he had one of the best insurances anyone could have. Yet when he had that awful crash, he had to take out a mortgage to pay the outstanding ten percent that was not covered; it was over two hundred thousand dollars. Other people we knew, despite having insurance, had to extend their mortgages to cover the cost of medical bills. Ever since hearing of the cost of visits in American hospitals, I have been so appreciative of our wonderful NHS. I worry when politicians espouse the American system, sneakily trying to privatise more and more of the service. Trust me, we do not want to go that way.

Early in the summer, we decided to walk along the road to visit some of Peter's friends. Our driving licences from our previous visits had expired and we were waiting to take our tests again. Turtles snapped at us from the ditches and beautiful butterflies floated around in the searing heat. The road was very long, straight and without shelter from trees. Peter was good at pointing out all the wildlife, but it was with a great sense of relief that we finally arrived at Auntie Wilma and Uncle Vincent's cool yard surrounded by trees. Under the welcome shade we sipped ice cold 'sun' tea and were very relieved to be offered a lift home.

At first, I would be astounded that people would drive from one end of the local town's Main Street to the other. It was such a short distance. As time went on, I began to understand. As the heat bounded from the white concrete pavements, blasting my senses, I would find even the short walk from the van to the shops taking all my usual boundless energy.

One time we were driving in the local reserve when I stopped. "Oh dear," I said, "I think I just ran over a snake." We got out to look. As we neared the prone creature, its tail reared up and started rattling. "It's not harmed," Peter answered, "Quick get back in the van." On relaying the story to Lillian, she recalled a story from years gone by.

"When I was a younger lass," she told us, "I was riding my horse into town. In those days there were no cars, the only means of transport was a horse or a horse and cart. Suddenly the horse got spooked and started racing off. I managed to look down and saw a rattle snake hanging onto the reins. If the snake bit the horse or me, I knew I was a gonner. I couldn't slow the horse down, as I would have to use the reins and I didn't want to do so. After a terrifying gallop, I managed to shake the snake off the reins and eventually calm the horse down."

I loved to hear Lillian's stories. She told us how she hated ice cream because the only time they could make it was in winter when they would dig a big ice pit in the garden. They would then whip up the cream from the cow's milk and place it in the pit to freeze. She would have to keep going out in the bitter cold to stir it and check on it. When it is icy cold, I can understand how ice cream is not appealing.

Over the summer we visited lots of friends, relatives and places feeling very much a part of life out there. As September came in, we realised we would have to head south soon before the winter closed in and shut the passes through the Rockies. We travelled in Peter's van. He had bought it on his previous visit and David had very kindly looked after it for him. Not being able to do the ceramics as we were travelling, I took on another project. One of my friends from school was typing up all my letters that I sent home. It was a mammoth task and I knew I could not afford to give her any money. I felt the best thing I could do was spend a lot of time and effort making her something in exchange. Over the winter and spring, as we travelled, I hand-stitched a star quilt for her, completing it on our return.

In Colorado we came across a beautiful town called Golden. Peter was thrilled to find a town of his namesake. It had a fabulous bronze statue of a dragon in the central park. We discovered that Coors Brewery was the main employer there, after the gold mine had dried up. We discovered that no-one called Golden actually lived in the town, although the police were very friendly and helpful. They even gave Peter one of their badges when they learnt of his name.

Crossing the spectacular Rockies, we discovered a town on the other side called Collbran. I could not believe it! A town with my surname (plus an "l") was on the west side of the mountain range (where I had more connections) and a town with Peter's surname was on the east of the range (where he had more connections). In Collbran they all moaned about having to spell it all the time for people. I fully sympathised, having had to spell my surname for years. The town had been named after a British born man called Collbran who was a railway engineer and entrepreneur. They wanted him to build the railway to their town and named it after him to encourage him to do so. An even further interesting co-incidence was that there was a romantic connection with Golden. The son of Mr Collbran married the daughter of the founder of Coors Brewery. Mr. Henry Collbran then went off to Korea where he became known as the 'King of Korea' because he built up their infrastructure of railroads. Another co-incidence is that my grandpa Colbran worked on the railways in England. Henry arrived in Korea in 1897, about sixteen years after my grandpa was born. I doubt there is any real connection, just an amazing set of co-incidences.

As we left and started driving down to Utah, an enormous rainbow formed a complete arch across the sky. We took a photo, Peter's little white van dwarfed by the giant curve of colour. It was a moment of pure happiness. Whenever I see a rainbow, it always lifts my spirits and gives me hope. I thought back to the visualised rainbow I had placed Matthew in, all those years ago and realised how far on my journey I had travelled since then.

From the splendid arch of colours in light, we moved on to the splendid arches of colours in rock, at Utah's National Park of Arches. The glowing red orange rock sculpted by nature into amazing shapes and forms was breath-taking. Clambering around and marvelling at them, we felt like children exploring a new playground. Little chipmunks ran amongst our feet, tempted into tameness by titbits from tourists. We spent all day there enjoying the beauty of our Mother Earth at her best.

Eventually, after a thousand miles of travelling, we arrived back in Arizona where I introduced Peter to all my friends from my first visit. It was great to see them all again. Peter finally met the beautiful Vanessa, whom he had seen pictures of but never encountered in real life before. He was thrilled when she was happy to be photographed with him. Vanessa is an amazing woman, constantly campaigning for the young people. Her latest achievement was organising fund raising events to build a centre for the youth to learn about their culture and heritage. I loved seeing her and her children again. Her little baby had become a lovely girl and her older children had grown into

255

wonderful young people, busy following their lives. I felt such love and warmth from them all. Going round to visit with Leona, I felt the same love and care, as we caught up with her life.

After some digging, I managed to track down Patti in Sante Fe. It was joyful to reconnect with her and her daughter, who had, also, grown into a beautiful little girl. I treasured my time with them. When I found out that her daughter had kept all the birthday cards I had sent her, I was very moved. Patti took us to lots of places in Sante Fe and the surrounding area. We reminisced and chatted about what had been happening in the intervening years. Sat in a Mexican bar, eating enchiladas and drinking tequila and lime from salt encrusted glasses, it felt very satisfying to be with my special friend again. Looking round the room, I thought back to when Patti had first mentioned Peter to me. At that time, he was thousands of miles away. Since then, I had been thousands of miles away from Patti. Now all three of us were together; it was like the completion of a circle.

Her new partner was from Taos and Acoma, so he kindly took us to visit the pueblos. I felt privileged to be taken as a guest to visit places that were normally only accessible by guided tours. After a lovely time with Patti, we moved on to Flagstaff.

On arriving there, we visited another of my good friends, who was now married. She kindly let us stay with her, meeting her husband and her daughter who had grown into a beautiful young woman.

Whilst we were in Flagstaff, we took the opportunity to visit Patti's mum, Eunice, who was incredibly warm and welcoming. I had met her a few times on my first visit and visiting her felt reassuringly familiar. She looked after us and made us feel at home. Her house felt like our safe base. We caught up with her life and that of her children and grandchildren. Because of my closeness to Patti, it felt like I was catching up with family.

Taking Peter up on to the mesas, I went to visit the father of one of my friends from Tuba, who was a moccasin maker. Sat in his stone-built home, we visited together, as the fire burned in the stove and the drying beans popped open in their cases. Time did not exist; just the calm quiet of now. After a while, Rex, who was then in his seventies or eighties, surprised us by saying he was going to his mother's for dinner and invited us to come. She was amazing. Over a hundred, she was very sprightly, living on the mesa without running water or electricity, very healthy and happy. She even had a letter from a former President saying she was a living legend. Sitting down to the dinner that she had prepared, we felt very humbled and honoured to be in her home. Wanting to show our appreciation and gratitude, I thanked her in Hopi (which I had learnt on my previous visit). Peter quickly asked me what to say, so I quietly told him the word to use. He spoke the same word and she nearly fell off her chair laughing. I did not realise that there are two languages, one for women and one for men. Peter had thanked her using the women's word and she thought it was hilarious.

Whilst we were up on the mesas, of course we went to find Tom. He was living in his home village again. It was good to find out how things had been going with the man whose visit to England had been the trigger for so much change in our lives.

After sharing all my special places and people with Peter, we moved on south again and stayed with my friend's dad in Phoenix. He very kindly said we could leave our vehicle at his house over the winter while we went south into Mexico.

CHAPTER 43

"To travel is to live." Hans Christian Anderson

Peter had never visited a country that that was not industrialised and wealthy. He was shocked and amazed at how people could be living in shanty towns that looked so squalid; yet emerge in pristine white clothes with a definite pride in their looks and bearing. It was great to travel together. We got on so well, laughed at the same things and appreciated the beauties of nature.

On one journey, we were travelling by coach over the hills when the wheel got a puncture. The pristinely dressed Mexican coach driver, in his white shirt and jacket, had to change the wheel. Disappearing into the restaurant which we were parked outside, he emerged in his vest and trousers. After changing the wheel, he was covered in oil and dirt. Retreating into the restaurant again for a very short time, he re-emerged looking spotless to drive us on our way. We were astounded as to how he did it.

For his first taste of the Pacific, I took Peter to Mazatlan, then on to Mexico City to sample the ruins of Teotihuacan and the Volodores. We were staying in a dingy hotel room in a small town, when I contracted 'Montezuma's revenge.' Depending on where you are travelling in the world, there is always a local name for the upset stomach. In India, I remember it being called 'Delhi belly.' I was in a bad way. Initially, I tried to deal with it using a standard over-the-counter remedy from the U.S.A., that I had brought down with me. All it did was turn my poo black but did not make me better. Then Peter suggested I ate some papaya seeds. "Where did you get that from?" I enquired.

"I've no idea," he replied. "It just popped into my head." In between bouts of stomach griping pain, I looked in my guidebook. "You'll never believe this," I said to Peter, "you were right. Look here." In the book it told me that if you were ever stuck in the wilds and could not get a remedy, to crunch up papaya seeds for the first day and drink water. The next day it recommended papaya seeds and papaya fruit, with pineapple, banana and papaya on the third day. All the lost vitamins would then be replenished.

I tried it. The seeds were foul. Whatever was in my intestine must have felt the same way, because very soon I started to improve. It was harder to crunch the seeds on the second day, as I was not feeling so bad, but the papaya was a delicious reward for having done so. My final day of fruit was bliss. Recovering rapidly, I then felt okay to travel onwards.

Our next destination was Merida to buy Peter a hammock. On the bus, we met an Italian woman, who had lived in Mexico for years. After chatting together, she invited us to come and stay with her and her family in a Mayan village in the Yucatan peninsula. We took her address. We parted saying, "We're going to an island just off the coast for Christmas, but we would love to visit you after that."

Merida is a lovely town which was gearing up for Christmas. Peter commented on how he had never realised how his skin colour would be a passport. Everyone assumed he was Mexican and would listen patiently to me struggle with my Spanish, then turn to him with a flourish and rattle away, as if he could explain it all. They were inevitably astounded when he had less Spanish than his floundering girlfriend. He was accepted by everyone. I found travelling a lot easier, with many more doors open to us, than when I was there previously.

After purchasing a few small things for each other, we boarded another bus to take us to the ferry for Isla Holbox (pronounced Holbosh). It was an overnight journey. On arrival at the ferry crossing, a low mist was enveloping the few huts that huddled around the jetty. No boat was in sight. A cock started to crow, as the dark faded into light and dawn approached. Sleepy figures swathed in blankets emerged from their homes and the odd swirl of smoke showed that the morning fires were being lit.

We had waited eight hours for a train earlier in our trip, so the wait did not seem long. As the sun rose and was beginning to burn off the mist, the ferry arrived. We set off and Peter nudged me, pointing to the sea. A school of dolphins were jumping around our boat. I was ecstatic and hugged the poor boatman who did not seem to understand why I was so thrilled.

On arrival on the island, which had no bank, we discovered that the prices were higher than our guidebook had led us to believe. We only had a limited amount of cash, so we realised it would be bread and jam for a couple of days, to afford a Christmas Day meal in the restaurant. On our first day we met a young Italian man called Antonio who was one of the other tourists on the island. There were only about fifteen of us altogether. He was sweet and obviously missing his home, so we invited him to join us on Christmas Day. He explained that the main celebrations on the island would happen at midnight on Christmas Eve.

After the bells for midnight mass sounded, the whole of the island surged in and around the church. We stood in the shadows, outsiders but still a part of it by being there. Suddenly a pick-up truck arrived carrying Father Christmas, dressed in green. (Mexico never followed the lead by Coca Cola to change it to red.) He handed wrapped gifts to the waiting children, who ran after the truck squealing with excitement and joy. It was a magical scene.

It was the simplest and one of the loveliest Christmases we have ever had. I found some driftwood to make a tree and we hung shells from the beach on it for decoration. Stockings were made from our socks, filled with a few very simple gifts such as soap and hair ties. Mum and Dad sent us some money and we had bought an Aztec woven calendar with it, which we admired and hung in our hut. Our gifts to them had been posted months earlier, hand painted ceramics from our summer with David.

Back in our wooden hut, Antonio arrived. We gave him a tiny gift we had made. He was thrilled. He told us he had some friends he wanted us to meet and asked if we minded sharing the table with them for lunch. By this time, we were looking forward to the fish dinner we had been saving ourselves for. When we met Antonio's friends, we were amazed. They were Canadian. The guy was Indigenous Canadian and the woman was Anglo Canadian. Out of the few tourists on the island, the chances of there being two couples of a similar racial heritage were quite amazing. Of course, we had lots to talk about and the meal passed in great spirits.

As we left the restaurant, we heard a commotion. One of the other tourists, a white Zimbabwean, was very drunk and hurling racist abuse at the local inhabitants. Antonio had earlier explained to us that the people on the island were descended from Italian fishermen who had populated the small place, although I have since read elsewhere that they are descended from pirates who married into the local Mayan population about a hundred and fifty years ago. Whatever their ancestry, we had no doubt that they would not take kindly to this offensive little twerp mouthing off. The testosterone was escalating, as some of the young village men started towards him. Within seconds fists were starting to fly, so Peter raced over, grabbed the Zimbabwean in a full Nelson arm-lock and lifted him bodily away. His friend came running over and we got him away from the fracas. Peter and the man's friend managed to calm him down enough to walk him out of range and back to his hut, where his friend stayed on guard.

Antonio meanwhile went to chat in Italian to the fishermen, who were obviously very upset. I think they realised that the offender was alone in his attitude. The rest of us were not of the same mind-set. Antonio later told us that the islanders were a tough lot who would not have taken his offences lightly. If we had not intervened, there might have been a nasty end to that interlude, probably for the Zimbabwean. We considered how rude the man had been and how unfair it was to behave like that to our hosts and spoil their Christmas, particularly when they were kind enough to allow us to stay on their island over such a special time. The next day we noticed he was on the first ferry off the island. He had been asked to leave.

We followed soon after, our money having run out. We never forgot that Christmas though and are still in touch with our Canadian friends.

Remembering the invitation from our other Italian friend, we made our way via Merida to a Mayan village in the middle of the Yucatan peninsula. On arrival we were warmly greeted by our friend Anneta, her husband Enrico and son Ivo. Considering we were complete strangers, they were very kind to us, sharing their one roomed concrete house for over a week. This one room turned into a five bedroomed house each night, when we slung our hammocks up to sleep in. They were based in the village, as they were helping to plant trees in the rainforest.

The Yucatan peninsula is limestone, so any trees take a long while to establish and grow. Over the centuries there had been a slash and burn culture in the rainforest. This had been sustainable because of the large territory and the length of time between each cut. However, more and more ranchers were moving into the peninsula and buying up land from the government, which was restricting the Mayan's traditional land use into smaller areas. The cycle was becoming increasingly shorter with the trees not having enough time to regrow.

Enrico had persuaded the villagers and the government to support a project of planting trees in the forest. The idea was to plant trees that would yield valuable crops for the villagers, thereby preventing the practice of slash and burn. Normally the plant debris around their homes was, also, burnt, so Anneta was teaching composting techniques and encouraging the women to use the composted soil to grow vegetables and food crops.

We were very interested and asked if we could help with some of the tree planting. The next day we observed how the team of about twenty local men were working to plant the tiny saplings. With their permission, we observed and photographed, then asked if we could help with the planting. The villagers were shocked and amazed that we would be willing to get our hands dirty. In turn, *I* was amazed that they were surprised. Their watering process was a skill to be admired. A bucket was drawn from a well deep underground. It was heavy work and required a few men to haul it up. Carefully, not losing a drop of the precious liquid, the water was transferred into plastic containers. The water was then carried to each new tree where the men used their fingers to create a spout. It was poured exactly where they wanted it to go, with not a drop spilt. I have never seen a more skilful operation with such crude apparatus. It made me very humble to think of our society which needs every modern invention to do anything, whilst these men could do so much with so little.

As we left the site, the men were saying that we needed rain to finish off the job.

The next day, Enrico took us to visit the neighbouring village that was, also, involved in the scheme. We hitched a lift with a village truck that was going in that direction. As we drove along the road there were exclamations from the driver and Enrico. The road for a few hundred yards was darkened. On looking closer we saw it had been raining. It was darker because of the wet, as was the forest on either side. "I don't believe it," he translated for us, "that was where we were planting yesterday. It has rained just on that bit and nowhere else!"

The truck dropped us on the roadside, so we walked down the track to the village. This settlement had no motorised vehicles in it, only bicycles. Our host, who was one of the planters from the day before, greeted us warmly, ushering us into his home of timber poles, thatched with leaves. Ensuring we were comfortably seated on the hammocks, he proudly delved into the large coca cola fridge standing incongruously in the corner. While we sipped our chilled drinks, he disappeared, leaving us with his wife and children. A short while later, he reappeared with armfuls of fruit, picked fresh from the tree outside. I have never tasted such delicious oranges. He indicated that we should dip the segments into chilli powder. I thought it would be horrid, but it was quite tasty.

The following day was New Year's Eve. Back in the village we were walking along the road when we saw a white cow tied up at the side of the road. Peter was very tall compared with the local inhabitants. Whether it was that or not, I do not know, but as we passed the cow, it looked at Peter and then fell over.

Anneta and Enrico then informed us we were invited to the mayor's house for New Year's Eve dinner with them. We felt honoured to be treated so well and arrived as the evening was settling in. The white cow, we learnt, had been slaughtered for the special feast and shared amongst the villagers. We were to partake of this treat for our meal. I felt sorry for the beast. I have always erred towards vegetarianism, and having seen our dinner earlier, did not help. The dishes were served up, but no-one was eating. The meat was floating in a sort of broth. Soon tortillas were brought out, but still no-one ate. I observed and waited, wondering what to do. Anneta explained we were all waiting for the son of the household to arrive from Merida with the bottle of alcohol. I was more than happy to wait, as my appetite was rapidly diminishing.

When he finally arrived, we started our food. I found that fat had congealed on the top. It was full of gristle. It took all my concentration to chew and swallow. Later Peter and I discussed how very spoilt we are in our culture with meat. We have the best cuts, then throw away the rest, whilst other societies are content with less

263

wasteful ways of processing their animals. Being aware of that was still no help. I continued to give all my attention to chewing, managing one slow mouthful after another. Each one seemed to take an age to consume.

Then Ivo started to gag on his meat. That was it. I could not sustain my own concentration any longer. I pleaded with my eyes to Anneta. "You don't have to eat it if it's gone cold," she said. Those words felt like release from torture. "They will heat it up for you," she added. The instant promise of release had closed in on me again, yet I knew in that moment I could not eat another thing. "I can't eat it," I whispered. "I feel so awful because I know what an honour it is, and I don't want to offend my hosts."

"Don't worry," she replied, "I'll deal with it."

When the others had finished, Anneta grabbed our plates and took them to the kitchen at the back. I followed with some more plates. I noticed Anneta surreptitiously throwing the contents of our bowls to the dogs in the darkness of the yard beyond. No-one else noticed, so I hope we did not offend anyone. At least the dogs were pleased that night.

In the street outside, the villagers were gathering for the piñata. A rainbow of brightly coloured paper covered a papier-mache donkey, which was being hit successively by the children. Suddenly the creation burst apart, sweets flying in every direction. Within seconds, little bodies were converging on the drops of confection grabbing what they could in a happy scrum. Collecting their booty, they returned to their parents for the midnight finale. As the hour tolled, the guy (similar to our Guy Fawkes) which had been suspended in the middle of the street all night was set on fire. Suddenly, his firework packed body started erupting, sending fiery explosions in every direction imaginable. I was astounded that no-one got hurt. Everyone was fine, laughing and joking. We all wished each other a Happy New Year and wandered off to our respective hammocks. A New Year to remember!

One other event stuck in my mind from our stay there. Every morning between seven and eight the water to the village was turned on. During that time all the water containers had to be filled, because after that, it was switched off till the next day. We helped Anneta to

264

fill the big tubs and carry them into the shade of the house. As in Thailand, I learnt to treat those tubs with care and respect. I could not wash my hands in a tub of clean water because that would pollute the precious liquid for everyone else for the day. I had to get a scoop, lift some water from the tub and wash my hands well away.

On one occasion however, a whole tub got polluted and for a very good reason. Ivo had a recorder and enjoyed playing it. I was doing something over the other side of the room when I heard a piercing cry. Anneta raced over to Ivo and thrust him and his recorder towards the tub of water. Then I saw why. Ants were swarming all over his mouth and floating in the tub. He had started to play, only to discover the recorder was full of ants, which started biting his mouth. Luckily, Anneta was well versed in remedies from living in Mexico for so many years. She soon calmed his mouth down, then dealt with Ivo's shock.

The trees had all been planted, Enrico had organised over a hundred thousand trees to be planted over three months between the two villages. It was some achievement for all involved. We went along to the presentation by local officials. Everyone looked very proud, speeches were made, Enrico and the villagers were all presented with a green tee-shirt and the press milled around, snapping for the local paper.

Soon after that, Enrico said they were ready for a break and suggested we went to the coast with them. He told us of a great beach they knew that was not very touristy.

We readily agreed. Taking the local bus to a point on the road, we then had to walk down a long dirt track to Xpu Ha beach. We would never have found it without their help. What a paradise! A white sandy beach stretched before us. A few thatched huts on stilts graced the beach, with smaller thatched huts for us to sling our hammocks in and sleep. A hut cost a princely of twenty pence each per night. Peter and I occupied one of the huts, whilst Enrico, Anneta and Ivo occupied another. Two Mayan brothers owned the beach and they had organised their life well. To the left, about thirty minutes' walk along the pure sand, was an azure blue lagoon. Fringed by craggy limestone, it was heavenly; the crystal-clear water bringing clarity to its depths. A few large private houses had been built on the ground behind the beach. One was owned by the local federale (policeman).

The Mayan brothers took people out in their boat fishing, then cooked the fish, for a fee, to eat in the restaurant. Being on a budget we tended to make our own food. By the Mayan brother's restaurant, they had an area to protect the baby turtles until they could get to the sea.

As we walked into the water, a fabulous coral reef opened a magical world before us. The next two weeks were blissful; swimming, snorkelling and sunbathing on this idyllic beach.

We kept noticing people walking along the beach with hospital style wristbands on. "Why are they wearing those?" we questioned. It transpired that to the right, further along the beach, the Mayan brothers had sold the hinterland and a scrappy bit of beach to an exclusive German tourist company called Club Robinson. People staying there were paying three thousand dollars a week, in comparison to our three dollars a week. Admittedly that included food and a luxury accommodation and armed guards and a plastic arm band, but they had to come on our beach for decent sand or to visit the lagoon.

Anneta, Enrico and Ivo stayed a few days then returned to their village. One incident happened before they left which has remained with me. From that, I always remember Anneta when I have a shower, particularly if the water is a bit cold. I will put my feet in first then my legs, gradually acclimatising my body to the temperature. One of the other beach residents came running up the beach asking if anyone had medical knowledge. Anneta immediately ran down to help. The person was very sick, almost passing out. Anneta called for some cold water and then started bathing the person, wiping their feet first, gradually working her way up the body, bathing each section in cold water. I do not know how it worked but it did. The woman very quickly came round and was incredibly grateful to Anneta.

Soon after this incident our friends went home. We were very grateful to Anneta and her family. Through their generosity of spirit and that of the villagers, we had been given a unique opportunity to share a small part of village life in the Yucatan peninsula, amongst people who were so warm and kind to us.

We were more than happy to stay and chill out in Paradise. Nearby our hut, was a camper van with a lovely American family. Like us, they were travelling for the winter in Mexico, had discovered this beach and were unwilling to leave. Larry, the father, was a brilliant masseur. He had set up his table on the beach and was offering massages in exchange for whatever anyone wanted to give. Sometimes it was a fish dinner (in the case of the Mayan brothers), sometimes it was a few pesos; sometimes it was in exchange for another treatment. Whatever it was, Larry accepted with no conditions and the massage was given freely.

Gradually, more and more people with hospital wristbands started to migrate across 'our beach' as we began to call it. The backpacking hut dwellers used to play games. They would take turns to see how long they could last in Club Robinson before the guards found them and threw them out. The longest on record at that point was three quarters of an hour.

Soon the Club Robinson inmates found Larry and his massage table. They paid him handsomely, he got fifty dollars for one session, then another day a hundred dollars. All the clients started to say how good he was and how much better than the person employed on site to massage. We have stayed in touch with Larry and his family. They told us that after we had left, Larry was invited into Club Robinson to do massages, so he won the game! He also did so well from the work that they ended up staying all winter, made a good profit and were able to continue travelling for a long while after.

Enrico and Anneta had told us of an area they used to live in around Lake Patzcuaro, which was on the opposite side of the country. After leaving Xpu Ha, we decided to go there. In the days of the Spanish invasion, a very enlightened priest had worked with the native people of this region. He had encouraged each village to specialise in a different craft. Some focussed on woodcarving, others focussed on weaving and so on. As a result, their local economies survived, keeping them and their culture intact over the centuries, as the invading culture took over. It also meant each village could trade with each other as well as the outside world, thereby growing the local economies rather than draining them, (an excellent example of permaculture at its best.) He encouraged them to retain their own languages as well as learning Spanish, thereby allowing the development of both cultures simultaneously. Enrico and Anneta had lived in the region for many years and were very fond of the area. On arriving there, we could see why.

Each village nestled in the hills around the beautiful lake. Visitors would find the different craft-ware on show outside people's homes. We were very attracted by the colourful wooden carvings, brilliantly painted. In Mexico they looked just right, but we imagined them in England and felt they would look out of place.

Enrico and Anneta had asked us to call and see their friends in one of the villages. We mounted the steep roadway, leading to the cluster of houses. Bright red geraniums and luxuriant bougainvillea adorned the walls and windowsills, making the place feel loved and cared for. At the far end was a walled in courtyard enclosing a brick-built house. We explained who we were, as best as we could in our poor Spanish, and showed them a note from their friends. What warmth and kindness greeted us! We were shown round their workshop and given some food and drink, which we ate in the shade of a large tree in the courtyard. Small children came and peeked at us, and the adults tried their best to communicate with these gringos who could hardly speak their language. We had already decided we would like to buy some chair backs, unpainted. We thought we would just get chair backs and arms because the full chairs were too low down for Peter to sit on. It was also easier to transport with our backpacks.

Following a week in this delightful area, we decided to start heading back up to the U.S. After several days journey and a few stop-offs, we arrived at the border. We passed through the barrier, checked by a pleasant young man, who suggested we should take it in turns to wait with our luggage while we each went upstairs to get our passports stamped. To do that, we had to walk back beyond the barrier again and up some stairs. I went first, and then Peter went. Whilst he was gone, the shift changed. A large brutish looking woman took over from our pleasant chap. Rubbing her hands together, she said, "Well let's see what shit we can kick today."

As I watched, a little Mexican man appeared at the border with all his belongings in a cardboard box. Having lived in Mexico for two months, I knew how precious a cardboard box is. Everything gets used and reused to a degree that shames the so-called recycling efforts in our country. In an economy where many people have very little; a box is incredibly important for carrying goods, storing things and all other manner of other uses. This bully border guard yelled at the little man to unpack all his belongings and threw the cardboard box in a corner. He scurried through the border, clutching his clothes and belongings in an untidy mess, as best he could. I stood, silently fuming at the woman. I hate bullies, particularly when they are from a richer and more powerful country and have the weight of authority behind them. Five minutes later another border guard came along. "We don't need to confiscate egg boxes anymore," he commented to the bully, "the salmonella scare is over."

"Oh, never mind," she retorted. She had no idea what she had done to that man's day and how she had made him suffer, through her lack of care, and her ignorance of her own country's rules and regulations.

Soon after, Peter came down from the immigration office upstairs. He had to pass through the barrier again. The beefy woman stopped him and rattled off in Spanish assuming he was Mexican. "I'm terribly sorry," he replied in the most cut-glass English accent he could muster, "I'm afraid I don't understand Spanish." He pointed at me, "I've already been through once and I'm with her." The look on her face was a picture. She was so confounded, she blustered out a reply with a hint of an apology in it, then ushered him through.

Unfortunately, we did not have any spare bags to give to the little man and by the time we had got through he was already on his way. I have never forgotten him, and often wondered what happened to him.

On returning to Phoenix, it was still winter elsewhere, so our friend very kindly let us stay at his place for a while. Phoenix never gets cold. He told us that in the summer it is so hot, construction workers must start at two or three in the morning, finishing by nine or ten in the morning because it is too hot to be outside after that.

It was bliss to stay in a house again. We tried to help by cooking meals and looking after him a bit in exchange for our lodging. During this time, we visited the Biosphere just south of Phoenix. We learnt that it was originally constructed as an experiment to see if people could live in outer space. It had all the climate zones of the world in three massive, sealed glasshouses, with a living area for humans and a growing space. The living area had a library, cooking, relaxing and sleeping areas. This is in the pre-digital age so there were no mobile devices available. Four scientists had agreed to be sealed in the

Sphere for a year. Each zone had a different climate in it. There was a rainforest zone, a desert zone, a Mediterranean zone, and a mini sea zone. The water was recycled round the Sphere as it would be on the planet, with wastewater from the living areas being cleansed and recycled by rainfall. Wind was created between the climate zones as the air moved from warmer to cooler areas. When they were designing it, they realised that the glass would break with the changing pressure inside the dome, so they built two tunnels from it, leading to two smaller domes, which housed a diaphragm, each one rising and falling with the changing pressures.

We were told it took four months to make a pizza, because the wheat had to be grown and everything made from scratch. It was very impressive and interesting; particularly when we discovered the experiment had to finish early because of a lack of oxygen. Scientists could not understand why. After many trials and tests, they discovered it was because the rocks in the Mediterranean zone and desert were made from concrete. Apparently concrete 'eats' oxygen for twenty-five years after it has been made. No wonder it always feels so airless in cities and your energy feels depleted. Our friend later told us that a large quantity of laughing gas had filled the Dome. No-one knew where that had come from either.

As an experiment for living in outer space, it had failed. The owners sold it to Bass Charrington and when we visited, it was being used to study the Earth and her ecosystems. Apparently by being in this microcosm it speeded up the rate of how things will develop on earth by twenty-five years.

A short while after, I ended up having an abscess on my tooth. We had not been able to afford insurance on a year's travelling as it would have been over a thousand pounds, so I had to pay to get my tooth seen to. All I could afford was the antibiotics to reduce it, and then the root removed with a temporary filling, until I could get home to our wonderful NHS and get it properly crowned. That delayed our departure for Flagstaff, because I had to go back and get it checked out. I was very conscious of over-staying our welcome. We felt we had impinged on our host's kindness and hospitality for long enough.

We crawled out of the warmth of Phoenix and took the road up through Sedona, the beautiful red rock town of 'wannabees,' to Flagstaff. There we reconnected with our friends, before heading up

270

to Tuba and then set out on our journey back north. The four hundred pounds spent on my tooth meant our travelling had to be cut short. Whilst we were staying with our friends in Tuba, I did a pregnancy test and discovered to my absolute joy and delight that I was finally pregnant.

On returning to South Dakota, Mom Alice and Sage were thrilled with our news. We spent a very pleasant week or so with everyone, catching up on events that had happened over the winter. Eventually we had to go, as our money was dwindling. We gave the van to Alice, as her old one had just died, then set off home from the new Denver airport. One of David's neighbours, Charlotte Wallingford, had a daughter in Denver, so she very kindly took us on the seven-hour trip to get there. We contributed to the petrol and she used it as a chance to visit her relatives.

CHAPTER 44

"Fathers are angels sent from Heaven." Unknown

We arrived back on the fourth of April, the same date I had left America six years previously. Our first night back we stayed with Jacqui and family, it was the Grand National and everyone was placing bets. I was too tired to think, never mind choose a winner. Having rested up a little at Jacqui's we continued our journey north, carrying our heavy bags through the underground stations in London.

Once home, we stayed with Mum and Dad for a few weeks till the lodger who was renting our home, could find new accommodation. Over Easter, I started to feel strange. Everything was a bit wobbly. I rested up in bed, but it was no good. Nothing could stop what was going to happen. All my rainbow promises turned to dust and disintegrated in a few awful hours. I had a miscarriage. I was devastated, so was Peter. We had really wanted this baby. Time was ticking on, and it seemed so unfair. I thought back to my other lost baby and wondered if this was payback for what I did before. We both grieved, but it was a strange feeling. It was almost as if we did not deserve to mourn because the baby had not even become a full baby. It had not been a reality in this world, just a promise.

Gradually coming out of the very unreal feeling of having nearly been a mum but not quite, I tried to focus on regaining normality by dealing with everyday things. The first step was to settle back into our home. I started teaching again and Peter found a job with a local landscaper to earn enough money to go back to America for the summer. One of his Lakota friends, who had pledged to take part in the Sun Dance, had asked Peter to support him. It was a real honour and Peter wanted to be there for him. It was not right for me to go and I did not feel up to it anyway.

He went for the summer, then on his return, he decided to start up his landscaping business again. I was beginning to be aware that my dad was not managing all the things he used to. Mum told me he had found it quite hard doing our paperwork whilst we were away, which had previously never been a problem for him.

In September, I started a long-term supply at a local school and in the following March I turned forty. Still childless, I felt it deeply when other women talked about their families and children. I started to feel resentful when people had a second child, particularly if they moaned about it. I became very sensitive to any comments that people made. One woman (then a mother of teenagers) said how she could not imagine having a baby at our age. It was a perfectly natural thing for her to say, but it cut like a knife into my sensibilities. Unless you have been in that situation, it is very hard to understand that desperate longing for the chance to start a family.

Later that year, around May, I had a phone call from Mum. "Please can you get over here quickly, your dad's really ill in hospital." It was then she explained how Dad had not been able to do lots of things he used to, how even putting a new cloth on the ironing board had really taxed his brain. This was a man who oversaw the structural welfare of all the government buildings in the northwest of England in his career. In his spare time, he used to scale down plans and build his own model steam engines that could pull up to five people. Dad had always been so capable and efficient. When the doctors took us in a room and told us that his brain was degenerating rapidly and there was nothing we could do, I felt devastated.

In the middle of all this I had to return to school for a week because OFSTED were arriving. Between school and visiting my dad, life was in a whirlwind. Dad was in and out of hospital, I felt bad for him, as he was not a man who liked institutions. When he first went in the nurses asked him to take his teeth out. He refused. They insisted and started to get cross with my gentle beautiful father, till he managed to get them to understand that the lovely full set of perfect teeth were his own, not a false set. Aged eighty-four he still had all his teeth from childhood.

Over Whit half term I spent my holiday at Mum's house, writing my reports and visiting Dad. One afternoon the phone rang, it was Peter asking how Dad was. Suddenly he started saying, "Well let's do it then." I had not a clue what he was on about.

"What do you mean?"

"You know what I mean."

"No, I don't otherwise I wouldn't be asking you!"

"You know, we may as well get married." A stunned silence came from my end of the phone. I had no idea he had been thinking in those terms. "Well? Are you still there?"

"Gosh, well yes, I suppose, yes, I'd love to," I replied.

"Right then," my Yorkshire bred husband to be answered in typical brief mode. "Okay." I came off the phone and walked upstairs in a daze to my mum in her bedroom. "Mum, Peter's just asked me to marry him."

"Oh, we were wondering when he was going to ask you, he asked us for our permission ages ago."

"What?" I shrieked. "When did he ask you?"

"When you both came over at Easter. I'm glad he's finally done it, we kept wondering if he'd asked you and you'd not told us." Looking back, I think Peter had kept waiting for the right moment, but with Dad being ill he wanted to make sure that Dad knew I had been asked.

Peter and I went to Harrogate to one of his oldest friends who managed a jeweller's shop there. It was the sort of shop where the clients sit at individual tables and they bring the pieces to you for inspection. It ended up a choice between two rings. I was split. One was a very practical and functional design with a solitaire diamond, the other was very beautiful with four rubies in the middle, surrounded by diamonds. I asked if I could use something as a pendulum to make my decision. His friend was quite surprised, no-one had ever chosen like that before in the shop. I held the pendant pendulum and asked if the solitaire was the one. The pendulum swung 'no.' I did the same with the ruby one, a very definite 'yes' swung across it. The decision was made.

We decided to get married in September, so Dad could be there. I started looking for dresses. I contemplated hiring one, then buying one, but even to hire, the prices were ridiculous. In the end I found my dream dress in a shop in Bramhall that sold good quality designer clothes second time around. It was half the cost of hiring a dress for

274

the day and exactly what I was looking for. Dad was at home during this time, the summer holidays had started, and I was staying over with them to help Mum out. I had to alter the dress, it was too small in places, so I took some material from the sash at the back, which I did not like anyway, and inserted it into the seams. Finally. it was finished. I stood in it, by the bed to show Dad. He smiled his wonderful smile and looked really pleased.

By August he was back in hospital and going downhill rapidly. Poor mum had to make the horrible decision on her birthday as to whether to force feed him to keep him alive. He was refusing to eat and knew his time was near. I was very proud of her, she decided against that last indignity for her beloved husband. After she had made the choice, the male nurse patted her arm and said she had made the right decision. He said how awful it is to have to put tubes into people who do not want it. We sat by my dad in turn, whilst he slipped in and out during those last days.

I knew I had to let him go, so one day I quietly whispered, "It's okay Dad, you can go." Often our loved ones need us to tell them. On my drive home I remember screaming and crying my eyes out, yelling at my sister Jill and Gran whom I knew were my Spirit Guides, "You'd better be there for him when he comes over! You'd just better be there!" In the middle of the night, he slipped away, quietly with no fuss, when no-one was there to hold him back and keep him here with their energies.

Mum had asked the hospital not to ring in the night. She had had one phone call like that for my sister and she never wanted another one. So, in the early morning we got the phone call, standing round the phone in the hall. My mum, my brother and I were without my lovely, wonderful dad in our lives anymore.

Peter made a fabulous wreath for the coffin, with flowers from our hillside intermingled with bought flowers. My Dad's funeral was very beautiful, like him. The church was full. He was very well respected and loved by everyone who knew him, a true gentleman in the real sense of the word. I managed to read a poem I had written for him, taking every ounce of everything I had got. Even Mum's critical friend from church said that Dad's funeral made her weep more than her own husband's. That was something from her.

When I was getting ready for the funeral, I was ironing the dress I was going to wear. Dad popped into my head and I heard him say quite clearly, "Well your ring matches the dress." That was exactly what he would have said. It comforted me loads to know he had seen my ring, even though it had not been ready before he died.

We postponed the wedding. I took Mum to Anglesey for a holiday. We had a lovely, gentle healing time visiting the places they used to go, reminiscing, and enjoying time together. We sat on the cliffs and watched seals, then found a beautiful ancient village hidden amongst mounded purples and gold of heather and gorse. I promised Mum I would take her on holiday every year and ring her every night. I knew how hard she would find it on her own.

CHAPTER 45

"Good relationships don't just happen. They take time, patience and two people who truly want to be together." Unknown

We rearranged the official wedding for the following April. Amazingly it ended up being the fourth of April. The same date that I'd left America on both of my trips there. We knew Mum would only want a small do, she was paying for it and it was only fair. We had about twenty guests, mainly close family or people who had been like family over the years to us. It was a very special day, with more family friends coming to the house on our return.

Just before the previous Christmas, we had attended the wedding of one of Peter's oldest friends, then in the New Year we had flown to Sorrento for our friends Charmaine and Pepe's wedding. A week after our own wedding, Peter and I attended Iestyn and Bev's wedding; with Peter being one of the three best men. I began to feel it was a bit close to the film "Four Weddings and a Funeral."

Although it had been a lovely ceremony for an official one, it was not the spiritual one we would have liked. Furthermore, we both had loads of friends and relatives whom we had wanted to invite but could not. So, we decided we would have another wedding on midsummer's day at the Bridestones, which are on the moors above us. This time we would invite all our friends. I wrote the ceremony and different people agreed to help us out. Lin, who found our house for us, agreed to conduct the ceremony, Ric read out Ted Hughes' poem about the Bridestones, my friend Ian from childhood read another poem out for us and Robert Hart could not be there but sent his Goddess of Mercy as a centre piece. Lu was my bridesmaid, our neighbour did the photographs, and many other friends played important roles in every part of the day.

The groom's party set off from the house, led by our friends Darren and Graham. Walking the route, they passed through the Golden Stones to get to the site. The bride's party accompanied me. We drove most of the way, just walking the last fifteen minutes from the road over the moors. I wore my white wedding dress, hiking boots and a headdress made of elderflowers picked from the garden. Everyone was asked to bring a stone. When we had assembled, we asked them to place their stones on the floor to form a stone circle. Standing outside the circle, Graham bound our hands in buckskin, then we entered the circle, which he closed behind us. Walking into the middle of the hundred people forming the circle, I felt very grateful to all our friends for being there for us. We made our vows to each other, and then Lin took the buckskin off. We were bound in spirit now and did not need the physical bonds. The ceremony ended and we went back home where more people turned up, two hundred in total over the weekend long party. The gifts people brought helped to create the day. Some friends had brought food, some friends helped to heat it up and serve it out. Other friends had brought drink: one friend had made bottles of home-made wine for us, which became legendary in the post party reminiscences. One friend told stories in the garden for everyone, whilst another couple played a violin concert for us. The generosity and kindness we received from everyone was unending.

I had not thought that Mum would want to come, but she decided she would. A friend from church brought her over and she had a whale of a time, running into the circle to photograph and running round the garden at home, with several of our friends chasing after this eighty-three-year-old, terrified she would fall. She was quite oblivious to all the watchful attention, loving chatting to all her nephews and nieces and to all our friends who made a real fuss of her. Bless her, she had been brought up as a strict Methodist by her minister father, yet she was open to our very different ceremony, which was probably 'pagan' in her eyes. She took it in her stride and made the most of it all. I so love my Mum for that.

As her gift to me for our wedding, my friend Jan had offered to give me a treatment on my feet, a few weeks earlier. She was a reflexologist and I had had a few excellent sessions with her through the LETs scheme, so I was really looking forward to the session. As she started, she said, "How would you feel if your dad came through?"

"Why?" I responded.

"Well, he's here and has been waiting for you to come for the last couple of hours."

"I would love to talk to him," I replied.

For the next few hours, I lost all track of time and space. It was the best gift I could ever have had, talking to my dad. He explained how he had died in hospital in this world, and then woken in the Spirit world in a sort of hospital, with his Mum and Dad on either side of the bed. After an adjustment period, he had then moved into a cottage with Jill, which had pink roses round the door. Mum always used to tell me how Jill loved pink. He told me how he was working on moving things and learning how manipulate objects in this world from there, so if things started being put in the wrong place it was him. He discussed his fears for Mum. He would watch her standing on the tall stool in the kitchen to reach things when no-one was there. He told me to tell her not to do it, that he was watching over her but would not be able to catch her if she fell. (When I later told her about that bit, she looked guilty and admitted to it. I think she still climbed on the stool though.) He explained the yellow rose in Mum's garden was his gift to her and that when it was blooming, he was there for her. From then on, that rose never stopped flowering. Even in winter there was still a bloom clinging to its stalks.

Next, he explained that over there they can watch films that have been created in this world. Apparently, he had watched the film 'Ghost' on the other side. It is certainly a film he would never have dreamt of seeing in his life. He said it was a good portrayal of the afterlife. "I used to think that much of what you said was a bit strange and I didn't believe you," he went on, "but now I know that you were right. I am so proud of you." He then went on to tell me that he, Mum, Peter and I had shared a couple of past lives together before. He showed Jan a beautiful green turquoise sea. She asked if it was Greece or in the Med. He kept saying no, until he finally managed to communicate it was in Atlantis. He then showed her images of another place till she got from him that in another life, we were in the School of Mysteries in Egypt.

Whenever I hear about exotic past lives, I tend to disbelieve it all, as they are so easy to romanticise and pick up on. However, I had no reason to disbelieve my dad, or Jan, who is one of the purest channelers I know. She would not make something up like that, she was too busy concentrating on the messages she was getting. Another thing that persuaded me it might have some truth in it, was that I love Ancient Egypt, but I had never come across the School of

279

Mysteries in anything I had read. Whenever anyone talked about Ancient Egypt, I would ask had they heard of it, but no-one had. It took fifteen years before I picked up any mention of its existence; first in a book I read, followed by the internet. Looking at internet articles they not only talk about the School but make a link with Atlantis, saying some of the teachers came from that mythical place. I decided to file that one away, but it was interesting to know that we had all shared past lives together and made me feel closer to Peter as a result.

I then asked if Jill was there when he passed over. Immediately Jill came in, "Of course I was there," she retorted, "he's my dad as well as yours!" Jill then went on to explain what she does. She helps teenagers pass over because she grew up in the Spirit world and she can understand how they feel. They then told me about our baby that we had lost. "You and Peter agreed on a soul level to let the baby incarnate in the earth world so that she could be born in the Spirit world. She was never meant to be born on Earth, that's why you had the miscarriage." I asked if I would ever have a child. Dad gave Jan a picture of a little blue teddy sitting on a crescent moon. It was a strong suggestion I would be a mum and have a boy. It gave me hope. They said our daughter needed a name and that we were to name her. Dad and Jill were calling her little Joan because she raced around like Mum, but the native relatives over there called her Butterfly. Peter and I decided to call her Butterfly Star. Dad said they would love to have had her with them, but she was being raised by Peter's relatives as they had the need to do so. Apparently, things happen in the Spirit world not from desire but need, which I thought was very interesting. I then asked about Peter's relatives who had passed. They came through to me and told me more things about the Spirit world. "It's great here, to dust you just wave your hand and it goes!"

I can only be eternally grateful to Jan for confirming so strongly for me that life does go on after death. It is not the end, our loved ones continue to watch over and look out for us, never stopping loving us. Love never dies, only the energy in our bodies changes its form. I truly believe that when we die, we go to the light. Our angels and relatives help us to find our way, so that we can, in turn, help the others left here. It is only a thin veil between the worlds and when we listen, we can sometimes hear their messages. They do not operate on the same time scale as us; in fact, time has no meaning, so that is why their visits can appear to be haphazard. I believe that whenever we need them, they will be there for us, whatever the time scale.

* * *

After our wedding, life continued as normal. I loved supply teaching in the town because it gave me links with the families here and made me feel part of the community. I would often get close to the teachers I covered, as I needed to work with them to make sure that I was delivering what they intended from the curriculum.

I think the biggest thing a teacher can ever be told is that they have inspired a child. A few years ago, I was thrilled to hear from the mother of a girl that I taught in the nineties. She told me that her daughter had recently had an interview for college. They asked her why she wanted to be a teacher. She replied, "I was inspired by a teacher as a child, and I want to do the same for others." I was incredibly touched when her mother told me that I was that teacher.

The year after our wedding, I took Mum for a week's holiday to Finland for the wedding of a young man from Bramhall. She had been like an adopted auntie to the family and was thrilled when she and I were asked to attend. It was a very special trip for me. It was to be our last holiday on our own together. Finland was very clear and clean, the cars drove with their lights on the whole time, the lights come on with the ignition, and there were saunas in every motel we stayed in. The wedding was in midsummer, and I revelled at the lack of night, it was still a dusky light at midnight.

There were all sorts of interesting Finnish customs at the wedding. The one I remember most was the breaking of the plates. At one point the bride and groom had to break some plates and the number of pieces the plates went into denoted the number of children they would have. Luckily for their sakes that did not come true. I think it broke into about twenty pieces!

281

CHAPTER 46

"We never know the love of the parent until we become the parent ourselves." Henry Ward Beecher

The following November, I finally thought I might be pregnant. Getting up in the middle of the night I could not wait any longer to do the pregnancy test. It faintly registered positive. I wanted more confirmation, so I asked for a sign. As I looked out of the window, I could see Orion's belt, a line of three stars. Whilst I watched, a star suddenly appeared and fell from the top to the bottom of the belt. That was my sign. I felt a wonderful thrill and joy to know I was going to finally be a mum. A few days later it was officially confirmed by the doctors.

I was so excited. I recalled the early days of my relationship with Peter. I had taken him round to Pat's and we were all sitting in John and Marilyn's garden. I noticed Pat scanning round everyone and later asked her what she had been doing. She told me she was looking round at everyone's true essences and when she reached Peter, she saw a pure brilliant star. As she spoke, I recalled what I had heard in that dream/vision all those years ago in Glastonbury, when I was there with Marianne. "One day you will carry a Star child." Some years later when I knew Peter better and felt I could confide this in him, he just looked at me and said, "Well of course. The Lakota Nation is the Star Nation."

In April, Mum, Peter and a growing-larger-every-minute-me went to Whitby for our holiday. Then in the summer our baby boy was born. Dad had been right with the blue teddy.

Nothing quite prepared me for the twenty-four-hour sole responsibility that comes with motherhood. People had passed on loads of stuff to me, so I thought we hardly needed to buy anything. I was wrong. I had nothing in which to put my baby down. Reading 'The Continuum Concept' whilst pregnant, I was determined my child should have human contact as much as possible. I dare not leave him on the bed, in case he fell off and did not know what to do when I needed to do a simple thing like going to the loo or peeling some potatoes for tea. I soon realised that a chair to rest him in while I did these necessaries, was essential.

Breast feeding was so painful, often sore and drawing blood, I used to kick the floor with my heels to get over the pain. I persevered and eventually it was fine. After waiting so long for him, I was determined to do it how I had always dreamed I would.

In those early months I would sit in bed nursing him and feel bewildered, yet happy at how different my life had become with his birth. I remember talking to Robert Hart on the phone around the time of the solar eclipse that summer. Everyone else was off walking up Stoodley Pike to watch it. I could not begin to imagine how I could accomplish that with this small baby. I felt totally incapacitated. Robert told me I must not look at the eclipse, it would be wrong for me and the baby. I stayed in and watched out of the window, my bedroom has a beautiful view of the hills, so it was no hardship.

Those first months were a very strange time for me. I did not feel me anymore, I was my child's mother and life revolved around him and his needs. My confidence disappeared and I found things that were no problem before I gave birth, turning into much bigger things. Simple things like doing the ironing became a mammoth undertaking; hanging out the washing with a child attached to me was so hard. Peter was hardly there in the early days. He had had time off for the birth and was desperately trying to finish a big landscape job, but in the meantime, I was home alone with my baby trying to do jobs that had suddenly become hard. My friend Catherine was wonderful, she came round and did some ironing and made me cups of tea. Of course, I could not expect my Mum to help, she was now eighty-six. I was forty-three when Mato was born, and she was that age the year I was born. She was double my age.

In the November, I suddenly got a phone call. Mum was in hospital. The man fitting the gas fire had taken up the floorboards, Mum had come running in from the garden to make him a cup of tea, not seen them and fallen through, scraping all the skin off her shins. I packed everything up and dashed over with Mato to stay. My baby hated travelling in the car, so it was a delicate operation to get him asleep, then place him carefully in the car seat. Peter would have had to bring the car up the track for me. Then I would drive the hour or so to my mum's, praying that he did not wake up. If he did, he would cry and cry. I would then have to stop, cuddle him, feed him, get him off to sleep again and set off. Sometimes it took me four hours to do the fifty-minute journey. Once I got there, I had a difficult balancing act of catering to Mum's needs and that of my three-month old baby. It was not easy, but I did it.

Christmas came and Marianne came to stay and help us celebrate Mato's first Christmas. Mum came over to us as well and we had our first family Christmas at home. Marianne could not believe the number of gifts and commercialism in an English Christmas. In Switzerland on Christmas Eve, they go into the woods and light candles and have a gentle celebration together. On Christmas morning there is not a mound of gifts hanging out of stockings and under the tree. Instead, the Christmas Angel places a few sweets on the breakfast plates and after the meal at lunchtime, simple small gifts are exchanged that people have made for each other. I have thought of that simpler, purer way to celebrate many times and wished we could change our country's customs to be more like that. I hate the commercialisation and debt trap caused by that time of year. It seems to be getting worse every year.

The New Year saw the arrival of the new millennium. Bev and Iestyn invited us to their friend's wedding do down in Cornwall. It was a brilliant idea. The happy couple, Dave and Helen, invited four of their friends, who then had to invite a couple each to join them. No-one knew everyone, but everyone knew someone. We stayed in a massive barn conversion and attached house, taking in turns to cook and getting to know each other. That holiday highlighted for me how I had changed. Normally I would have revelled in getting to know everyone and discussing issues of the day. I felt almost like a hermit. I dreaded the journey down, worrying how we would cope with Mato's dislike of car travel when he was awake. It took hours and hours, even with an overnight stop at my brother's. On arrival, I scuttled into the house section, where all the families with children were staying. Luckily, the other families were Iestyn and Bev, with their son Ben and Dave and Helen with their daughter Amber. I found it hard to come out of the house to meet everyone else. My baby's needs came before everything and I was not happy unless he was with me. Eventually over the few days, I managed to get a balance and ended up enjoying it, but it took me a while. I admired people who seemed to manage two children. I had no idea how anyone could give both children the same amount of time and attention that they seem to need.

Gradually I got into the swing of being a mother. I loved the role and talked to my baby boy, sang to him and communicated with him as much as possible. It paid off. He started speaking at quite an early age and friends and relatives remarked on his good use of language and ability to converse. One thing he did not do was crawl. From school, I remembered some research that had been done about children who were on the dyslexic spectrum who did not crawl, just went straight into walking. The research suggested that crawling was crucial to link up the left brain and right brain. I found every opportunity I could to make him crawl. Any tubes in playgrounds or tunnels in playgroup equipment, I encouraged him along them. I modelled crawling with him and soon he would enjoy playing and crawling.

Another thing I loved to do was read to him. I have always loved children's books, so it was great to have the excuse to read them all, time after time.

After his first birthday, our lives became focussed on lots of different activities. I was aware of him being an 'only one' in a small, isolated community with no other children. To make sure he met and interacted with other children we went to Tea and Biscuits, a rotational weekly meeting at each other's houses (a great way to be legitimately nosy about other people's houses), playgroup, (another chance for parents to chat and children to play), gym tots and swimming. I met lots of other local mums and built friendships, further cementing my feeling of belonging in the community.

Remembering my promise to Mum, we went on a holiday each year, which I always enjoyed, mainly to Anglesey or the Lake District. One time when we were on Anglesey, (Mato was about two at the time) we decided to visit one of mum's friends who was a vicar there. As we drove away from the cottage Mum exclaimed, "Turn round! We must go back. I've not got my friend's address." I drove back to the cottage. She leapt out, catching her leg in a handle of her bag on the floor. She fell and lay on the dirt of the road.

"Oh Mum, are you are alright?" I jumped out of the car.

"It really hurts…" It was still pre-mobile days, so I ran over to the house opposite and knocked on the door. Explaining the situation, I asked if there was a doctor nearby. She got the doctor on the phone and he said to call an ambulance. The lady was very kind, she held Mato for me, while I ran in and got blankets to cover Mum and toiletries for hospital. I kept trying to reassure her until the ambulance arrived. The men lifted her carefully in. Mum was trying so hard to be brave, but she could not help letting out a yelp of pain. I felt for her so much. We followed the ambulance as it raced off to Bangor hospital.

* * *

Mum really liked Bangor hospital, "It's much nicer than my local place," she confided on my first visit after her operation. Soon reinforcements arrived as a succession of relatives came to see her and help me out; my Auntie Pat, cousin Sian, Peter and Jeremy. As usual she apologised for troubling everyone. "Oh, don't apologise," said Sian, "we've had a lovely little unexpected holiday out of it." Mum, in her typical selfless way, was happy that out of her misfortune she had given others happiness. Jeremy came at the end of the week to run her home, as I could not manage with Mato, all the luggage and Mum. I think she also wanted a more peaceful journey than it was with us.

Next time we went to Anglesey, Auntie Pat came as well. After we had booked the cottage, Mum discovered she was going to miss a church outing to visit the sites of the Commonwealth Games in Manchester. She was upset about it. Auntie Pat agreed to run her back in the car, for the night, returning on the Friday for the last day of the holiday. On that Thursday, Mum had another fall bruising her face and hurting her leg. Undeterred, she decided to go to Manchester as planned, which caused a lot of comments and concern from her church friends. Whilst at home overnight, she took the opportunity to consult her neighbour, who was a nurse, about her injuries. The neighbour said she should really go to hospital. Because Mum liked Bangor hospital so much, she persuaded Auntie Pat to take her back there to be checked out, before returning to the island for the rest of the Friday.

A year later she had another fall. This time she was in the middle of Bramhall village. I had a phone call from an ambulance man, telling me not to worry but my mum was on her way to hospital. Her other hip had been broken. Each time she was amazing at recovery, demonstrating a real lesson in will power and determination. She hated being dependent on anyone and was eager to mend as quickly as she could to get back to her normal life, so she could help everyone else.

It did slow her down a bit though, which was a relief for everyone around her. One time I took Mum and Mato down to Jeremy and Heather's. They let me stay at their house writing up my school reports whilst they took Mum and Mato canoeing. When they returned, they were shattered. "How do you do it?" Heather asked. "Mum runs one way and Mato runs the other and we don't know which one to go after first, Mum to make sure she doesn't fall or Mato to make sure he doesn't run into danger!" "And there were two of us," she added.

* * *

For her ninetieth birthday, Mum said she wanted to go up in a balloon. However, on looking into it, we discovered that the landing is not always guaranteed to be upright; the basket can sometimes roll over. Bearing in mind her broken hips, she reluctantly decided not to do it. Looking for different alternatives we opted on a barge holiday for the weekend instead. Apart from initially finding it a bit slow, "I could have driven a hundred miles on the motorway by now," she gradually relaxed into it and enjoyed having a weekend afloat with all her family around her. The peace of the Macclesfield canal, the views of the countryside afforded by the gentle pace and memories of earlier times when we used to take the canoes there with Dad, made it all worthwhile.

Despite everything, I absolutely loved those early years with Mato and did not want them to end. When he finally reached his first afternoon at the school nursery, I took him down the hill, left him and cried all the way up the hill wondering how my little three-year old boy would cope without me. They were very good and let me just have him there for three afternoons a week for his first year. The following year in Reception I had to let him attend full time, but by then I was doing supply in the school, so it was not so bad. And he was that little bit older.

CHAPTER 47

"We could never have loved the earth so well if we had had no childhood in it." George Elliott, The Mill on the Floss

When Mato was five, I had a full year of supply work covering an older class. At the end of it we went to America for the summer. On arrival, we stayed in New York State with Janette and Bob, where Mato got to fly Bob's two-seater plane. It did have dual controls I must hasten to add, although Bob let him be in charge for quite a while, encouraging him to do a wing-over. They were wonderful hosts. They took us to the Finger Lakes canoeing and visiting their local town's sights.

One day we drove out into the country to have lunch with their Mennonite friends. It was quite bizarre for me. Last time I had been there, the mother of the family was only a child. She was one of the eight children who had come with their parents to meet Mum, Dad and myself at Janette's house. After the meal, which we ate outside on tables under the trees, we drove over to her parents, who remembered me from before. Again, I was impressed by the Mennonite lifestyle. Everything is done the old ways. Children help around the farm; the family is very important, and the clothes and food are all handmade. Television is not allowed. Mato was relieved to find another family like ours, from that point of view.

After our wonderful stay with Bob and Janette we went up north to visit my Mohawk friend from Akwesasne. It was great to see Norma again, meet her family and introduce Peter and Mato to them. Peter was very interested to see how different Akwasasne was from Pine Ridge. He and Norma kept comparing notes.

We flew to Colorado and bought a second-hand car, then drove up through Golden where there were even more beautiful bronze statues everywhere than on our previous visit. I could now feel it was my town since I had gained that part of Peter's name with our marriage. The police gave us another badge and showed Mato all their guns. A dream for a little boy whose mother is a pacifist. I have since discovered that the brother of one of my school friends lives there, a fellow previous inhabitant of Bramhall. Small world!

After the long drive through the grain belt and cattle ranching sand hills, we arrived in South Dakota. We were greeted with much love and warmth by all our friends and family. David very kindly let us stay in his trailer home, even though he was not there, leaving keys with his sister for us. We did not know how to use the air conditioner, so rather than fry in the midday temperature; we got into the habit of going to the bowling alley which was air conditioned and cool.

Mato loved going out to Housing where Grandma Alice and all the family lived. He had loads of children to play with there and we could allow him the freedom to go off with them, knowing that they would have had strict instructions from Grandma to keep him safe. We chatted to Mom Alice and enjoyed visiting with her and all the family. I loved her stories of the past and of how things were. One day she told me something which made me really think about how life must have been like for her as a child. "One time," she said, "we went on a school trip to the Little Bighorn cemetery. On the way we stopped off at a Fort in Wyoming. I can't just remember the name of it now. As we approached the Fort, on either side was a Butte, towering over the fort. Atop each Butte was the statue of an Indian. I looked up there and was scared. In that moment, I realised how it must have felt to be a white person. Through films and schooling and everything, we were told that the Indians were the bad guys. For a split second I forgot who I was. Then I thought, wait on, I'm an Indian. Why am I thinking that the Indian is scary and the bad guy? He is my relative. From then on I started to see how we had been taught to fear our own people and felt very sad."

It must have been very hard, being taught to think one way in school, then realising that was totally wrong. It is bad enough teaching children to be fearful of another race, but it is ten times worse to teach them to be fearful of their own race. I felt for Mom Alice, imagining the conflict that caused inside her head.

Since our last visit, Grandpa Sage had died. One day, Frankie (one of Peter's sisters) said she would take us out to visit his grave on the Nature reserve. We got out there and Frankie told us to close the car doors. "Why?" I asked. "Surely it would keep the car cooler?"

"Rattle snakes will sneak in when we aren't looking," was her reply.

We had just found Sage's grave in the graveyard when suddenly Nano, a boy of eleven now (he was a baby at our last visit), yelled out. Two rattlesnakes were coiling around each other in a beautiful mating dance, in the middle of the road. I grabbed Mato and told him to stay close to me, then picked up one of Frankie's little girls who was toddling towards them with no fear. The boys and men threw stones at the snakes till they moved off into the undergrowth, then we all leapt in the car. Frankie then explained how dangerous it was. We were over forty minutes' drive away from the nearest serum at the hospital. If one of us had been bitten, we would have had no chance of survival. I cuddled Mato close and thanked all my guides for keeping us safe.

Soon after that David returned from his trip and we got to spend some time with him. We had ten years of catching up to do and spent lots of time chatting and reminiscing. After a few days, we decided to go travelling to visit some more friends. We drove up to Wanble to see our friend Larry and then on into the Badlands. Mato loved the steep multi-coloured dry mud slopes with all its crevices and mini canyons. As in many natural landscapes in America, there is a feeling of so much freedom and space.

After the Badlands we went onto Rapid City to visit another of David's sisters. Marilyn and Larry looked after us very well, taking us to visit a gold mine, where we 'panned for gold,' then round some of the old-style saloons in Deadwood. It felt strange to be in similar scenes to those of the big screen. Mato was thrilled when a gun battle was re-enacted in the saloon bar.

The big Harley event at Sturgis had been the week before, so we missed it, but Larry took us all out on his Harley, in turn, to make up for it. Peter and I had caught the Sturgis rally on our last visit, and it was quite amazing. They call it Thunder in the Hills and it truly is. The sound of throbbing engines reverberates around, as thousands of people and bikes descend on this small town once a year, transforming it into a mecca for motorbikes. Every style and outfit imaginable can be seen, from the practical to the outrageous.

One place Grandma had told us we had to go when we were in Rapid City was a restaurant which had a talking fox. We could not believe

290

it. As we sat down, a mechanised fox, taller than a child, rolled over to us on tracks that went all round the tables. Then out of the fox, a human voice had a conversation with us, asking us questions, discussing what we wanted to eat, finding out we came from England then asking us whether London had big red buses and so on. Mato was entranced.

On returning from Rapid, Shirley, another of David's sisters gave us a room in her motel. The combiners had been there when we first arrived but they had left now and so she kindly let us stay. Both Marilyn and Shirley take after their mum, showing so much kindness to others. During the summer, the massive combine harvesters work their way across the grain belt of America, travelling from town to town to stay for a few weeks while they cut the wheat. The sight I love in South Dakota summers is the acres of sunflowers. Nothing in this country can match the swathes of golden heads going on forever.

Mum was sending letters to Grandma Alice's address for us. When we returned from one of our trips out, Alice said she had accidentally thrown some papers on the tip only to realise later that my Mum's letter was amongst them, as yet unopened by me. She had been so worried about it, that two of her teenage grandsons had gone on the tip and spent ages delving in the filth and dirt till they found the letter. I was so touched and impressed by that. There are not many young people who would do that. I did not know how to thank them enough. Grandma was very proud of them. The local press gives the young native kids a very negative image, yet the majority are well meaning, kind and helpful, particularly to their elders.

We took Mato to both Pine Ridge and the local Pow-wow. Grandma Alice came to the local one and we enjoyed being there surrounded by family. Mato loved the Veteran's parade in the Grand Entry, eyeing up all their guns, running on with all the other kids to collect the used cartridges after they fired the gun salutes. Formality does not exist for the children. I love the way children can dance in with the adults if they feel like it, coming and going as the fancy takes them. The Lakota understand that children learn by doing. In Pine Ridge we did not know so many people but had a good time watching the dances, hearing the drums and singing and watching the skills on display in the rodeo.

291

Our all-too-brief summer was finishing and when we were leaving, Grandma Alice and all the family organised a big cook-out at the park for us. It felt very special to be there with all the family, the big kids looking after the little ones, some of them playing basketball, some eating, chatting and enjoying being together. At the end of the evening, Alice gave us some very precious gifts. She must have saved up for ages for us. As usual I was overwhelmed with all the family's kindness and generosity. It felt so hard having to say goodbye again. We did not know when we would next be over.

Sadly, this time we could not leave the car with them because we needed it to drive to Denver. Our friends from England, John and Marilyn, have a son who lives near there who is married to a lovely American girl. We met up with them and spent a great couple of days together. He very kindly said he would sell the car for us, after we had left, putting the money in Peter's bank account. As we could not leave the car for her, Peter used the money to make sure Grandma's fuel tank was filled up to keep her warm during the bitter cold of winter, which is always a big worry for her.

CHAPTER 48

"All that I am or hope to be, I owe to my angel mother." Abraham Lincoln

It was exactly ten years previously that we had visited the States. When we got back to Mum from our trip, we were so happy to see her, especially Mato. She was really pleased he felt like that. As the conversation went on, I began to pick up from her comments that she had been worried that we were having such a good time out there, that we would not want to come home. I felt awful. I loved her so much and would never dream of leaving her like that, particularly in her nineties. I had tried to make sure she was okay while we were away; Heather and Jeremy had been up during the summer and had taken her on a holiday to her favourite home from childhood in Whitley Bay. Auntie Pat had been around, she had had visits from friends, but I knew something was not quite right with her.

Gradually, it came out. She had been having stomach pains and had not been eating well. She said she would pay me the money I would have earned at school if I could be around her a bit more. Of course, I did not take the money from her, but I knew then that she needed me to spend more time with her. I asked the Head if I could just do PPA cover that year, so I was able to visit her more often. Christmas came and went. She seemed to be getting worse. I took her for appointments with the doctors and specialists. It gradually became clear that she was very poorly, although no-one told us directly what it was. The specialist told her she had a little growth in her tummy, he was keeping an eye on it and he would see her again in September. He asked if she wanted an operation on it. She refused. She said she could not cope at her age. When he said that it might help for a short while but not for long, she felt she had made the right decision.

My Uncle Norman had died the previous year and his ashes were waiting to be scattered. My cousin was organising for them to be placed on the Isle of Wight, where he used to live, so we arranged a holiday there. Mum kept going, hardly complaining of the pain, so I had no idea how bad it really was for her. She was focussing all her attention and hope on the holiday and my niece's wedding in the summer, so we went to get outfits for both events for her.

On the holiday, she became very poorly, I called a doctor and helped her as much as I could. She kept insisting that our holiday should not be ruined, making us go out on little trips, while she stayed in the cottage. I never wanted to be out for long, not happy to leave her alone.

In one sense it was rather amazing, because she got to see many of her nieces and nephews who had all come over for the ashes. Jo, my cousin, was staying with us, who had been like a sister to me as a teenager; her youngest and favourite sister, Auntie Pat, was also with us. Carrie and Tom, her grandchildren, came over by ferry for the day, and her other surviving sister, Auntie Marjorie, happened to be on holiday with her daughter and son-in-law. We all met up with more of Auntie Pat's children and grandchildren on a lovely sunny day at the beach. It could not have been better from that point of view; she got to see many of her relatives in one week.

Auntie Pat was worried about the drive home because Mum was so unwell. Auntie Pat prayed and I asked my guides to help us out. It was a Saturday after the Whit week holiday. The motorway should have been crowded. It was virtually empty. We sailed through, stopping only a couple of times at service stations, getting Mum home without much trouble.

After that Mum's health went worse. Jeremy kept nipping up to visit, trying to balance being there for his mum and back in Bristol for his wife, Heather, who was undergoing treatment for cancer. On one of the visits the lovely local doctor asked to speak with us both. I remember sitting talking to her on Mum's swing seat in the garden. Warm sun shone down on us, the newly cut lawn stretched in front, Mum was sitting beyond earshot in the lounge with the French windows open, and the birds were singing. It was too lovely a scene for the words the doctor was saying. "Your mother is terminally ill," she told us. "She has pancreatic cancer. What do you think about whether or not she should be told?" It seemed so sudden. The garden that had been my solace and comfort over the years was the birthplace of the end of it all. It was so matter of fact. Ever practical, my brother and I discussed it and decided she would be better off not knowing. I am sure she was aware deep down, but as Jeremy said, if

294

she knew, all hope would be gone and she would find that harder. We asked how long it would be. "I'm not sure, a matter of weeks, maybe a month or so. It depends on so many things."

We were determined to keep Mum at home, she hated being in hospitals and always dreaded being in a Nursing Home. I kept trying to organise care between myself, her friends and Auntie Pat, being very aware that Jeremy had Heather to care for and worry about, as well as being two hundred miles away.

Three weeks after our return from the Isle of Wight, I went home for the weekend, as I needed a break and felt that I had been neglecting Mato and Peter. One of my mum's friends stayed with her and on my return on the Monday, Mum told me she had had an angel looking after her, referring to her friend. I have never got over how many older people are so grateful for any little thing you do for them. It is a very gentle stage in life and a privilege to be with someone who delights in your company.

On the Tuesday, she had a hair appointment. I took her for that, aware that she looked almost ghostlike. Her skin was yellow, and she was so thin. Then I asked if she would like a drive out, so we went for a drive round all her old haunts; Mellor, Marple, New Mills, where her sisters and parents had lived for many years. We had a lovely day together and she settled down well for the night. In the morning, I had to go back to teach for the afternoon, but I had secretly organised for another friend from church to visit. Mum did not want to think people were coming, because she felt she had to tidy up, but if they turned up 'unexpectedly' she was always happy to see them. Before I went, Mum was talking about when she died and made me promise that Jeremy and I would not argue over anything in the house. She wrote a cheque out for each of the grandchildren and made sure all her affairs were in order. She knew that she did not have long.

Jeremy had business in Warrington that day, so he was coming to stay the night, which relieved me from dashing back over. After school I took Mato to his football practice, and then got him to bed. At quarter to eleven Jeremy rang. "Do you know the doctors number? Mum has a lot of pain in her chest." I told him to bypass the doctors and ring the ambulance.

A short while later the phone rang again. "Mum has died. I think she's had a heart attack." My scream brought Peter rushing upstairs.

I could not think. I told Jeremy I would be over and went into a blind panic. Peter calmed me down. He rang our friend John, who immediately said he would drive me over because Peter needed to be there for Mato. I will never forget the strangeness of that night-time drive to Mum's and the kindness of John, dropping everything to take me there.

Somehow, just over an hour later, I found myself in Mum's hall hugging Jeremy, with him quietly telling me there was a policeman in the dining room. The house which always felt so warm and loving felt bleak, cold and empty. The stark light in the back room made everything look hard and uninviting. The policeman apologised but said that in a case of a sudden death at home, they had to come and ask questions. It was all wrong. He mentioned the Doctor Shipman case and I realised it was the doctor he was questioning. Mum would have hated her lovely young doctor to have come under suspicion. We answered him and finally he left.

"Do you want to see Mum?" Jeremy asked carefully. I went up with him. She looked so small, tucked under her sheets. I did not want to touch her. She looked as if she was asleep. I did not want her to feel cold, that lovely mum who had held me and cuddled me with so much warmth and fun throughout my life; that strong woman who had always been there for me, no matter what, whether she agreed with me or not; that kind, loving, considerate and thoughtful person who had such a sense of fun and was always ready for a dare; that vibrant life force with boundless energy who could wear us all out; that wonderful mum who had finally worn herself out.

Her funeral was a testament to her. She wanted the crematorium first, so her coffin was not in the church, because she wanted her funeral to be a celebration of her life. She had even told me the hymns and the particular tunes, "Not that version she had said, it's too slow and morbid." Peter made the wreath and as I stared at it in the crematorium, it glowed with Mum's energy. She loved yellow because it was bright and happy. The flowers were a glorious mound of yellows. As it sat on the coffin, sunlight streamed onto it and I felt Mum was there with us, lively and happy as ever.

Bramhall Methodist church, her second home for so many years, was so full they had to find more chairs for people. Through my haze of grief, I felt so proud of my mum, who in her ninety-third year could fill a big church like that, with people of all ages. I had written another poem, for Mum this time, and again just about managed to get through it with the support of my favourite minister from mum's church, just behind me to take over, in case I could not finish it. Her two oldest grandchildren, Carrie and Tom both contributed beautifully, as did other friends and relatives. It went very well, even though the tune she did not want was accidentally played for one of the hymns. "Mum will kill me for that!" I whispered to Jeremy. A lovely touch that the minister did was to go round the church asking people for their memories of Mum. One friend commented on how wonderful the flowers were in her window. She always had flowers in a vase facing outwards in the big picture window, so that everyone passing could enjoy them. The funeral is such a blur when it is a close relative. I was very touched to read about all the people who had come from all over the country to pay tribute to Mum. It also meant a lot that our friends John and Catherine had come over from Todmorden, even though they had not really known Mum that well.

Although her death had been hard to take, I was very comforted by the fact that she had died at home, Jeremy had been beside her and the heart attack had taken her quickly. She did not have to suffer the lingering pain of the cancer. She had seen many of her relatives recently and had had some dear friends from church close to her in her last weeks. I felt that I had done everything I possibly could for her, which helped with the inevitable feelings of guilt after a death. I still wondered if our trip to the States had precipitated the cancer, but friends told me not to go there. Mum always said she never wanted to reach a hundred, she never wanted to end up in a care home and she hated being in hospital. She died at home, with her son beside her, just before her ninety third birthday, so she was happy.

Peter and I had travelled in America the year before I was forty, then Dad died. This time it was Peter, Mato and I who had travelled to America the year before I was fifty and then Mum died. I was beginning to feel a bit worried about our trips to America.

A few weeks later we were all down in Bristol for Carrie's wedding. There are some uncanny parallels between Carrie and me. It is a comforting feeling and makes me feel closer to my lovely niece. I have discovered that Carrie and I ended up behaving in very similar ways as teenagers towards our parents. Comments Heather makes about those times are very similar to the comments my mum used to make. Then our husbands are both very different from our fathers yet are often similar in temperament and their behaviour towards us. We both ended up with the same career, as primary teachers. I got married the year after Dad died; Carrie got married just after Mum died. When we get together, we compare notes.

Carrie and Tim's wedding was a lovely day and I knew Mum and Dad would be there in spirit, so proud of their beautiful granddaughter. Dad had told me when he came through before, that he was there for our wedding, so I was sure they would both be there for Carrie. Mato was a page boy and loved riding in the wedding cars which 'bounced' with their hydraulic suspension, at traffic lights. After the brief interlude of Carrie's wedding, we returned north to start the sorting out.

Packing up my home for fifty years, was almost as hard as losing Mum. I had been born in that house, in the front bedroom, and had always known it as home. I still called it home. Every time I went over to sort out another part, I would open the front door and call out "Hello" to Mum. It made it seem like she was still there. I am sure on one level she was. I loved being there because it made me closer to her. Jeremy and Heather were very good at clearing out, we kept having blitzing weekends. We did not argue over anything, Jeremy and I tended to want different things. Interestingly Carrie and I had similar tastes in what we wanted. We still did not argue. We all realised that our relationships were much more important than possessions.

The house was finally cleared and ready for sale. It sold the first day on the market, in fact two people were fighting over it, so it had to go to sealed bids.

After it had been sold, I had a dream that upset me. I dreamt the new people were there and Mum was looking out of her windows. She could not understand why the house was not hers anymore and was very upset. I woke feeling I had taken it from her, and she was now homeless. It took me a while to realise she did not need it anymore.

Near Christmas I had a lovely experience. I woke from a dream around midnight, something I rarely do. Because I had just woken up, the dream remained clear in my head helping me to remember it. I was walking down one path and Mum and Dad were walking on a path towards me but on the other side of a fence. They were holding hands and looking so blissfully happy, with pure joy, beyond anything we feel in this world. I knew, then, that they were together and happy. I have felt at peace about them ever since.

CHAPTER 49

"Give light and the darkness will disappear of itself." Desiderius Erasmus

Over the years of being in Todmorden, so much has happened. I have lived a very ordinary everyday life with moments of happiness, sadness, joy, anger and gratefulness to be living in such a beautiful place. I have learnt how to fight for rights and to protect ourselves and others. I am sure like all towns, it is a microcosm of the outside world. Whenever things have got too much for me, I retreat to the garden or hills around. Walking or being near nature has become part of my life blood. When I have been in a city, which is rare these days, I yearn for the green hills, to see down the valley and watch the weather approach and to hear the trickling streams dance and gurgle through the fields above. It is a valley of rainbows. Often when the weather blows in, sun succeeds rain and an arch of colour floods the hillside.

Living an ordinary life in this town is surprisingly eventful. We often say that our Fold alone could provide a wealth of drama for a soap opera and there are only six or seven households. As at home in Bramhall, some of our neighbours have become like family, particularly our friends, Sam and Vonny.

A few years previously I had seen a woman sitting by the road, waiting for a bus, with her small young son. At the time, I had thought to myself, I like the look of her, she could be a friend. Just before Mum had died, this lady had moved into the houses below, reached by a footpath through the fields. Her son was at the same school as Mato and we got to know each other. Sandra and I have become good friends over the intervening years, not least because she understands my spiritual perspective. We share many views and understandings of the world.

When Mum died, Christmas became a big thing to overcome. We always focussed it round Mum. She loved it, so it felt very odd not to be with her. Jeremy and Heather are so far away and besides, they have their own children and grandchildren now, whilst Mato enjoys his Christmases at home. We decided Christmas was for the friends who are like family, so have spent it with Sandra, Jack, Vonny and Sam over the years.

Nearly every event that happens in our town has a personal link through someone I know. Tragedies and triumphs that would just be an item of news in a bigger place, become very vivid, and I learn the human cost of each one, on many levels. Todmorden has given me a wide and all-encompassing understanding of humans and how they can operate, showing me many scenes. I have quietly prayed for lots of people, asking my guides for help with many situations and they have always delivered.

I often look at Spiritual 'gurus' who advise and direct people. I sometimes think to myself, it is all very well being spiritual, when you are surrounded by lots of others with similar views, but how about applying it daily with real people in a real world? I suppose we need both. We all have a role in the world. If we could all follow our hearts and be valued for what we truly love to do in our work, then society would work like a dream. Sadly, the money driven economy is not like that, but I do believe we can dream and the more we dream, the more chance there is of turning it into a reality. Money certainly is not everything.

On several different occasions I have found something that someone else has lost. It seems to me that the joy they will get in retrieving their lost possession will far outweigh any thing I would get from keeping their valuables. In fact, I feel that if I kept something, knowing that someone else's loss is attached to that object, it would not give me any happiness. The older I get the more I think that 'things' are a burden. Our house seems weighed down with 'stuff' and I wonder whether we need any of it. Inevitably, however, if I get rid of something, it immediately becomes needed or is discovered to prove valuable. I think it is called 'Sod's Law.'

When Peter decided to go to America early in our relationship, he had cleared all his stuff out. Jez, his friend, was a DJ in his spare time, so Peter gave him all his old records. Tucked in amongst the 45rpms were some little pieces of paper with scribbles on. Jez obviously did not know what they were and did not place any value on them. The papers had a story behind them.

301

As a teenager, Peter had left school and gone as an apprentice gardener in Lister Park (now Manningham Park) in Bradford. Leaning on his spade one day, he was contemplating some sculptures which had been erected all over the grass. "What do you think of them?" this voice said.

"To be honest, I think they're a load of crap," Peter replied to the man beside him.

"Well, I made them," the man said.

"That doesn't change my opinion," said Peter, "I still don't like them." Ask a Yorkshire man a question and you will get the truth. The man, whose name was Henry Moore, then took Peter into his temporary office to explain what the sculptures were. In there he showed Peter the original little models that he himself had made. "I like those," Peter conceded, as Henry Moore then went on explain what they all meant with scribbles and drawings on several pieces of paper. After hearing the explanations Peter could appreciate what the artist was doing but he still preferred the little models to the big cast sculptures outside. He gave Peter the sketches and Peter kept them, later storing them amongst his vinyl records.

After Henry Moore died, Peter began to think that these might be worth something and kept trying to remember where he had put them. Finally, he recalled his record collection and contacted Jez. By this time Jez had had them a while and he could not recall the papers either. This went on for a few years. Finally, we got a call from Jez, "My wife remembers what she did with those papers, she used them as firelighters." We had a good laugh about it, particularly when our son looked up the only drawing ever sold by Henry Moore on the internet and discovered it had gone for over a hundred thousand pounds. The most expensive firelighters ever! Our philosophy is there is no use crying over spilt milk. What is gone, is gone.

Whilst Mato was a baby, I could not do my tai chi like I had. As he started to become older, I started to revert to being able to do my daily morning stint. It keeps me supple and focusses me for the day. I am pretty rubbish at it. The short form, which should take twenty minutes, is over in five most mornings, but I do the breathing and it does me good.

For a while, that was my only source of spiritual comfort. Of course, I talked to my guides, but not a lot. In the early years of the twenty first century, I experienced a lot of difficult and hard times. Going to see Mum was always a sweet relief, her lively and positive view on life always helped me. By the time she had died, the worst of those times had passed, but I still missed her dreadfully. Gradually others have taken her place, Jeremy and Heather, my Auntie Pat and good friends are there for me but of course no-one can fully replace her, ever.

Various people helped through what I class as the darker times. I was going through a lot of stress and my body was reacting by making me quite poorly. Luckily, I had a good homeopath who helped. She liked one of my strategies for coping, when I explained it to her.

In autumn, Mum would always say, "Catch a leaf and you will have a happy month!" Then the story of her friend would get trotted out. Mum and her friend, who was engaged to mum's brother, were all catching leaves one autumn. Her future sister-in-law caught three. She had three happy months with my uncle, then he broke off the engagement. Mum always sited this as proof the leaves worked.

At the time I was worrying about many things and my greatest fears were for Peter and Mato. I decided that one way to deal with it was to catch twelve leaves. My happiness was dependent on their well-being so if they were fine, I would be happy. I had a lovely time going out catching the falling leaves. It is not as easy as it first appears to be. They often fall in a completely different way than you are expecting them to. I discovered I had to get into an almost meditative zone, focussing all my attention on the tumbling, drifting colours. Standing on soft layers of crunchy leaves, under a canopy of red, oranges and gold, with the sun shafting through the branches was very peaceful. I forgot my problems for a while. Every leaf caught gave me a thrill of achievement. It felt as if I was taking my own destiny back. I was not a victim of the nastiness being directed at us anymore. I was in charge and doing something to ensure the well-being of my family for the next year.

Since then, I have used it as my insurance policy every year and it has worked. Every autumn presents a different challenge of where to catch the leaves and when. It has enabled me to appreciate many different woods and trees from Northumberland to Devon, as the leaves tend to be easiest to catch during the half term holiday. I have even convinced others to have a go, although I stress it is only my interpretation that makes it necessary to catch twelve. It can be done just for fun.

* * *

My friend Catherine and I kept each other going with the odd spiritual experience. We went to a few Spiritualist church meetings, but nothing really grabbed me. I had one or two readings from psychics when I was desperate, but none matched the clarity and beauty of the reading I had had with Jan all those years ago. Catherine started developing her psychic gifts more through the Spiritualist church, but I felt I was floundering. I had lost a strong and powerful link with spirit but did not realise it. I felt adrift. The worries and troubles of everyday life had swamped my clarity of connection.

I continued subscribing to Cygnus Book Club, an alternative book club, and as I pulled out of the dark times, their monthly newsletter used to remind me of what I used to have. As Mato grew up and I began to have more time for me, I felt the loss of my very active spiritual days but did not know how to get back there. I wondered about going to one of Helen's workshops but did not feel that was the answer. Then one day in Cygnus, I saw an article about this woman called Anastasia who lives in the northern forests of Russia, in the Tiga. I was hooked. The whole set of books was called the Ringing Cedars series and they were expensive. Over seventy pounds for the set of nine, but they were worth every penny. It took me over a year to read them because some of the ideas were so different and mind-blowing that I had to read them slowly, for each new concept to settle. A bonus was that in one of the books I came across the very first mention I had ever seen of the School of Mystery in Egypt. I immediately recalled how Dad had told me of our past lives there. The Ringing Cedars series was the very first place I came across the term 'co-creative' which has become widely used since then.

Gradually I became fired up. The Earth became a magical place full of endless possibilities again, the history of the Earth could be understood from a new and exciting perspective and links with the plant and animal kingdoms could be very different from our mundane and boring understanding of how the world works. She presented a

304

blueprint for a wonderful new way of living across the planet, connected to a simple yet beautiful way of life, being close to earth and growing our own food. It tied in with all my previous understanding but took it to a new and exciting level of possibilities. I began to feel alive again.

I had kept in touch with my friend Jan, through Christmas cards, phone calls and the odd email. They had moved away to Ireland where she had eventually married her partner. Then the marriage had finished. She returned to England and was living in Manchester. She told me she had started doing readings again and was working on the phone lines for a psychic reading company.

About a year or so later, she suddenly turned up at Peter's yard with another friend. We had a good chat, catching up on the missing years. It was great to see her again and she told me about the psychic development groups she ran. She had asked me a few years before to run a trance session, releasing trapped souls, with her group, but it had not felt right to go. Now however, it did feel right to go along, not to do trance but to join her meditation group.

I went to the first session, and I was hooked. Going weekly, over the past few years, I have rediscovered and developed my skills at reading auras, listening to my guides and sending healing. Jan is, and always has been, a very safe person to work with. She is very pure and does not put her ego into the messages she gets. She gives them as they are. Because she works with Spirit daily, doing readings for people, she has developed fine skills and is very clear. She has lots of interesting and amazing stories about her psychic experiences.

One time she told us about a previous member of the group who was a young man, very keen on experimenting and wanting to explore the psychic world. On this occasion there was just the two of them meditating. Suddenly Jan was psychically aware of two alien beings in the room. They were either side of her and about eight feet tall. Having no reference point with anything she knew, the only way she could describe them was as gigantic ant people. Jan mentally reached out to them and felt their energy. They had no emotion as humans do, they were beyond that. She felt they were watching over us as guardians but with an absence of any feelings that humans could relate to. They were concerned for our well-being, and she felt they were monitoring us and there to guide us if we asked for help. She asked them to leave. They respected her wishes, so then she knew they were on the positive energy spectrum.

When they had finished the session, she asked her companion if he had seen them. "Oh yes," he responded, "I invited them here."

"Well next time give me some warning," Jan retorted, "I would like to know if you're going to invite aliens to our group, it's sort of courteous!"

As Jan relayed this story, something clicked in my head. "Oh my God!" I exclaimed. "It all makes sense now."

What do you mean?" the others queried.

"In the Hopi legends it talks about them having lived in four worlds. The first world was destroyed by fire, the second by ice, the third by floods and we are now in the fourth world. Each time people were out of balance with the Earth, so she cleansed herself. Tom's father was elected by the Kikmongwi, to tell the world of the Hopi prophesies, how we are approaching the end of the fourth world if we continue to abuse, pollute and destroy our beautiful Mother Earth. He did his task; then in the nineties he was told to return. If people weren't listening that was their choice, but he had fulfilled his duty."

I continued, "In the legends that I read about, each time the Earth cleansed herself, the true Hopi, who had remembered how to live in balance, were taken underground by the Ant people. This was the part I have always found hard to understand. I obviously thought that the Hopi had observed the ants and had somehow learnt from them. When you, Jan described these beings, it all made sense. The Ant people who were your alien visitors seem likely to be the Ant people referred to by the Hopi, a superior race of beings who look after us, watch over us and protect the people with true hearts so they can survive to continue the human race." I must admit I was quite blown away by the idea. I was very excited about my discovery. However, when I mentioned it in the staffroom at school, I did get a few funny looks.

I decided to be more circumspect about my experiences in meditation. Nevertheless, the weekly sessions helped me to fine tune my spirituality in everyday life. Every morning after my tai chi I pray for people in my healing book and all the places where my family and I will work or be that day. I send love and light down the Fold and around the world, particularly to places of conflict and sadness. After a while, I was getting so much out of the group that I took Catherine. She too began to find it a great source of strength and insight.

Another thing I must share with you from the group is the white petals. One year, I was going to visit one of my good friends in London. She suggested taking my son and me on a tour of the House of Commons. It was in 2012, just after the Olympics. On the drive down, I was musing about the impending visit and contemplated using the opportunity to have a go at spiritually cleansing the House of Commons and the House of Lords. Remembering Findhorn and all the 'holier than thou' confused souls lodged in the Universal Hall, I rationalised that there must be even more confused souls in such an important place of government. Obviously, I could not sit and do trance work in the place itself, my son and my friend would have thought I had completely lost it. I decided to memorise an image of the place and talk to the rest of the meditation group about how we could work on it on my return.

We duly arrived there and had a great tour. My friend is very knowledgeable, and it was interesting to see all the famous places. No cameras are allowed after the first main hall, so we had to record everything in our hearts. In the Atrium outside the House of Commons there is a statue of Churchill, one of Thatcher and several busts of previous Prime Ministers. I went over to Stanley Baldwin's bust. I touched his head and explained to my friend about our family's connection with him.

My paternal grandma grew up in Rottingdean on the south coast. Pictures of the village, as it used to be, adorned the walls of her granny flat. Looking at them, I would ask her to tell me about her life there as a child. I remember her relating to me about my great grandpa, who was German. He had come over from Germany to stay with a rich uncle. On arrival at his house, the butler had shown him into a room and told him to wait. Hot tempered and impatient by nature, he could not stand the indignity of having to stand around until his uncle was ready to see him. Apparently, he stormed out, deciding he would make his own way in this foreign country, without his uncle's help. I am not sure how he met my great-grandma and married her but by the time they had children, he was in and out of different labouring jobs which were rather unreliable and spasmodic.

To keep the household together, my great-grandma found work looking after the house of rich folk. Whilst the wealthy family were up in London during the winter season, my grandma's family lived in the large house to keep it aired and clean. It, also, provided them with lodgings. Then in the summer they would find rented accommodation.

I believe the rich family was that of Burne-Jones, the artist, and his wife, Lady Burne-Jones. I know my grandmother was friendly with her because we have correspondence addressed to Grandma from the wife of the artist. They date from the turn of the twentieth century when Grandma had gone out to Canada to work as a dental assistant, so I think I am right in assuming that the house they looked after was hers.

In the same village of Rottingdean there lived Rudyard Kipling. Grandma used to tell us how he was very shy of the public. He had doors in various places in the wall around his garden. Often, he would sit on the cliffs, looking at the view and watching the children playing on the beach. Suddenly voices of visitors to the seaside settlement could be heard enquiring after Mr Rudyard Kipling. Next moment he would be scuttling back to the village and diving through a door to escape. He was very shy and disliked all the attention his books brought him.

Another time she told me how the whole village turned out to celebrate the relief of Mafeking in the Boer War. Rudders, as his aunt affectionately referred to him in her letters, led the triumphal parade. His aunt was Lady Burne-Jones. She was one of the Macdonald sisters. Her other sister was mother to Stanley Baldwin.

On his visits to his aunt and cousin, Stanley Baldwin decided he really liked the place, so when he was getting married, he requested that it should be in the village church, even though he did not live there. He probably thought it was very quaint. I presume his aunt became involved with the arrangements and must have suggested that some of the local children could be the couple's flower girls. All I know is that my grandma, as a young girl, ended up walking in front of the couple, scattering rose petals in their path. Over a hundred years later, looking at his bust in the atrium, I felt a warmth towards this man, at whose wedding my grandma had played a part.

My friend was a great tour guide and full of interesting information. I had not realised that the House of Commons was burnt down in the War, that's why the room is a lot plainer and less ornate than all the carved and painted splendour of the House of Lords. I quietly registered that it also meant there was going to be fewer generations of confused souls stuck there.

* * *

After our trip down south, I could not wait for the next meditation group to broach my idea. "If I hold an image of the place in my head, then that should be enough of a connection for our energies to go in and clean," I suggested. Rachel was not there; it was just three of us that week. At the end of the meditation, we always send out love and healing, so at that point we visualised ourselves cleaning and scrubbing the darkness in the Houses and replacing it with light. We all did it in our own different ways.

None of the others knew about my grandma and her connection with Stanley Baldwin.

After we have closed our connection with the guides, we tell each other what we have seen. Catherine said she had seen us as nineteen-fifties cleaning ladies, with our heads in scarves; Jan was sweeping, I was mopping, and she was scrubbing. I saw us putting light everywhere, pushing away darkness. Jan said she had been working at the cleaning very hard, then found we were not getting far, so she asked the angels for help. When she looked up, the sky was a mass of the fittest, most muscular 'don't mess with me' angels she could imagine. They came in their hordes, carrying baskets of white rose petals. They placed a petal on each crown chakra of everyone who works there, from the clerks, to the cleaners, to the MPs. The guides told her that we had to keep a good watch out because from now on, the MPs would start to say things they did not intend to reveal. They thanked us for initiating the idea.

After Jan had told us about her vision, I told her about Grandma. She was amazed. She could not believe that my ancestor had scattered rose petals in front of one of the prime ministers all those years ago and now the angels were using the exact same tool. I know we should get used to these things, but it is always quite exciting when synchronicities like this occur.

309

Since then, we have discovered that the white petals are a great thing to use, particularly when the situation is too big for us or when the energies of the people involved are a bit nasty and we do not want our energies to get tangled with theirs. Anyone can use the idea. If you have a situation that you find hard to handle or someone is particularly unpleasant or in great need, visualise white petals covering them. Be pure in your intention and ask the angels to help sort the situation or heal the people. I always find it important to 'white petal' both the victims and the perpetrators. The ones doing the bad stuff need as much, if not more, healing than the people receiving it. We are all connected. Healing one strand of the web will not work unless we heal all the strands. The other brilliant thing about the petals is that if they get attacked or negative energies try to destroy them, they multiply. If one gets removed, five take its place. How good is that?

The visions we receive in mediation are wonderful. We always ask for full protection and guidance from our own guides, the angels and the Source of love itself. We leave nothing to chance. If you feel tempted to go into this work, it is very important to ensure you protect yourself properly. It always worries me when people play with things like Ouija boards and séances when they do not know what they are doing. The Spirit world is just like the human world, there are good and bad out there. It is stupid and irresponsible to make yourself open to all of it without safeguards. Your guides are always there for you. You will know it is right if it feels good to you and others around you. Their energy is pure love. You cannot experience it without feeling that it is totally right.

A recurring vision, particularly a few months ago, was seeing many points of light, all representing people on this planet, with me being one of them. I kept being shown these lights in different ways, all linked together forming a wonderful network of glowing light that encircled the world. Sometimes it can feel very hopeless, as if we are working in isolation. I can easily think to myself what difference can I do? I am so little. No matter how much goodness and light and love I send into the world and ask the guides and angels to send in, it is very small. It is not. Every time someone sends good thoughts, feelings or kindness to others, it feeds into this wonderful grid of light that encompasses the world. Think of it like an energy grid, supporting all the good in the world.

Most people in the world want to live in a peaceful, happy place where they can bring up their children in safety with enough food to eat and clean water to drink. Sadly, a small minority want to spoil all that for everyone else and they are the ones who are constantly reported in the media. I always loved the comment made by the grandpa in 'Outnumbered.' He's got a touch of Alzheimer's and has watched the TV all day. He reports with concern to his daughter, that there have been ten plane crashes all happening in the same place today. It is a very good point. We are constantly bombarded by the news, hearing the same story ten times a day. Whatever radio station or TV channel, the same gruesome stuff is brainwashed into our minds, till all we can think about is the terrible condition of the world and how awful everything is. Luckily, not all the media are so negative. There are lots of programmes about the positives in the world and I have gradually noticed how things have progressed since I was younger.

CHAPTER 50

"The secret of change is to focus all of your energy, not on fighting the old but on building the new." Socrates

Many wonderful people have fought long and hard over the years to change things. No matter how hard the negative camp tries to dismiss all the good things and argue against them, there have been many positive improvements since I was a child.

A couple of years ago we sadly attended a funeral of a beautiful friend of ours. She was very stylish, full of fun and believed everyone should be equal. As we parked up and approached the church, lively trumpet playing could be heard, as a band paved the way for a glass encased coffin, pulled by a stunning pair of horses, with feathered plumes waving. In the packed church, friends and family gave moving and fitting tributes to her, then we followed the hearse over to the other side of Manchester to Southern Cemetery. There I learnt how the Afro-Caribbean community show their love to people who have passed on. The grave had been dug but the dirt was left by the side with shovels. After her coffin had been laid inside, the women started singing and the men took it in turns to gently shovel the soil onto her grave. They explained to me that you would never allow strangers to put a loved one to bed, so why is it any different for the final big sleep? When the mound was completed, bunches of flowers that people had brought were opened and each individual flower was planted, with love, by the women. Soon the mound was ablaze with colour and beauty, reminding us of the lively beauty of our friend in her life.

At the funeral tea, in a very stylish hotel in Didsbury, I got chatting to one of her aunties. "You know things have moved on a long way in this country from when I arrived here in the fifties," she commented. "An occasion like this would never have happened then, all these white people and black people mixing together and treating each other as equals. We wouldn't even have been welcome in the same bar." I reflected that she was right. Things have changed massively in all sorts of areas.

Children are treated with more respect and care by the system in general, particularly in schools. In the fifties my brother, as a child, came home having a dreadful headache. My mother later discovered that the teacher had bashed his head against the coat pegs because he had walked the wrong way round the cloakroom, when the class was being punished for some small thing. My brother was a quiet, incredibly well-behaved boy, who would never have done anything wrong on purpose. He did not even tell Mum about the incident, his friend told her some days later. That would never happen nowadays. The teacher would lose their career for that now. I am not saying things are perfect in schools, but physical abuses like that have been eradicated. Children are treated as people nowadays, instead of objects to be disciplined and inculcated with facts.

There is more awareness of abuse on all levels and visible channels to find support and help. Sadly, it still goes on, but it is not so hidden. There are more opportunities and encouragement for victims to speak out. Teachers and other professionals are trained in identifying victims and hopefully there is more understanding and a willingness to listen.

Medically there have been massive advances. Mum and Dad watched a programme about an operation that cured a little girl of the problem that Jill was born with. In the fifties, the operation resulted in Jill losing her life, but now it is done safely and successfully. As well as advances in allopathic medicine, alternative medicine is more widely accepted and used. A whole range of therapies and treatments are used in beauty salons and health clinics across the country. Many of these practices were generally unrecognised thirty years ago, with people looking at me strangely when I mentioned them in the 1980s.

Twenty-five years ago, when I started learning about permaculture, I kept going on to others about how important it was to grow food as close as possible to where it was needed. At times, I felt as if I was a lone voice shouting in the wilderness. In the 1980s and early 90s allotments were lying abandoned, with people preferring to fill their gardens with colourful bedding plants. In those days maintaining vegetable plots, chicken rearing and beekeeping was something that few people did, even in the country. Now there is a massive movement to grow your own. Our local town has a scheme called Incredible Edible, where many public places are planted with food crops for people to help themselves to, which has attracted both royal and world-wide interest. Round the country, allotments are all taken, with waiting lists of people hoping for a place to grow their own food. Urban as well as country gardens resound to the sound of chickens and many a lawn has been dug up to be replaced by vegetable beds. Several programmes on the radio and TV promote the movement, expounding on the physical and mental health benefits of growing food and being close to nature. It is a fabulous development and one that was only a dream for many people like me a quarter of a century ago.

In the 1970s, wind, waterpower, solar panels and all different forms of renewable energy were modelled on a small scale in the Centre for Alternative Technology in Wales, with the vision of them one day becoming a reality for the country. Forty years later and with much work, publicity and caring effort from many people, part of that reality is now here.

Rainbows bring a promise of hope and there is hope for the human race. Not only can we make a better future for ourselves, we are on the way to doing so. I know there are still horrendous conflicts, wars and abuses. However, there are many good humans working against all these things with love and care, believing in a better future for all of us. It is important to remember the positives. Whatever form your beliefs take, keep putting out love and light to everyone and asking the pure, loving and beautiful energy force of the universe to help us in this task. We can do it. We can create a beautiful future for ourselves on our wonderful and ever-loving Mother Earth, our home.

A film that inspired and helped me to realise what humans have the potential to be, is a fabulous film called La Belle Verte. It can only be found on YouTube. Although it is funny, inspirational and has an amazing vision, it was never allowed on general release. If we work towards a future that is envisioned there, we cannot go wrong.

I know that people argue about the world and that it must have positive and negative to stay in balance. I believe in the cycle of ages and that every two thousand years a different background of stellar influences affects our planet. It is in reverse order to that of the annual progression through the star signs. From the year 0 to 2000 A.D. (roughly) has been the Age of Pisces. The symbolism of Christianity reflects this, as one of the dominant and governing religions of that era, particularly in the Western world. The symbol of the fish abounds, referring to Jesus as and his disciples as 'fishers of men,' with the fish carved and inscribed across the globe, wherever the power of Rome has had a hold. Islam and Buddhism have, also, been major religions that were birthed and developed during these years and the fish symbol holds importance in those religions too.

The two thousand years prior to that was the Age of Aries. The Old Testament relates to this time when the ram, ewe and lambs were important symbols in the Jewish religion, as well as in other beliefs that were around at the time.

From 2,000-4,000 B.C. was the Age of Taurus, the bull. The Minoan culture dating from around 3,000 B.C. is known to have focussed on bulls, Hinduism was founded around the same time which relates to cows as being sacred and I know that one of the earliest Egyptian religions was called Apis or the cult of the bulls.

The Age of Pisces is described as swimming in the waters of emotion, with no clear vision of how the world can be, just going along with the flow. The culmination of all this was Hitler, who manipulated a nation with the mindless wave of emotion, doing terrible things to other humans.

The present two-thousand-year changeover is moving into the Age of Aquarius. In the 1970s the musical 'Hair' heralded the birth of this age in one of its songs. Aquarius is the water carrier, carrying the waters of emotion and controlling them, heralding the balance between male and female and is supposed to be an enlightened age. Hopefully, it will be a time of greater understanding, thought and reason; people will become more rational and less easily persuaded by mass hysteria. I have heard that it is a forty-year change over period, which is why there have been so many vast changes in the last four decades. The old Gods of Pisces will not release their tyrannical hold easily, so there has been much turmoil and distressing times during these years. It is important to hold onto hope and remember that better times are coming. My narrative has spanned those years, reminding me of how different things were in my younger life. If, like me, you believe that this is how it is, it heralds a positive and exciting future for us all.

A year or so after coming back to my full-blown connection with the spirit world, a friend of mine was desperately ill in hospital, so I asked my guides to use me to send her some healing. As I did so, it felt right to visualise her in a ball of light, which was one of the colours of the rainbow. Next time I wanted to channel some healing I tried it again. This time I found myself visualising a different colour. Then after doing this a few times, I got a message in meditation that each colour relates to a different planet and that when we channel remote healing, we can ask for additional support from the different planets. The colours that come through are vibrantly beautiful and seem to change depending on what people need.

We get a lot of insights and understandings in meditation. Recently, we got a message about light workers. There are many people on this planet working to make it a better place, full of good intentions, love and light. If you have got this far in the book, I can guarantee you are a light worker yourself. You may be only starting to recognise it in yourself, you may have been doing it for years or you may be somewhere in between. Whatever the case, it is important to remember that the more you develop your abilities the more you need to stay positive. Each one of us is like a drop in a pond. If we feel angry, that anger ripples out in every direction around us, passing negativity to others. If we feel kindness, that also ripples out, passing positivity to others. When I was younger, I used to get very angry and want to stand up for every injustice around me. Now I have realised that anger is not the way. Compassion, love and understanding are what everyone needs, even the bullies of this world.

Sometimes in meditation, I meet up with Jill and Butterfly Star and we have a great girly time together. Occasionally Mum and Dad are there, or they give messages through the others in the group. My gran sends her love and warmth both in meditation and my life. At other times, I get understandings of how things work. Sometimes my 'feathery' guide works with me and takes me on a journey. During the meditation, time can expand or contract, we seem to be in a very different place or even dimension at times. All I do know is that however I receive it, I get valuable and useful ideas to help my everyday world flow well. It is like a recipe for life, giving me a hint of hope and a dash of rainbows to help me on my journey.

This book was born in that group. Jan and the others kept getting messages for me, telling me to write it and giving encouragement, till now it has come to fruition. I hope the words in here will help in some way; maybe there are ideas that might suggest a new way of looking at the world or just entertain. Whatever you get out of it, if it helps you in one tiny way, I will have achieved what I set out to do.

Looking back over my life so far, I feel very privileged to be on this beautiful Earth, to have met the people I have and to have had the experiences that have helped me to grow. As I quoted earlier from the first line of the Mohawk Thanksgiving prayer, 'To be Human is truly an Honour.'

ACKNOWLEDGEMENTS:

First, I thank Jan, Catherine and Rachel and all their guides for the idea to start writing and then for their messages, unstinting support and encouragement to keep going.

Peter and Mato for allowing me to get on with writing, giving me their support and love.

Iestyn Davies for his brilliant idea for the book cover.

Ben Davies for an amazing translation of his dad's ideas into a work of art for the book cover.

Sara Simpson for the wonderful layout and design of the cover.

Sandra Macleod, Bev Davies and Pat Williams for their belief in me, their individual encouragement and their capable proof reading of successive versions of the text.

All my friends and relatives mentioned in the book who have read and commented on their part in the book, then given me their permission to use their real names.

Thomas Banyacya Jr: Hopi Independent Nation

Norma Sunday for all her support and advice in relation to the title and ensuring my facts were correct about the Mohawk Nation.

Patti and all her wonderful family, who treat me as one of their own.

Vanessa and Leona with all their lovely families, who welcomed me into their lives with so much warmth.

Nia Francisco: Dine poet and weaver (author of Blue Horses for Navajo Women)

Alice Two Bulls and all the family who are always there for us and have given us so much love over the years.

Francisco Coll: English office IPM of UK PO Box 380 Worcester WRZ 5ZL

Dr Helen Ford: Stourbridge, West Midlands. Author of 'How to Create the Life You Want for Yourself'

'The Path of Power' by Sun Bear

'Rolling Thunder' by Doug Boyd

Statement declaiming Sun Bear and Rolling Thunder by traditional Native Americans:

https://www.culturalsurvival.org/publications/cultural-survival-quarterly/united-states/spiritual-hucksterismthe-rise-plastic-medicin

'We Are All One Planet' song by Molly Scott

'Awakenings' by Tim Wheater

'Hidden Meanings' by Laird Scranton. Laird Scranton youtube(http://www.tragnark.com/187/the-language-and-symbols-of-the-dogon-tribe/)

'Living Energies: Victor Shauberger's work explained by Callum Coats(translator)'

'Fingerprints of the Gods' by Graham Hancock

'The Sign and the Seal' by Graham Hancock

'The Man Who Planted Trees' by Jean Giono

'The Permaculture Manual' by Bill Mollinson

'Forest Gardening' by Robert Hart

'Beyond the Forest Garden' by Robert Hart

'The Farmer, the Plough and the Devil' by Arthur Hollins

'The Ringing Cedars of Russia' series by Vladimir Megre

'La Belle Verte' written and directed by Coline Serreau

Thanks to Mike Feingold, Permaculture expert (check out his video on youtube) for permission to use his quote.

All my amazing family and friends for all their love, support and nurturing over the years, particularly my dear, lovely parents who no doubt will be doing their best from the other side to help my book come to fruition!

319

Lightning Source UK Ltd.
Milton Keynes UK
UKHW041130200722
406121UK00001B/66